Praises to a Formless God

SUNY Series in Religious Studies
Harold Coward, editor

Praises to a Formless God

Nirguṇī Texts from North India

David N. Lorenzen

State University of New York Press

Published by
State University of New York Press, Albany

Printed in the United States of America

For information, address the State University of New York Press, State University Plaza, Albany, NY 12246

Production by Bernadine Dawes • Marketing by Nancy Farrell

Library of Congress Cataloging-in-Publication Data

Lorenzen, David N.
Praises to a formless god : Nirguni texts from North India / David N. Lorenzen.
p. cm. — (SUNY series in religious studies)
Includes bibliographical references and indexes.
ISBN 0-7914-2805-2 (ch : acid-free). — ISBN 0-7914-2806-0 (pb : acid-free)
1. Religious poetry, Hindi — Translations into English. 2. Hindi poetry — To 1500. 3. Hindi poetry — 1500–1800. I. Title. II. Series.
PK2040.2L67 1996
[PK2141.E3]
891'.4310080382 — dc20 95-20931
CIP

Dedicated to three very different teachers
who have shared the ability and the will to inspire others to think,
and sometimes to disagree:

N. O. "Nobby" Brown

A. L. Basham

and

Bipan Chandra

CONTENTS

A NOTE ON TRANSLITERATION

Diacritics have been used for most Sanskrit and Hindi words. Diacritics are *not* used, however, for the names of places and rivers, for the names of persons and institutions with "official" English spellings, for Hindi/Sanskrit words in the titles of books and articles written in European languages, or for Hindi/Sanskrit words commonly used in English or that are partly anglicized. These latter words include: Brahmin (the social group), Krishna, pandit, puranic, Purana, raja, Ram or Rama, sadhu, sannyasi, Shaiva, Shaivite, Shiva, Shudra, tantric, Upanishad, Vaishya, Vishnu, Vaishnava, and yogi.

The standard transliteration system for Sanskrit is used except for a few modifications to aid in pronunciation. For Hindi, the mute *a* at the end of a word is dropped. A final *a* is kept when it is preceded by two consonants (exceptions: *granth, panth, mahant*). Within words, the mute *a* is retained ("Tulasī" not "Tulsī") to preserve the original spelling. Nasal consonants written with an *anusvāra* are changed into the appropriate class nasal, except before *v, s,* and *h* where *ṃ* is used. This *ṃ* is also used in the case of nasalized vowels *(anunāsik)*. The words *pad* (a type of song) and *pada* (a quarter verse) are distinguished, although the Hindi word is the same.

Other changes include the following:

च and छ = "cha" and "chha" respectively

ड and ड़ = "ḍa" and "ṛa" respectively

PREFACE

The praises to a formless god that this book illustrates and discusses are those composed by low-caste saint-poets of the *nirguṇī* or *sant* movement of Hindu and Sikh devotion in North India. Most of the sects that make up this movement were founded in the sixteenth, seventeenth, and eighteenth centuries. Many of these sects are still active today, but, with the exception of the Sikhs, they are being increasingly marginalized by the march of modern civilization and popular mass culture. Nonetheless, the words and ideas of the best of the *nirguṇi* poets such as Kabīr, Dādū, and Gurū Nānak continue to provide pleasure, inspiration, and solace to many millions of persons well beyond the bounds of their immediate devotees.

Only a few works of *nirguṇi* literature have received translations that really work well as poetry in English: Linda Hess and Shukdeo Singh's selection of songs from Kabīr's *Bījak;* John Hawley and Mark Juergensmeyer's anthology that includes songs by Raidās, Kabīr, and Gurū Nānak; and Rabindranath Tagore's now somewhat dated translation of one-hundred songs attributed to Kabīr. Also important are Winand Callewaert and Peter Friedlander's translations of Raidās, Charlotte Vaudeville's and V. K. Sethi's translations of Kabīr, and Monika Thiel-Horstmann's (now Boehm-Tettelbach) translations of selections of Dādū Panthī material. Nonetheless, major poet-singers such as Gurū Nānak, Gurū Amar Dās, Dādū, Palaṭū, and Sundaradās have yet to find translators to put the major part of their compositions into an English that is accurate and readable at the same time. Perhaps the task is impossible. The words of songs are meant to be sung. Separated from their original language and from musical performance, how can we expect them to survive intact?

The texts that are translated, edited and discussed here in this book are not all great works of art. They are presented as historical documents rather than as literary texts. Nonetheless most *are* texts that I have found aesthetically pleasing, and I have tried to translate them in a way that gives at least some suggestion of their style and art.

In the case of the songs, I have usually attempted to give the translations a regular rhythm based on set numbers of feet per line and using mostly iambs and anapests. This is not quite the way the original Hindi meters work, but it does seem to me to give a better idea of the style of the original texts than rendering them in modern free verse with irregular line lengths as is often done. The original Hindi texts also are rhymed, but no attempt has been made to rhyme the translations. The struggle to find rhymes makes it impossible to closely follow the original text, and the results usually sound ludicrous in any case. The refrains of the songs are italicized. In performance they are repeated after each verse.

Two longer works presented in this book have been translated into prose. Jan Gopāl's *Prahilād charitra* tells the famous story of the pious demon Prahlād, son of the evil Hiraṇyakaśipu. It is written in a solid narrative verse that makes few claims to a true poetic style, except for a few songs or hymns that are included in it and have been translated in metrical form. Although Jan Gopāl's text was once quite popular, it is difficult to know exactly how it was originally performed. Probably it was recited rather than sung and also given an improvised commentary in spoken prose.

The second longer composition is Sain's *Kabīr-Raidās kā saṃvād*. It is cast in the form of a religious debate between Kabīr and Raidās about the relative merits of *nirguṇ* and *saguṇ* conceptions of the Divine. Its basic style is didactic verse rather than poetry. Like the *Prahilād charitra,* probably it was originally recited together with a spoken commentary.

Chapters 5 and 6 of this book are based in part on Spanish language articles earlier published in *Estudios de Asia y Africa,* a journal of the Center of Asian and African Studies of El Colegio de México. None of the other material has previously appeared anywhere.

Two colleagues actively participated in the preparation of this book: Shukdeo Singh of Banaras Hindu University and Uma Thukral of El Colegio de México. The translation of Jan Gopāl's *Prahilād charitra* was done with Shukdeo Singh during his visit to Mexico in June and July of 1991 and my visits to India in January and February of 1992 and 1994. The translation of Sain's *Kabīr-Raidās kā saṃvād* was done with Uma Thukral in Mexico, mostly in 1991. She also gave constant help and advice during the preparation of the rest of the book, particularly chapters 1 and 3. Dr. Narayan Das, a former student of Shukdeo Singh, helped with many of the translations found in chapter 6.

Other colleagues who from time to time offered valuable comments on earlier drafts of parts of the book include John S. Hawley of Barnard College, Linda Hess of the University of California, Harjot Oberoi of the University of British Columbia, David Swain of the University of Chicago, and Thomas Trautmann of the University of Michigan. Thanks are also owed to my wife, Barbara Martiny, and my children, Matthew and Rebecca, for putting up with time spent in my books when I should have been doing chores or helping with homework.

Economic support for research and writing was provided by El Colegio de México where I work and by three short-term fellowships from the American Institute of Indian Studies that enabled me to visit India in 1990, 1992, and 1994.

Illustrated manuscript of Prahilād Charitra (6.5–9) from Dādū Panth monastery at Narena. (Photo courtesy of Monika Boehm-Tettelbach.)

INTRODUCTION

Hey God, God don't never change
He's God, always will be God

God in the middle of the ocean
God in the middle of the sea
By the help of the Great Creator
Truly been God to me

God in the creation
God when Adam fell
God way up in heaven
God way down in hell

He spoke to the mountain
Said how great I am
Want you to get up this morning
Skip around like a lamb

God in the time of sickness
God in the doctor too
In the time of the influenza
He truly was a God to you

God in the pulpit
God way down at the door
He's God in the Amen corner
God all over the floor

— Blind Willie Johnson, 1929

The religious current known as the *nirguṇī* or *sant* movement arose in North India about the middle of the fifteenth century of the Common Era. Its early exponents include both Hindus and Sikhs. Among the more famous poet-saints of the movement are Kabīr, Raidās, Gurū Nānak, Dādū Dayāl, Haridās Nirañjanī, Gurū Amar Dās, Rajjab, Sundaradās, Palaṭū Sāhab, and Jan Gopāl. These and other *nirguṇī* poets composed thousands of songs, couplets, verse dialogues, and verse narratives in which they preach a religious message of *nirguṇ* bhakti, devotion to a God without attributes, coupled with reverence toward the saints and gurus of the movement and toward the *guru vāṇī,* the words of these saints and gurus. This religious message is combined with a social message that rejects, with greater or lesser directness, the hierarchical ordering of society into inherited castes.

The *nirguṇī* texts translated and discussed in this book have all been popular at one time or another among the followers of the *nirguṇī* movement, but none of them have so far received much attention from modern scholars. In the cases of Jan Gopāl's *Prahilād charitra* and Sain's *Kabīr-Raidās kā saṃvād,* I have included new critical editions of the original texts as well as translations. In my discussions of the texts, I have paid particular attention to the relation between their religious and social messages. I also hope that the translations convey at least some idea of the value of the texts as literature.

Scholars outside *nirguṇī* tradition, both Western and Indian, have often noted the logical contradiction inherent in a religious movement that insists on offering heart-felt devotion to a God without attributes, without even any definable personality.[1] How is it possible for anyone to feel devotion to such a God? Even in Judeo-Christian and Muslim tradition, God has at least a definite personality (and an incarnate form in the case of Christianity). In the mainstream Hindu tradition of *saguṇ* bhakti, God becomes solidly anthropomorphic, or theriomorphic, and takes a variety of physical forms, each with its own personality. Whatever the logical difficulties, however, mountains of *nirguṇī* literature testify to the reality of this personal devotion to an impersonal object. As Galileo said after being forced to recant his finding that the earth moves around the sun: *Eppur si muove* ("And yet it moves").

I first began my study of *nirguṇī* religion in 1974 when the American Council of Learned Societies awarded me a short-term grant to do research in London on the early history of the Kabīr Panth, the sectarian movement organized by Kabīr's followers. In 1976 I got another short-term grant, this one from the Indian University Grants Commission, to continue my still fledgling studies on the Kabīr Panth in India. In Banaras I met the American scholar Linda Hess who was working on a translation of the *Kabīr bījak* with Shukdeo Singh of Banaras Hindu University. She introduced me to Singh and to Āchārya Amṛt Dās, the late head of the Kabīr Chaurā monastery.

The Kabīr Panth has been a central part of my life ever since. Without ever becoming a devotee, I have come to consider myself as a sort of honorary Kabīr Panthī. Many sadhus and lay followers of the Kabīr Panth and related movements have become my friends, as have many of the small band of academic scholars who study and teach about *nirguṇī* poets and sects.

This long association with the Kabīr Panth in India and my many years in Mexico have brought me a long way from my early life in Connecticut, but these changes have constantly impressed upon me one simple lesson: human sentiments and human ideas are, when all is said and done, pretty much the same everywhere. Human cultures are certainly different, but not so different that we cannot grasp what other peoples feel and think.

Anthropologists and cultural historians rightly earn their living explaining the differences between cultures, but often they go too far. The anthropologist Louis Dumont (1986), for instance, has proposed that, culturally at least, Indians belong to a radically different human species, homo hierarchicus. McKim Marriott (1989, 17) has suggested that Indians live in a mysterious world in which the "Hindu postulations of mixing, unmarking and unmatching . . . in effect constitute the universe as a set of 'antiequivalence relations.'" A. K. Ramanujan (1989) has argued that there is a distinctive, context-sensitive "Indian way of thinking," a view that updates older speculations about "the Indian mind." Owen Lynch (1990) has argued that even our basic emotions are constructed out of concepts that are culturally specific, so that the emotions of Indians are in some senses fundamentally different from those of Americans, Europeans or Chinese.

Dumont, Marriott, Ramanujan, and Lynch are brilliant scholars who have each had a strong influence on the academic study of Indian culture, yet all my own experience and instinct tells me that it just isn't so. Indian society and culture are certainly organized in unique ways, as are all societies and cultures, but the basic structures are human, not Indian. Likewise, the typical thoughts and feelings of Indians often differ from those of other peoples in terms of their interests and emphases, but not in the way they operate. Somehow all these arguments for radical difference among national cultures are — like the reports of his death that so amused Mark Twain — greatly exaggerated. One of the basic premises of this book is that the social and religious values embodied in *nirguṇī* texts can be understood by persons outside the movement, even by non-Indians, without the need of more than a judicious amount of commentary.

One essential part of this commentary is, of course, translation. In one sense, any translator necessarily creates a new text, but this new text should be one whose sense and form are intimately related to those of the original text. Despite all the cultural and linguisitic obstacles, the aim should be to convey a reasonably accurate idea of both the immediate sense and the social and cultural significance of these texts from one language and one audience to another.

For both Dumont and Marriott, despite their many disagreements, a major corollary to their idea that the social and cultural values *among* different national cultures are radically different is the idea that the values *within* any given national culture, or at least within Indian national culture, are quite uniform. John Leavitt (1992) has aptly described this monolithic aspect of their otherwise competing models of the cultural values of Indian society as "cultural holism": the idea that all castes, classes, and factions within this society share the same basic values. As I have argued elsewhere, this idea is curiously similar to the older Marxist idea that every society has a "dominant ideology," equivalent to the ideology of its ruling classes.[2]

Here again my own life experience, somehow spread across three separate national cultures, tells me it isn't so. What I prefer to stress — and what the *nirguṇī* movement illustrates — is the existence of *alternative* value systems, or social ideologies, based on caste and class. Sociocultural models like those of Dumont and Marriott, as well as that of Marx and Engels, seriously underestimate the importance of such alternative value systems or ideologies within any given national society.

In the case of India, John Leavitt (1992) has identified one set of such alternative value systems as that of *regional* cultures based on local languages, customs and beliefs. There is much to be said for Leavitt's hypothesis, but it tends to simply replace one big national value system with many little national value systems, although Leavitt does introduce the complication of both systems operating simultaneously in the same populations.

In North India, a more significant alternative value system is embodied in the religious and social ideology of the *nirguṇī* movement. *Nirguṇī* poets sharply contest the dominant social ideology of mainstream Hinduism, the hierarchical ideology of *varṇāśramadharma,* and propose a more egalitarian social model that I have elsewhere described as "non-caste Hinduism" (Lorenzen 1987a). This alternative set of values necessarily operates under the hegemonic influence of mainstream values since the purveyors of mainstream values wield the lion's share of economic and political power. Insofar as it is feasible for the followers of *nirguṇī* ideas and values to dissent and resist, however, they do so.

Looked at from a comparative perspective, the basic egalitarian emphasis of *nirguṇī* social ideology bears a definite resemblance to that of Judeo-Christian and Islamic tradition, a resemblance that suggests the possibility of historical influence. But how could such influence be transmitted? The *nirguṇī* movement appeared in India at a time when cultural and commercial contact between India and Europe was minimal. One can point to the obvious link provided by Islam, particularly Sufism, but the extent to which Islam influenced the *nirguṇī* movement is uncertain and still quite controversial.

As an initial epigraph to this introduction, I have transcribed a song by a gospel and blues singer named Blind Willie Johnson that illustrates how the artistic form and theological message of typical *nirguṇī* songs are not completely alien even to Christian tradition. Here it is not just social ideology, but also art and theology that link together East and West. Before turning to a summary of the main arguments of this book, I would like to digress for a few pages to discuss Johnson's song and various possible explanations for its resemblance to its *nirguṇī* counterparts.

The chances of the Texas singer and guitarist Blind Willie Johnson having read or heard any songs by *nirguṇī* poet-saints of India such as Kabīr and Gurū Nānak are remote at best.[3] Nonetheless, Johnson's 1929 song "God Don't Never Change," is remarkably similar, both in form and content, to many *nirguṇī* songs of India. Logic suggests three possible explanations: indirect historical diffusion, universal genetic predispositions, and similar socio-economic preconditions. All three factors must have contributed to the resemblance, but how much is owed to each is difficult to estimate.

By indirect historical diffusion I mean historical borrowings that take place through the agency of third persons. Both Blind Willie Johnson and the *nirguṇī* poet-saints were heirs to larger cultural traditions that at various times had been in contact and had influenced each other. We know that people speaking Indo-European languages spread into India about three and a half thousand years ago and into America about five hundred years ago. In addition, there were important contacts between India and Europe, via the Middle East, during Roman times and more constant contacts between India and America, mostly via Europe, for the last three hundred years.

By universal genetic predispositions I mean the universal tendency of human beings to express similar thoughts and emotions in similar ways. Where do we draw the line between what we learn and what we inherit? In recent years the geneticists and social biologists seem to be gaining back some of the ground earlier lost to social scientists, but no general consensus is even remotely in sight. At the least, however, the human predisposition to express thoughts and emotions in song and poetry must have some genetic basis.

By similar socio-economic preconditions I mean the similarities of family structure, socio-economic class, education, political rank, and history that can foster the creation of similar cultural products. One obvious common factor is the biologically determined condition of prolonged dependence on one's parents that plays a key role in the creation of fantasies about one's mother, father and siblings, fantasies that are similar, in a "family resemblance" sort of way, in all human societies. At a less biological level, the similarities include such things as the contrasting influences of the royal court and prison life on the form and content of artistic creations.

The most striking similarity between "God Don't Never Change" and a typical *nirguṇī* bhajan of, say, Kabīr is that of form. First of all, they both are songs, meant to be sung, each with a specific melody, rhythm and musical structure. More than that, they both have poetic lyrics structured in almost identical fashion: a repeating refrain followed by verses of two lines each marked by a regular meter, end rhyme, and a division of each line into two parts. Likewise, in both songs the function of the refrain is to summarize and recapitulate the basic message of each verse.

Our genetic predisposition to express ourselves in song is somehow related to the ability of music and poetry to give us pleasure and to help us remember the words. It is these functions that partly explain the prevalence of common features such as the repeating refrain and rhymed couplets. Nonetheless, it is also likely that the similarities of linguistic structure between Hindi and English and the common cultural heritage of the Indo-European language family played some role in creating this similarity of poetic structure. It is also significant that both "God Don't Never Change" and *nirguṇī* songs have a comparatively *simple* musical and poetic structure. Both are created by and for a poor and relatively uneducated social class. They are decidedly not the artistic products of a royal court or scholastic academy.

Rather more puzzling are the similarities between the theological contents of "God Don't Never Change" and those of many typical *nirguṇī* songs. A particularly close comparison can be made with the well-known *nirguṇī* song "Moko kahāṃ ḍhūṇḍhe re bande" ("Where will you find Me, my friend?"), attributed to Kabīr.[4] Both songs are songs of praise to a *formless* God, a God who is everywhere and nowhere, within all things and apart from all things, a supreme God without arms, legs, beard, eyes, sex, or even a recognizable personality.

More specifically, both songs emphasize God's *omnipresence*. God, they claim, is present in the whole of the physical world and cannot be circumscribed by sacred spaces such as churches, temples, and mosques. In "Moko kahāṃ ḍhūṇḍhe re bande," Kabīr resorts to a typical *nirguṇī* strategy, the *via negativa*. God is not everywhere but nowhere, which is, if God exists, much the same thing. The real sense of the song is not that God is nowhere, but rather nowhere in particular. His presence is not limited to or circumscribed by any specific holy place or person *except*, that is, for the human heart of each and every one of us. God says: "Not in idols or sacred spas,/ not in secret places,/ I'm not in temples or mosques,/ not in Kāśī or Kailāś. . . . I'm found in faith." Johnson's God, for His part is in the ocean, in the creation, in heaven, in hell, in the doctor, in the pulpit, at the door, in the amen corner,[5] all over the floor.

The common emphasis on God's omnipresence does undoubtedly conceal important differences in the nature and history of Christian and *nirguṇī* conceptions of this concept. Historically, omnipresence plays a much larger role in Hinduism and Buddhism than in Christianity. One classic Hindu depiction of omnipresence is the upanishadic analogy that compares the relation between Brahman and the physical world to that of salt dissolved in water.[6] A variety of monistic and pantheistic conceptions of omnipresence stand, of course, at the very center of the different schools of Vedānta.

In Christianity, on the other hand, omnipresence is the least emphasized of a number of divine attributes that include His omniscience, omnipotence, infinitude, goodness, mercy, transcendence, spirituality, and personality. Since this God is pure spirit, Christian theologians generally carefully distinguish God from the substance of His creation, the physical universe, and, less consistently, tend to reject the idea that God is identical with, or resides within, the human soul.

Whether or not Johnson's song can be said to transgress the line that divides the orthodox Christian concept of divine omnipresence from the heretical one of divine immanence, and thus to dissolve the distinction between God and nature, there is no doubt that "God Don't Never Change" expresses theological sentiments that are remarkably similar to those of *nirguṇī* songs such as "Moko kahāṃ ḍhūṇḍhe re bande." What inspired Johnson to sing such a song?

Johnson's song is evidently a longer version of a traditional hymn that appears in the famous Frank C. Brown collection of North Carolina folklore.[7] This at least shows that the song is not simply the idiosyncratic creation of Johnson himself. The other religious songs he recorded, conveniently collected on a recent compact disk set (Johnson 1993), are taken from a variety of published and unpublished sources. Their themes include modern disasters such as the 1918–1919 influenza epidemic (also mentioned in "God Don't Never Change") and the 1912 sinking of the Titanic; the Old Testament story of Samson and Delilah; personal laments such as "Motherless Children Have a Hard Time" and "Lord, I Can't Just Keep from Crying"; Jesus' crucifixion in Johnson's famous rendering of "Dark was the Night, Cold was the Ground"; and songs such as "Can't Nobody Hide from God" and "The Soul of a Man" that share at least some of the flavor of "God Don't Never Change." Many of Johnson's songs also display a dark fascination with death that finds a notable parallel in the *nirguṇī* songs attributed to Kabīr.[8]

First let us consider the possibility that the thematic similarities between "God Don't Never Change" and *nirguṇī* songs are the result of historical diffusion. Johnson's Christianity probably had three basic sources: African religion, Protestant Christianity, and the Bible itself. All three traditions often claim that a quite intimate relation exists between God and Nature. To the extent that this intimacy borders on a concept of divine immanence, the underlying theology can be described as something close to pantheism.

Although the white masters of the African slaves brought to the United States consciously tried to suppress their slaves' African cultural heritage, some elements of this heritage obviously made an important contribution to the creation of what is now called African-American culture, including African-American Christianity. The extent to which this heritage included pantheism, however, is unclear. Certainly it included phenomena related to pantheism such as spirit worship and spirit possession. Nonetheless, it is noteworthy that major studies of African-American culture such as those by E. Genovese (1974) and L. Levine (1977) do not characterize African-American Christianity as being pantheistic. Moreover, in countries such as Brasil and Cuba where African cultural traditions have been better preserved, African-American religious beliefs tend more toward polytheism than pantheism.

A second possibility is that the pantheistic flavor of "God Don't Never Change" was influenced by American Protestant tradition. At the time it was passed to the slaves, however, this tradition had a strong conservative bias that did not easily admit pantheistic ideas. Nonetheless, Emerson and Thoreau and other leaders of the religious and literary movement known as American transcendentalism often displayed a sensitivity to nature that sometimes flirted with pantheism. Emerson even explored religious ideas derived directly from India through his study of English translations of Sanskrit texts such as the *Bhagavad-gītā*.

Although this movement was most prominent in New England in the period from 1830 to 1855, its considerable influence on later American culture is seen in the works of Whitman, Hawthorne and Emily Dickinson. Nonetheless, the extent to which transcendentalism could have influenced Johnson, even indirectly, is uncertain.

A rather different Protestant tradition that undoubtedly did have a direct influence on Johnson's Christianity was that of the Baptist sects, both black and white. These sects were more open to the expression of religious emotion than more mainstream Protestant sects. Practices such as spirit possession and speaking in tongues were common among both white and black Baptists. The Holiness and Spiritualist sects that gained many adherents among African-Americans from about 1900 on also contributed to these tendencies.

Another possible source for the pantheism of "God Don't Never Change" is the Bible itself. Most African-American Christianity has relied heavily on the Old Testament, particularly the narrative books such as Genesis, Exodus, Deuteronomy, Joshua, Judges, and Samuel and, in a different vein, the psalms. Although the narrative books do show the God of the Hebrews constantly meddling in human affairs, they are hardly pantheistic.

The psalms, however, are more problematic. Several of them closely associate God and Nature, particularly powerful natural forces like thunder, wind, rain, fire, and the sun. In psalm 18 we read:[9]

Then the earth reeled and rocked;
    the foundations also of the mountains trembled
    and quaked, because he was angry.
Smoke went up from his nostrils,
    and devouring fire from his mouth;
    glowing coals flamed forth from him.

Psalm 104 — almost certainly inspired by Ikhnaton's hymn to the sun — identifies God with the sun:[10]

Thou art clothed with honor and majesty,
    who coverest theyself with light as with a garment,
who has stretched out the heavens like a tent,
    who hast laid the beams of thy chambers on the waters,
who makest the clouds thy chariot,
    who ridest on the wings of the wind,

who makest the winds thy messengers,
fire and flame thy ministers.

Whatever influences may have contributed to the pantheism of "God Don't Never Change," we also need to ask why Johnson chose a song that seems to reject the dominant Christian tradition of sharp division between God and Nature. Here social factors may well have played an important role. If Protestant Christianity was a rebellion against Catholicism, then African-American Protestantism was, at least in part, a rebellion against aspects of European-American Protestantism. Johnson's song carries that rebellion still one stage further. The last verse uses pantheism to undermine the pretensions of even African-American churches to act as intermediaries in the direct relation between God and his devotee. God is found not only in the pulpit but also "all over the floor." He is everywhere and needs no church to make Himself known to us.

By a rather roundabout route, this brings us back to Kabīr and the poet-saints of the *nirguṇī* movement. In this book, one of my principal aims is to show how the marginal socio-economic situation of these poet-saints contributed to their choice of mythical heroes, to their hostility to the dominant *varṇāśramadharma* ideology of Hindu society, to their attempts to legitimate their religious beliefs through the historical example of earlier saints, to their reinterpretation of the content of typical Hindu rituals, and to their use of vernacular languages and literary forms to express their message.

The word *nirguṇ* literally means "without qualities or attributes." In its religious context, it refers to a God who is without form, sex or personality, a God who is best described by what He is not: not here not there, not male not female, not matter not spirit, not moral not immoral, a God who "does not sing and dance" as Kabīr puts it in his debate with Raidās. In the context of a movement of the devotees of such a God, it is inevitable that even He, or It, becomes associated with other things that bear more concrete and positive attributes. The immortal soul that dwells within our bodies is said to be either identical with or a part of this God, as are the Guru and the Words by which the Guru reveals Him. His very Name comes to be regarded as somehow identical with His Self. This God, His (or Its) Guru, His Guru's Words, His Name, and the company of His saints become the source of our final salvation and our sole refuge against the merciless world of transmigration.

The theoretical opposite of *nirguṇ* is *saguṇ*, a word that literally means "with qualities or attributes." In its religious context, *saguṇ* usually refers to a high God that has attributes such as form, sex and personality: a God such as the fierce ascetic Shiva, the great Goddess, and above all the many avatars of the benevolent god Vishnu. Although the relation between the worshipper and this *saguṇ* God tends to be more suffused with pious emotion, this God, like the *nirguṇ* God, also offers salvation through the mediation of His Guru, His Guru's Words, His Name, and the company of His saints.

Underlying the theological division between *saguṇ* and *nirguṇ* devotion is a basic social division. The *nirguṇī* saint-poets and their followers were almost all from the lower classes of Indian society. A small but significant minority were converts from Islam. The leaders of the *saguṇī* movement, on the other hand, were mostly Brahmins, though their followers came from a variety of castes and classes, including even some Untouchables. The social ideologies of these two movements were both more liberal than that of the more orthodox proponents of Vedic and *śāstrik* Hinduism, but it is also true that *nirguṇī* poets generally spoke against the *varṇāśramadharma* norms of Hindu society and the *saguṇī* poets generally spoke for them.

The first part of this book discusses the curious case of the pious demon Prahlād, son of the cruel king Hiraṇyakaśipu. Prahlād's unnatural decision to worship Vishnu incites his father to try to kill him, but Vishnu's Man-lion avatar saves Prahlād, bursting forth from a pillar of the palace and ripping out Hiraṇyakaśipu's heart. By about 1000 C.E., this story had become quite popular through its retellings in the *Viṣṇu-purāṇa* and the *Bhāgavata-purāṇa,* two quintessentially *saguṇī* texts.

Rather surprisingly, this *saguṇī* story also held a considerable fascination for the poet-saints of the *nirguṇī* movement. The story is featured in several songs by Nāmadev, the most important precursor of the *nirguṇī* poets, and later in songs attributed to Kabīr, Raidās, the Sikh Gurū Amar Dās, and others. In the first part of the seventeenth century, a longer *nirguṇī* retelling of Prahlād's story was composed by Jan Gopāl, a disciple of the Rajasthani poet-saint Dādū Dayāl. The first chapter of this book discusses how and why these *nirguṇī* poets took up Prahlād's story, while the second chapter presents a translation and critical edition of Jan Gopāl's "The Deeds of Prahlād" *(Prahilād charitra).*

The second part of this book is mostly about texts composed by Kabīr and his followers. In chapter 3 I discuss the question of how and why *nirguṇī* poets chose to compose hagiographic songs about earlier saints, particularly historical saints of the present Kali Yuga such as Gorakhanāth, Nāmadev, Kabīr, Raidās, Sain, Pīpā, and Dādū. This recourse to historical precedent for the legitimation of religious authority bears a particular affinity to the bhakti movement in general and *nirguṇī* tradition in particular, while it is quite alien to more orthodox Vedic tradition. Most of these hagiographic songs by *nirguṇī* poets have themes that can be described as eulogistic, testimonial or egalitarian.

Chapter 4 presents a translation and critical edition of a *nirguṇī* dialogue entitled "The Kabīr-Raidās Debate" *(Kabīr-Raidās kā saṃvād)* attributed to their fellow-disciple Sain. This work is an important example of a class of *nirguṇī* texts called *saṃvāds* or *goṣṭhīs* that feature debates between an important historical guru, most often Kabīr, and a leader of one of several competing *nirguṇī* and *saguṇī* sects such as Gorakhanāth, Śaṅkarāchārya, Rāmānanda, and Gurū Nānak. Like the hagiographic songs, these *saṃvāds* and *goṣṭhīs* appeal to the legitimating authority of events and persons that are thought to be historical.

Chapter 5 presents a sort of hit parade of twenty songs attributed to Kabīr that are today best loved by a sample of persons mostly from eastern Uttar Pradesh and Bihar. What is most significant about these songs is that they are mostly *not* the songs that appear in the older collections and anthologies. In addition, the songs that are most popular today tend to contain less of the sharp social and religious criticism for which Kabīr is famous. Despite their more muted and pessimistic tone, however, these songs express much the same oppositional religious and social message as that found in the older *nirguṇī* songs.

Chapter 6 discusses and translates many of the songs sung during the rituals of the Kabīr Panth, particularly the occasional rite known as the *chaukā.* The version of this rite celebrated in honor of a person who has recently died presents a vision of the journey of the soul that stands in rather sharp contrast to the journey described in the more orthodox texts of *saguṇī* religion.

The texts of *nirguṇī* tradition offer striking testimony to the futility of any attempt to construct any unified, holistic model of Indian religion and social ideology. *Nirguṇī* tradition is clearly an alternative tradition, one that inverts and subverts basic elements of mainstream Hindu tradition. In important respects it is at odds with Vedic Brahmanism, with *śāstrik* Hinduism, and with *saguṇ* bhakti. At the same time, however, *nirguṇī* tradition is clearly an Indian tradition, a historical creation derived from the concepts and sentiments associated with the same Vedas, Upanishads, and Puranas that underlie all of modern Hinduism. The question is how and where should we draw the lines?

– I –

The Demon Prahlād

1

Prahlād the Pious Demon

The story of Prahlād, the pious demon, is a narrative about the transgression of religious and social categories.[1] Although Prahlād is the son and heir apparent of the demon king Hiraṇyakaśipu, he becomes, by an accident of fate, a devotee of Vishnu, the Lord of the gods. His father and gurus repeatedly try to correct Prahlād's inversion of traditional religious and social norms, but to no avail. In the end, Hiraṇyakaśipu decides to kill his errant son, but the Man-lion avatar of Vishnu emerges from a pillar of the palace and kills the demon king instead, tearing open his chest with his nails.

This story is one of the great favorites of puranic literature. Most of the major Puranas tell often quite different versions of it. By far the most popular and influential version, however, has been that of the *Bhāgavata-purāṇa*. Largely through the medium of this text and texts derived from it, the story has become a basic part of bhakti religion. In North India the story has long been popular not only among the followers of *saguṇ* bhakti, those who worship anthropomorphic and theriomorphic deities, but also among the followers of *nirguṇ* bhakti, those who worship an ineffable divine Absolute.

The story of Prahlād is, on the face of it, an unlikely theme for a *nirguṇī* storyteller, since this demon devotee is ultimately saved by one of the quintessential manifestations of the *saguṇī* conception of the Divine, the Man-lion avatar of Vishnu. Nonetheless, many well-known *nirguṇī* authors such Kabīr, Raidās, Bhīkhā Sāhab, Gurū Amar Dās, Rajjab, and Jan Gopāl not only often mention Prahlād in passing, they also dedicate entire songs and narratives *(charitras)* to telling his story. Why did the Prahlād story appeal to these *nirguṇī* authors? And what changes did these authors introduce in their versions of the story to adapt it to a *nirguṇī* context?

Nāmadev, the well-known Maharashtran poet-saint, is a transitional figure whose songs are revered by the followers of both *saguṇī* and *nirguṇī* traditions. Most scholars believe he flourished in the first half of the fourteenth century, but a somewhat later date is also possible. Many of his songs contain passing references to Prahlād. Three of them are mostly or wholly dedicated to telling Prahlād's story. The oldest surviving version of the best known of these songs is found in the Sikh *Gurū Granth Sāhib*. Both the narrative incidents mentioned and the specific vocabulary used in this song attributed to Nāmadev suggest that it served as the model for other songs about Prahlād by later *nirguṇī* poets:[2]

Śaṇḍa and Marka went to complain:
"Prahlād won't study. We're worn out trying.
He calls on Ram and claps his hands,
all our students are getting corrupted;

Over and over he recites Ram's Name;
Hari alone he keeps in his heart."

The queen went to plead with her son:
"The king controls all the earth,
You are his son, Prahlād, yet you
reject his word and resolve on another."

The evil ministers met together:
"To the years he's got left let's fix a limit."[3]
The terrors of mountains,[4] water and fire,
King Ram repelled their magic power.

(The demon) drew his sword and sneered:
"Tell me, who will protect you now?"
"Hari, the yellow-clad Lord of the universe,
Dwells within the pillar of stone."

His claws tore Hiraṇyakaśipu apart.
The Lord protected both men and gods.
Says Nāmadev: the Man-lion fills my thoughts
It's Ram who grants me freedom from fear.

Probably the oldest song about Prahlād by a fully *nirguṇī* poet is a *pad* attributed to Kabīr. It appears, with some textual differences, in both the Rajasthani *Kabīr granthāvalī* and the Sikh *Gurū Granth Sāhib* collections. It is also found in Gopāladās' *Sarvāṅgī* collection and in several unpublished manuscripts containing miscellaneous songs by Kabīr and other *nirguṇī* poets. A modern collection of Kabīr bhajans contains yet another version.[5] The *Kabīr granthāvalī* version reads as follows:

"Sir, I'll not give up Ram's Name.
Why should I study other things?"

Prahlād set off to class to study,
taking with him many classmates.
"Why do you teach me silly nonsense?
Write on my slate just *Lord Gopāl*.

Śaṇḍa and Marka told the king,
who had them fetch Prahlād in chains.
"Stop this habit of saying 'Ram.'
Respect what I say and I'll let you go."

"Why do you threaten me time after time?
Ram made the water, land and mountains.
Go ahead and tie me, beat me, burn me,
to abandon Ram would insult my guru."

His angry father drew his sword:
"Tell me, who will protect you now?"
Vishnu burst out from within the pillar,
and clawed Hiraṇyakaśipu open.

The Supreme Being, the highest God,
became the Man-lion for the sake of bhakti.
Kabīr says: No one can reach His shore.
Time and again He rescued Prahlād.

Another of Kabīr's songs, this one found only in the *Gurū Granth Sāhib,* contains the following verse about Prahlād:[6]

Hari is the sole Lord of all bliss.
The Guru has given me His Name.
He saved Prahlād's saintly vow,
And clawed Hiraṇyakaśipu open.

The fact that neither of these two songs occurs in the more strictly *nirguṇī Kabīr-bījak* collection of the Kabīr Panth is probably significant. As Linda Hess (1987: 111–41) has shown, the *Kabīr granthāvalī* and *Gurū Granth Sāhib* are somewhat more open to the influence of *saguṇ* bhakti than is the *Bījak*. It also seems to be the case that many followers of *nirguṇ* bhakti in Rajasthan knew the *Bhāgavata-purāṇa* well and often adapted its stories, including that of Prahlād, to their own purposes, as will be argued in more detail below.

A somewhat longer composition (13–15 verses of four lines each) about Prahlād is attributed to Kabīr's brother-disciple Raidās. It is sometimes called the *Prahlād charita*. W. M. Callewaert and P. G. Friedlander have recently edited and translated this text.[7] It identifies Hiraṇyakaśipu as the king of the city of Multan, and Prahlād as his son. The father asks his son what he has learned in school. Prahlād says the only thing worth learning is the name of Ram, all else is simply entanglement in earthly existence. This response angers Hiraṇyakaśipu, and he tells Prahlād to abandon all worship of Ram. Prahlād refuses. Hiraṇyakaśipu calls his courtiers, and they recommend that Prahlād be killed. Prahlād is put in fire and in a well but is not harmed. Hiraṇyakaśipu boasts of his possession of a boon of being indestructible by day or by night, on the ground or in the sky. Prahlād tells him that Ram is in everything, in me and in you. Hiraṇyakaśipu replies: "If Ram is in this pillar, then why doesn't he free you?" In the twilight, the Man-lion lifts Hiraṇyakaśipu onto his thigh and tears him open with his nails.

Prahlād's story was particularly popular among the early Sikhs of the Panjab. In addition to the already cited songs of Nāmadev and Kabīr, the *Gurū Granth Sāhib* contains three songs by the third guru, Amar Dās (1552–74), that narrate the story of Prahlād.[8] Many other songs by Amar Dās and other Sikh gurus contain passing references to Prahlād's story. It is also retold at some length in the Sikh *Dasam Granth Sāhib* (1983–86, 1:388–95). Amar Dās' first song makes an interesting comparison with those of Nāmadev and Kabīr:

"On my slate write 'Hari Govinda Gopāl.'
    Anything else and Death will snare you.
The Satguru gives me his protection.
    Hari, the giver of bliss, is with me."

As taught, Prahlād repeats the Name.
The child doesn't fear any threat.

His mother tells him: "Dear Prahlād,
    give up Ram's Name and save your life."
Prahlād says: "Listen, mother, I'll never
    abandon the Name my guru taught."

Śaṇḍa and Marka went to complain:
    "Prahlād corrupts himself and his mates."

In the evil court a plot was hatched,
but the Raghus' king was Prahlād's protector.

The arrogant demon raised his sword:
"How will your Hari save you now?"
The fearsome form burst from the pillar,
clawed the demon and saved Prahlād.

Hari cares for the needs of his saints.
He saved generations of Prahlād's descendants.
Says Nānak: The guru teaches the cure.
Ram's Name saves his saints.

A fourth song by Gurū Amar Dās, though dedicated only in part to the Prahlād story, contains two verses that help explain the fascination of *nirguṇī* poets with the story of Prahlād. These verses compare Prahlād's identity as a demon *(daitya)* with the low-caste identity of two other famous devotees, Kabīr and Nāmadev:[9]

Nāmadev the tailor and Kabīr the weaver,
obtained the goal through the perfect guru.
They recognized the word of Brahman
and lost their egoism and their caste.
Gods and men sing their songs.
Brother, no one is able to destroy them.

The demon's son knew only the One
and wouldn't study karma and dharma.
He met the guru who made him pure.
Every day he recited the Name.
He studied the One; he learned the Name.
No other thing entered his mind.

As I will argue in more detail below, this comparison between demon and low-caste status, is present, at least implicitly, in all *nirguṇī* retellings of Prahlād's story and is implied even in the more socially conservative retelling of the *Bhāgavata-purāṇa*.

Although collections of *nirguṇī* poetry from Eastern India contain many passing references to Prahlād, more detailed allusions to his story are rare. The following lines from a song of Bhīkhā Sāhab (on *gaddī* 1760–91 C.E.), a poet of the Bhuṛakuṛā (Ghazipur district) monastic lineage, constitute the only detailed reference I have found in an eastern collection:[10]

O Ram, do me this kindness now.
Do it for me as you always do.

Hiraṇyakaśipu tormented his son,
But Prahlād firmly held on to the Name.

With anger he raised his sword to kill him.
The Man-lion appeared and burst his belly.

It is among the followers of the Dādū Panth of Rajasthān that Prahlād's story attained its greatest popularity in a *nirguṇī* context. We have already noted the inclusion of a song about Prahlād in the *Kabīr granthāvalī,* a Dādū Panthī collection of Kabīr's songs and verses. Similarly, the early Dādū Panthī poet Rajjab often refers to Prahlād, as in this verse in *chhappay* meter that describes the cruel ordeals that Hiraṇyakaśipu inflicted on Prahlād:[11]

For the saint water held no danger.
    Buried under ground Prahlād felt no pain.
He was thrown from the mountain and didn't die.
    The many perils had no effect.

With the Name on his lips as an antidote,
    the poison's evil had no effect.
Prahlād shone like gold as he sat
    with auntie Ghūnghachī in the fire.

When the sword [hit] the pillar the Man-lion emerged
    and killed [the demon], a father and foe.
Rajjab says: "He gave his darshan
    and easily saved his young devotee.

One of the most ambitious and most popular *nirguṇī* retellings of the Prahlād story is the *Prahilād charitra* of Jan Gopāl, a Dādū Panthī sadhu who lived in Rajasthan in the early part of the seventeenth century. Jan Gopāl also wrote a *Dhruv charitra* and a *Jaḍ Bharat charitra,* as well as a hagiographical life of Dādū Dayāl and many shorter compositions. Manuscripts of most of these texts, particularly the three *charitras,* are quite numerous in the manuscript collections of Rajasthan. A critical edition and translation of the *Prahilād charitra* is included in this book.

Why would a writer of the Dādū Panth — one of the principal bastions of *nirguṇī* tradition — choose to compose major retellings of the stories not only of Prahlād, but also of Dhruv and Jaḍ Bharat, all three puranic legends closely associated with the *saguṇī* tradition? In his *Dhruv charitra,* Jan Gopāl explicitly states that he based his account on the archetypal *saguṇī* text, the *Bhāgavata-purāṇa.* From the close correspondence of the plots and several specific passages, it is clear that the *Bhāgavata-purāṇa* was also the principal source for Jan Gopāl's *Prahilād charitra* and for his *Jaḍ Bharat charitra.*

One factor that helps explain why Jan Gopāl chose these three *saguṇī* heroes is suggested by his biography, sparse though it may be.[12] From it we learn that Jan Gopāl was already some sort of begging sadhu when he first met Dādū, and that he apparently came from a Vaishya family. Taken together these "facts" suggest that Jan Gopāl was originally a follower of *saguṇī* Vaishnava tradition and was probably well-acquainted with the *Bhāgavata-purāṇa* before becoming a follower of Dādū. Apparently this *saguṇī* background continued to influence Jan Gopāl's religious beliefs and preferences even after his becoming Dādū's disciple.

A second factor in Jan Gopāl's fondness for Prahlād is, as we have seen, the general popularity of this story in *nirguṇī* as well as *saguṇī* tradition, particularly in western India. To a somewhat lesser extent, the story of Dhruv also appealed to both *saguṇī* and *nirguṇī* poets. Although complete songs about Dhruv similar to those about Prahlād are not found in *nirguṇī* collections, both these mythical devotees are frequently mentioned in them. The complete word index to the large collection of the songs of Dādū, Kabīr, Nāmadev, Raidās and Haradās, Sundaradās, and Gorakh recently published by Winand Callewaert and Bart Op de Beeck (1991) lists twenty-seven references to Prahlād (Nāmadev 9, Kabīr 7, Raidās 4, Haradās 2, Dādū 1, Sundaradās 4) and twenty-two references to Dhruv (Nāmadev 9, Kabīr 2, Raidās 2, Haradās 3, Dādū 2, Sundaradās 4). Often the two are named together.

A third possible factor has to do with the social ideology espoused by the *Bhāgavata-purāṇa,* the main source for Jan Gopāl's *nirguṇī* retellings of the stories of Prahlād, Dhruv and Jaḍ Bharat. In the context of *saguṇī* bhakti, the social ideology of the *Bhāgavata-purāṇa* is exceptionally liberal and much closer to *nirguṇī* ideology than most other *saguṇī* texts. An excellent article by Thomas J. Hopkins (1968) collects together many passages from the *Bhāgavata-purāṇa* that demonstrate this liberality. Hopkins does, however, somewhat overstate his case.[13] Although *Bhāgavata-purāṇa* does offer salvation even to Shudras, women, and Untouchables, it also strongly supports the hierarchical social ideology of *varṇāśramadharma.*

In the *Bhāgavata-purāṇa* (1971), the story of Prahlāda occupies most of book seven. This book is divided into fifteen "Discourses" and has a total of 750 verses.[14] The portion of book seven actually dedicated directly to the Prahlāda story ends at verse 47 of discourse 10, making a total of 492 verses. My critical edition of Jan Gopāl's *Prahilād charitra* is divided into eighteen sections (the division into sections varies somewhat in the different manuscripts). The base text has a total of 207 verses and the text with all interpolations added has 304¾ verses.[15] In other words, the *Bhāgavata-purāṇa* version of the story contains considerably more verses than even the interpolated text of the *Prahilād charitra*.

The *Bhāgavata-purāṇa* telling of the story of Prahlāda was, as has been noted, almost certainly the main source for Jan Gopāl's *Prahilād charitra*. The close correspondence between the content and order of the individual episodes in the narrative portions of the two texts as well as the presence of several parallel passages in the didactic sections are clear indications of Jan Gopāl's dependence on the *Bhāgavata-purāṇa*.[16]

In the case of the songs of Nāmadev, Kabīr, Raidās, Gurū Amar Dās, Rajjab, and Bhīkhā Sāhab, it is likely that their ultimate source is the *Bhāgavata-purāṇa*. The poets also borrowed from each other, however, with Nāmadev's song being the first of the series. They may also have borrowed from other, now lost, vernacular and oral sources. The narrative incidents mentioned in the songs are too few to be certain about the exact relation of the songs to the *Bhāgavata-purāṇa*, but almost all the incidents that appear in the songs also occur in the *Bhāgavata-purāṇa*. One interesting exception — found in Kabīr, Raidās, Gurū Amar Dās, and Jan Gopāl, and apparently not in *any* Sanskrit Purana — is the reference to Prahlād writing one or more names of Vishnu on his schoolboy's slate.

The many retellings of Prahlād's story in Sanskrit texts have been compared and analyzed in historical, structural and religious terms by Paul Hacker (1959), Madeleine Biardeau (1975), and Deborah A. Soifer (1991). One common denominator of all these retellings is what Sheldon Pollock (1991a, 38) has aptly called "an established constellation of mythological components: an ensuing threat of cosmic evil; the intervention of the divine and its transmutation into a preternatural form that circumvents the boon's apparent all-inclusiveness. . . ."

Where the *Bhāgavata-purāṇa, Prahilād charitra,* and *nirguṇī* song versions of the story most dramatically depart from this constellation of mythological components — and from most earlier versions of the story — is in the central role played by the paradoxical figure of Prahlād, the pious demon.[17] Earlier versions of the story mostly narrate the struggle between Hiraṇyakaśipu and the Man-lion. Several of them omit or barely mention Prahlād's role. In the *Bhāgavata-purāṇa* and the various *nirguṇī* retellings, however, it is Prahlād and not the Man-lion who becomes both the victim and the hero of the story. The Man-lion is little more than a *deus ex machina* who comes in at the end to put an end to Prahlād's suffering.[18]

According to the *Bhāgavata-purāṇa* (1971, 7.1–10), the story of Prahlāda begins with a curse made against Jaya and Vijaya, two heavenly attendants of Vishnu, by the childlike sons of Brahmā led by Sanaka. Jaya and Vijaya are cursed to become incarnate first as the demons *(asuras* or *daityas)* Hiraṇyakaśipu and Hiraṇyākṣa, then as the demons *(rākṣasas)* Rāvaṇa and Kumbhakarṇa, and finally as the Kshatriya villains Śiśupāla and Dantavaktra. Each of these figures will be killed by an avatar of Vishnu: Hiraṇyākṣa by the Boar avatar,[19] Hiraṇyakaśipu by the Man-lion avatar, Rāvaṇa and Kumbhakarṇa by Rama, and Śiśupāla and Dantavaktra by Krishna.

Hiraṇyakaśipu decides to declare war on Vishnu and his human devotees after the Boar avatar kills his brother Hiraṇyākṣa. Hiraṇyakaśipu first goes to Mount Mandhara to practice asceticism. Meanwhile Indra invades the world of the demons and carries off Hiraṇyakaśipu's pregnant wife. The sage Nārada prevents Indra from killing her and takes her to his ashram where he teaches her divine wisdom. She eventually forgets these lessons, but her unborn child also hears them and is born as a great devotee of Vishnu. This child is Prahlāda.

The power of Hiraṇyakaśipu's asceticism eventually begins to upset the universe. The gods go to Brahmā to warn him against what is happening. Brahmā goes to Hiraṇyakaśipu and offers him a boon. Hiraṇyakaśipu chooses a boon that he hopes will make him immortal and unconquerable. After Hiraṇyakaśipu returns home, Nārada returns his wife to him and Prahlāda is born.

Meanwhile, Hiraṇyakaśipu attacks the gods, occupies heaven, and takes over the palace of Indra. The gods go to Vishnu to complain, and he tells them not to worry (ibid., 7.4.28): "When the demon seeks to harm his own high-souled son, Prahlāda, . . . I shall slay him. . . ."

Hiraṇyakaśipu appoints Śaṇḍa and Marka, the two sons of his own guru Śukra, to be the teachers of Prahlāda and the other demon boys. One day Hiraṇyakaśipu places Prahlāda in his lap and asks him (ibid., 7.5.4–5): "Tell me, my child, what you regard as good." Prahlāda replies that "one should go to the woods and take refuge in Śrī Hari."

Prahlāda is returned to his two teachers with the warning that they had better see to it that he is properly instructed (ibid., 7.5.7) "so that his intellect may not be perverted by Brahmins devoted to Vishnu." Prahlāda cannot be swayed. When he is again brought before his father, Prahlāda once more praises Vishnu. This time Hiraṇyakaśipu becomes enraged and orders him killed. The demons find that their attempts to kill him are unsuccessful, however, and Prahlāda's teachers convince Hiraṇyakaśipu to give them another chance to teach Prahlāda the doctrines appropriate for a demon prince.

One day when the teachers are out, Prahlāda teaches devotion to Vishnu to his fellow students, the demon boys. They accept his teaching and ask him how he learned it. Prahlāda tell them the story of his pregnant mother's capture by Indra and her stay with the sage Nārada, a secret he had refused to tell both his two teachers and his own father.

The two teachers report Prahlāda's continuing bad behavior to Hiraṇyakaśipu, who again calls Prahlāda and asks him: "By what power have you defied my command? . . . If (Vishnu) is present everywhere, why isn't he seen in this pillar?" (ibid., 7.8.7,13). The Man-lion appears in the pillar, fights with Hiraṇyakaśipu, puts him in *his* lap (as Hiraṇyakaśipu had put Prahlāda in his lap), and splits open Hiraṇyakaśipu's heart with his claws.

After Hiraṇyakaśipu's death, the destructive energy of the Man-lion strikes fear in the hearts of the gods. Brahmā asks Prahlāda to pacify the Man-lion which he does by means of a long eulogy to the avatar. The Man-lion offers Prahlāda boons, but Prahlāda refuses all but the wish that his father Hiraṇyakaśipu be absolved of sin. The Man-lion tells Prahlāda to perform his father's funeral rites and then: "Mount your father's throne, set your mind on me, and, devoted to me, perform your acts as the followers of Brahman approve" (ibid., 7.10.23). Prahlāda does so and the Man-lion vanishes.

In terms of the actual events of the story, its retelling in the *Prahilād charitra* is mostly similar. This version does differ, however, in the omission of several minor details of the plot, the greater elaboration of the description of the tortures that Prahlād is forced to endure, the omission of much of the didactic material (long speeches by Prahlād and other major characters), and several key changes in the theological and ideological messages of the didactic passages that remain.

Common to both the *Bhāgavata-purāṇa* and *Prahilād charitra* versions of the story is a psychological parable of a conflict between father and son. If there is indeed an Indian Oedipus, Prahlād clearly has a strong claim to be he.[20] It should be noted, however, that Prahlād's mother plays only a small role in the story, although she does try to convince her son to save himself by obeying his father in the above quoted songs of Nāmadev and Gurū Amar Dās. Prahlād's only true love seems to be for Vishnu, the *good* father figure. There is also an interesting duplication of the bad father/good father roles of Hiraṇyakaśipu and Vishnu in the figures of Indra (who wants to kill Prahlād) and Nārad (who saves him).

But Prahlād is more than simply an unjustly punished son. It is also important that Prahlād is a demon, a category of beings set apart from both gods and men. As Sheldon Pollock (1991b, 68) notes, the demons of Indian mythology "offer a specific vision of the Other in traditional India." Prahlād's demon identity automatically makes him one of the Others, an outsider vis-à-vis the divine society of the gods and also from its counterpart here on earth, the human society of *varṇāśramadharma.*

Nonetheless, it is important to note that Prahlād is not a *foreign* Other in the same way that Rāvaṇa and the *rākṣasas* of the *Rāmāyaṇa* seem to be. Prahlād is the Other within the social order, not beyond it. Particularly in *nirguṇī* texts such as the *Prahilād charitra,* Prahlād clearly serves as a character with whom the members of the lower orders of Hindu society are intended to identify. This pious demon serves as a metaphor for all the downtrodden and marginalized victims of human society, for the pious and moral persons who have become the oppressed victims of the rich and powerful. It is this that makes him an ideal victim-hero for the mostly low-caste followers of *nirguṇī* tradition.

It is, of course, one thing to make such a claim and another to prove it. Prahlād's demon status is a *metaphor* for the marginalized social status of those who have listened to his story and identified with him. It is not a direct didactic statement of such an equivalence. As we have seen, however, at least one text does come close to making this equivalence explicit. This is Gurū Amar Dās' song that juxtaposes Prahlād's demon status with the low-caste status of Kabīr and Nāmadev.

Another way to unpack this metaphorical equation of demons and low-caste persons is to note the close equivalence between the relation of gods and demons, on the one hand, and high-caste and low-caste persons on the other. As gods and high-caste persons are commonly said to be noble, honest, chaste, brave, vegetarian, and clean, so demons and low-caste persons are said to be base, dishonest, libidinous, cowardly, carnivorous, and dirty.

It is also true, however, that the caste system is "replicated" within demon society. Great demons such as Rāvaṇ and Hiraṇyakaśipu are described as the kings, and presumably Kshatriyas, of demon society.[21] Prahlād's demon teachers Śukra, Śaṇḍa and Marka, on the other hand, are specifically called Brahmins. This sort of replication of the caste system within demon society does not, however, negate the more general equation that demons are to gods as low-caste persons are to high-caste persons. Indeed, the situation is closely similar to the replication of high-caste customs by low-caste persons that Louis Dumont and Michael Moffatt have described in relation to village society in South India.[22]

Also interesting in this context is the *Bhāgavata-purāṇa* story of Jaya and Vijaya that provides the "historical" background to Prahlād's story. Owing to a fault committed against the mind-born sons of the god Brahmā, the heavenly attendants Jaya and Vijaya are cursed to be reborn as first the demons Hiraṇyākṣa and Hiraṇyakaśipu, then the demons Rāvaṇa and Kumbhakarṇa, and finally as the "demonic" human Kshatriyas Śiśupāla and Dantavaktra. In other words, just as an evil deed produces bad karma that will cause a high-caste person to be born as a low-caste person, so an evil deed will cause a god to be reborn as a demon.

Finally, we can draw an analogy from an example from William Sax's anthropological study of the buffalo sacrifice in the Garhwal region of North India. In Garhwal and elsewhere in India, the buffalo sacrifice re-enacts the struggle between the buffalo demon Mahiṣāsura and the Goddess, a myth narrated in the *Devī-māhātmya* and many other texts. In locally told versions of this myth, Sax found that the tellers often referred to the "demon caste" of the buffalo. Sax concludes (1991, 128): "The myth of the buffalo demon is concerned mainly with caste relations. Not only is the buffalo explicitly said to be of low caste, but the inferior status of the lowest castes is reproduced by the buffalo sacrifice." Here as elsewhere demon status clearly serves as a metaphor for low-caste status.

This is also what makes me somewhat skeptical of Pollock's (1991b, 70) claim, made in the context of a discussion of the *Rāmāyaṇa,* that so specific a historical identification "obstructs any view of what the *rākṣasas* might signify in the imaginative world of the epic poem itself." To me it seems clear that although the metaphorical identification of Prahlād with the lower classes of Hindu society rarely becomes explicit, even in the *Prahilād charitra,* it is in fact consciously intended by the authors of both the *Bhāgavata-purāṇa* and *Prahilād charitra* and is central to the meaning of these versions of the story. In the final analysis, this is a story that refers to a real and quite specific human society, as the didactic passages that accompany the narration make abundantly explicit. Pollock's (1991b, 71) insistence that the demons "yield their richest signification" when they are regarded as "generalized imaginative representations, large symbolic responses to important human problems" seems too abstract and literary an approach, at least in the context of the story of Prahlād.

Although Pollock emphasizes the Otherness of demon society, he also points out that it is not simply "the antiworld usually associated with monsters" (74–75). The demons are the rivals of the gods, not their radical opposites. Pollock (75–82) identifies the three principal "deviations" in the character of the demons as their propensity for violence, their ambiguous and frequently metamorphizing physical nature, and their "intemperate and aggressive sexuality." On the other hand, demons such as Hiraṇyakaśipu are also capable of practising asceticism (although mainly to get boons to use against the gods), of learning the Vedas, and even of having a certain nobility of character.

As we have seen, even the division of society into *varṇas* exists in demon society. Prahlād's demon teachers Śukra and his two sons are specifically called Brahmins in both the *Bhāgavata-purāṇa* and the *Prahilād charitra*. Hiraṇyakaśipu is king of the demons, and presumably he and his son Prahlād are Kshatriyas, though neither the *Prahilād charitra* nor the *Bhāgavata-purāṇa* specifically calls them such. It is important to note, however, that the *Prahilād charitra* — and in much more ambiguous fashion the *Bhāgavata-purāṇa* — are largely written for the benefit of the lower orders of Hindu society. There is no doubt whatsoever that the audience of the Prahlād story was meant to identify with Prahlād as a victim. It is also significant, however, that Prahlād's immediate enemies and oppressors, the villains of the story, are identified as his Brahmin teachers and his own royal father. The demon Brahmins and kings represent human Brahmins and kings in their more disagreeable personae, those who unjustly appropriate an unjustified share of the status, wealth and power of society.

The story of Prahlād is a myth. Like most such texts, it serves as a vehicle for conceptualizing and expressing the key ideologies of the society in question. This is what Pollock (1991a, 41) seems to be driving at when he describes myth as follows:

> When I use the term "myth" here, I have in mind a patterned representation of the world, with continuing and vital relevance to the culture, which furnishes a sort of invariable conceptual grid upon which variable and multifarious experience can be plotted and comprehended. It is this essential power to interpret and explain reality — and I mean social reality in the first instance — that has gone largely unappreciated in previous mythic interpretations of the *Rāmāyaṇa*.

What Pollock perhaps forgets to add — but does make more explicit in his discussion of kingship in the *Rāmāyaṇa* — is that in a complex society stratified into social classes like that of India, many myths have an inherent, and often intentional, bias in favor of certain classes and against certain others. Furthermore, even allowing for such biases, different versions of the same myth can utilize the same "invariable conceptual grid" to express quite different religious doctrines and social ideologies. Such is the case with the myth of Prahlād and its retellings in the *Bhāgavata-purāṇa* and the *Prahilād charitra*.

The authors of the *Bhāgavata-purāṇa* and *Prahilād charitra* make their own religious doctrines and social ideologies most explicit in the several religious, theological, moral, and social discussions and comments found in both texts. This is particularly true of the *Bhāgavata-purāṇa* where such didactic passages both frame the story as a whole and also occur at key moments within the narration. I like to think of such passages as a sort of commercial message or advertisement that pays for the entertainment of the story itself. Similarly, the different religious and ideological messages expoused in the *Bhāgavata-purāṇa* and *Prahilād charitra* versions of the Prahlād story can be compared to a change in the sponsors of the entertainment.

One of the more curious features of the studies of Hacker, Biardeau, and Soifer is that they all almost completely ignore these didactic passages. In terms of the historical, structural, and religious analyses that these scholars attempt, such a procedure may have some justification. In terms of any attempt to analyze the full intentions of the authors of the texts, however, these passages obviously represent essential material.

A comparison of the more didactic passages in the *Bhāgavata-purāṇa* and *Prahilād charitra* versions of the Prahlād myth reveals many of the significant differences between the religious and social projects fostered by the religious movements associated with *saguṇ* and *nirguṇ* bhakti respectively. I have discussed the principal differences at length elsewhere (Lorenzen 1987a; 1987b; 1995a). Here I want to discuss mainly the issues of the choice of *nirguṇ* and *saguṇ* conceptions of the Absolute and the attitudes toward salvation for women and low-caste persons expressed in these two versions of the Prahlād myth.

To some extent the choice of *nirguṇ* and *saguṇ* conceptions of the Absolute is arbitrary, but not entirely so. As is well known, the *saguṇ* bhakti movement first became important in Tamilnadu with the devotional hymns of the Āḷvārs and Nāyanārs. Gradually it spread to Karnataka, Andhra, and Maharashtra before reaching the Ganges valley and adjoining regions of North India. The *nirguṇī* movement, on the other hand, first became important, at a considerably later date, with the *nirguṇī* followers of Rāmānanda led by Kabīr. Since the *nirguṇī* movement was created largely in opposition to the *saguṇī* movement with its *saguṇ* avatars and *paurāṇik* mythology, a logical step was to resort to a *nirguṇ* conception of the Absolute. Such a conception had in fact already been developed by Advaita philosophers led by Śaṅkarāchārya. Kabīr and his early followers were certainly not systematic philosophers, but the great prestige of Advaita metaphysics undoubted influenced their choice.

Another factor was the presence of Islam. Even though Allah retained a definable personality, Islam was strongly opposed to any anthropomorphic or iconic representations of Him. Kabīr, Dādū, Rajjab, and several other important early *nirguṇī* saints were raised in Muslim families. The question of the extent of mutual interaction between the *sant* and Sufi movements remains quite controversial, but few scholars deny that some such interaction took place.

A third factor in the choice of a nirguṇ conception of the Absolute was the possibility to use it to deny the ultimate reality of caste and class differences. If everything is grounded Brahman, and the physical world is in some basic sense illusory, then the differences between human bodies, between Brahmin and Shudra, are also finally illusory. This argument, logical enough, is in fact frequently wielded by *nirguṇī* poets and writers. Although this egalitarian corollary of the concept of Brahman appears to be congruent with the doctrines of Advaita Vedānta, Śaṅkarāchārya and his followers generally insist that this ultimate identity of all persons is valid only from the perspective of full enlightenment and should have no effect on one's behavior in the context of everyday reality (Lorenzen 1987b).

In both the *Bhāgavata-purāṇa* and *Prahilād charitra,* Prahlād largely displaces the Man-lion from the central role he plays in earlier versions of the myth, but there is little getting round the fact that God here appears in the thoroughly *saguṇ* form of an avatar. For the *Bhāgavata-purāṇa* this presents no problem. For Jan Gopāl the question is somewhat more difficult.

Like most *nirguṇī* authors, Jan Gopāl accepts the existence of the pantheon of gods including Brahmā, Vishnu, and Shiva as minor emanations of the *nirguṇ* Absolute. He generally refers to the one Divine Reality above these gods by the name "Ram" (but sometimes "Hari," "Gopāl," "Vishnu," and other terms). Although all these names are closely associated with Vaishnava tradition, the Ram or Hari of the followers of *nirguṇī* tradition is not a form or avatar of Vishnu, but the undefinable Supreme Godhead. Nirguṇī poets including Jan Gopāl also often speak of God's Name as somehow being identical with the Godhead Itself. The most impressive evocation of the impersonal *nirguṇ* Absolute in the *Prahilād charitra,* however, is a hymn of praise that describes this Absolute exclusively in terms of what it is not:[23]

No bottom no constraint, say all the saints.
No limit no defeat, say all traditions.

No end no number, say all the saints.
Unplumbed and unfathomed, they call you unreachable.

Unseen and invisible, say the gods and Śeṣ.
Undivided and uncut, say all the Vedas.

No boundary no support, they call you formless.
no movement no weight, they call you priceless.

No duality no fear, say the songs of praise.
No chant no image, they call you measureless.

No body no opening, they call you homeless.
No limbs no companion, unbroken, unbroken.

Although the supreme God of *saguṇī* tradition is also often given a transcendent character, a *via negativa* eulogy such as this would be highly out of place in a text such as the *Bhāgavata-purāṇa*. The corresponding eulogy in the *Bhāgavata-purāṇa* is much longer and covers a number of different topics. One of its central purposes, however, is to praise the embodied avatars of Vishnu, something that would be equally out of place in a *nirguṇī* text such as Jan Gopāl's.

In practical terms, the most basic difference between the *nirguṇī* and *saguṇī* devotional movements is not their metaphysics but their attitudes toward caste divisions and social hierarchy. It should also be kept in mind, however, that *both* the *nirguṇī* and *saguṇī* bhakti movements generally fostered more liberal social attitudes than those held by more orthodox Hindus, particularly the Brahmins who followed Advaita Vedānta, Mīmāmsā, and other traditional *darśanas,* as well as scholars of the Vedas, *vedāṅgas* and *dharmaśāstras.* The most important exceptions among these more orthodox Hindus were the Brahmin proponents of Viśiṣṭādvaita Vedānta and Dvaita Vedānta, many of whom played important roles in the philosophical systematization of the *saguṇī* bhakti tradition.

The attitudes of *saguṇī* bhakti poets and theologians toward caste and hierarchy are naturally quite complex and varied, given the enormous historical depth and geographical spread of the movements they led. On one question, however, most seem to have been in agreement: heartfelt devotion to the Lord will allow anyone, *even* Shudras and women, to achieve salvation. The base text of this view is the *Bhagavad-gītā,* where Krishna says (9.32): "Those who take refuge in me, Arjuna, even those who have had a sinful birth as women, Vaishyas and Shudras, will reach the supreme goal."[24] Several passages in the *Bhāgavata-purāṇa* version of the story of Prahlāda express similar sentiments. Most striking is the conclusion to Prahlāda's long speech to the demonless boys (7.7.51–55):

> O sons of the demons, neither the status of being twice-born, nor of being a god, nor of being a sage is sufficient to please Mukunda, not good behavior, nor learning, nor charity, nor asceticism, nor making offerings, nor ritual purity, nor religious vows. Hari is pleased by pure bhakti. All else is imposture. For this reason, O demons, you should practise bhakti to Lord Hari, the Lord who is the Self of all beings, by everywhere [regarding] the identity of the Self and others. For [this reason, even] Daityas, Yakṣas, Rākṣasas, women, Shudras, herdsmen, birds, wild animals, and evil persons have attained salvation. This is to be remembered as the highest goal of man: exclusive devotion to Govinda, which [means] to see him in everything.

Such passages clearly represent a much more inclusive and liberal view of the possibilities for salvation than that of more conservative thinkers such as Śaṅkarāchārya who generally limit the right (if not necessarily the capacity) for salvation to male Brahmins alone, or at most to twice-born males. Nonetheless, these passages also reveal a decidedly patronizing attitude toward women and low-caste persons: salvation can be obtained *even* by women and Shudras.

Other passages in the *Bhāgavata-purāṇa* retelling of the Prahlāda myth make it clear that the author or authors strongly support the Brahmanic ideology of *varṇāśramadharma.* Above all, the text stresses the necessity of offering respect and charity to the Brahmins. The final five discourses (11–15) of book seven of the *Bhāgavata-purāṇa* that follow the narration of Prahlāda's story mainly consist of a lengthy dialogue between Nārada and Yudhiṣṭhira on the virtues of *varṇāśramadharma.*

Jan Gopāl's *Prahilād charitra,* on the other hand, promotes the more egalitarian and generally anti-Brahmin ideology commonly found in *nirguṇī* texts. Verse three of the first section does contain a perfunctory obeisance to the four *varṇas* and the four *āśramas*, and other verses briefly pay respect to the Vedas, cows, and Brahmins. More typical, however, are statements such as Jan Gopāl's final comment when Indra asks Nārad how it came to pass that the great devotee Prahlād is to be born in a family of demons: "The Brahmin [or "Brahmā"] and the low-born are of one essence. Gold cannot become something different. Jan Gopāl says: For the Lord of the World, family (status) has no meaning."[25] The final verses of Prahlād's speech to the demon boys make the same claim from the point of view of the devotee:[26]

> For service to Hari, nothing is needed. When one has offered [this service], one obtains food, wealth, and clothes. Material things are not needed for service. Love of devotion alone gives sustenance. No other god has authority. Kshatriya, Vaishya, Shudra and women: for devotion to Rām all have authority. Everyone from Brahmin to Untouchable should think about this. If one sings the virtues of Hari with love, one will get that most difficult to obtain goal.

Here the words bear a definite resemblance to the parallel passage in the *Bhāgavata-purāṇa*, and also to the famous *Bhagavad-gītā* passage, but the patronizing word "even" is missing. All the varṇas are, in fact, treated equally.

In many respects this comparison of the retellings of the Prahlād myth in the *Prahilād charitra* and the *Bhāgavata-purāṇa* represents an extreme test of the hypothesis that *saguṇī* and *nirguṇī* traditions differ significantly both in terms of theology and social ideology. On the one side we have a *nirguṇī* author whose choice of this story and whose religious and caste background suggest that his commitment to *nirguṇī* tradition was somewhat equivocal. On the other side we have a classic *saguṇī* text that is noted for its liberal social attitudes and was evidently the principal source for Jan Gopāl's telling of the story. Nonetheless, as I have tried to show here, the authors of these two texts differ markedly with respect to the way in which they conceptualize the Godhead, in their attitude toward the possibility of salvation for low-caste people and women (although both accept this possibility), and in their attitude toward the hierarchical social ideology of *varṇāśramadharma*. These differences are, I think, illustrative of a whole range of theological and ideological oppositions between the *nirguṇī* and *saguṇī* traditions that ultimately reflect the different religious, social and psychological needs of the persons who belong to these movements, on the one hand, and those who direct and control them on the other.

Appendix

Prahlād charitra attributed to Raidās. It is transcribed from Rājasthān Prāchyavidyā Pratiṣṭhān (Jodhpur) manuscript no. 1882, folios 69–70. This is roughly the same as Callewaert and Friedlander 1992, 224–25.

राग धनसी ॥ अथ प्रहलाद चरित लिष्यते ॥
पूर म(?)ढ(?)न [27] मुलतांन तहां हिरनांकुस राजा ।
पुत्र भये प्रहलाद सरै सबहि।न के काजा ॥
जोसी जाय र पूछी यौ भये सुत राज
कुमार या बालक सम को नहीं ऐ असुर सिंघारन काज ॥ 1 ॥
कै धौं रै प्रहलाद कहा गुन तू पढ्यौ ॥ टेक ॥
पढ्यौ रांम कौ नांम आंन हिरदै नहि आंनौं
र रौ म मौ दोय आंक और तीजौ नहिं जांनौं ॥
कहा पढावै बावरे और सकल जंजाल ॥
भौ सागर जम लोक मै मोहि कौंन उतारै पार ॥ 2 ॥
राम गुण मैं पढ्यौ ॥ टेक ॥
सुनि राजा परजरयौ रोस मन मैं अति कीनौं ॥
मेरौ बैरी रांम सो तैं हिरदै धरि लीनौं ॥
ए पढिबौ तू छाडि दै रे कह्यौ हमारौ मांनि ॥
टूक टूक करि डारि हौं रे जब र सुनौं हरि कांनि ॥ 3 ॥
जौ बरजै सौ बार कह्यौ तेरौ नहि मांनौं ॥
छांडि सिंघ की सरन गीध कै गवनिन(?) लागौ ॥
पूरन ब्रह्म सकल मई जा कौ ऐ । बिसतार ॥
जा कै रांम सहाय हैं ताहि कौंन सकगौ(?) मारि ॥ 4 ॥

सभा लई बुलाइ कहौ धौं कहा बिचारौ ॥
लै देषौ परतीति जाय गिर वर तैं डा।रौ ॥
सकल सभा मिलि लै चले लै गये सैल चढाय ।
पंछी हू की गम नहीं तहां दीयौ छिटकाय ॥ 5 ॥
जब पिरथी आधीन दीन होय दुरसन आई ॥
मस्तक चरन छुवाई लीये हिरदा सौं लाई ॥
कहा भगत कौं त्रास है आदि अंति नहिं और ॥
अब कै सेवा चूकि हौं तौ नहि तीन लोक मैं ठौर । 6 ॥
हसत हसत प्रहलाद पढन जब साल पधारै ॥
उचरत रं रं कार सकल तजि सव परहारे ॥
परषि लेत परचौ भयौ मु(?)नि उपज्यौ बिसवास ।
सकल सभा आनंद मई इक राजा फिरत उदास ॥ 7 ॥
असुर भयौ मति हीन जाय लै पावक दीनौ ॥
अंगि ज्वाला परजरी तहां द्रिढ आसन कीनौ ॥
सकल देव रिछ्या करैं पावक निकट न जाय ॥
पठयौ सीत सहाय कौं(?) मांनौ मीन मकर मैं न्हाय ॥ 8 ॥
ना जांणौ कछु जंतर मतर नट नाटिक कीनौं
अज हूं न समझत अंध जाय लै कूपै दीनौं ॥
सुर नर मुनि जन जांनहीं ध्रु(?)व नारद सै साषि ।
जा कै रांम सहाय है रे ताहि कौं हौ लै राषि ॥ 9 ॥
प्रफुलित है प्रहलाद मंदिर मांहीं जब आये ॥
षोजत षोजत असुर जाय प्रहलाद संताये ॥
तो कौं राषै जो कहां अब र छाडि हूं नांहि ।
कोमल बचन कुंवर जब बो(?)ल्यो मो पति षंभा मांढि(?हि) ॥ 10 ॥

रे मो मृत अब हू न आय षडग बांण नहिं भेदै ॥
जल ज्वाला मैं मरौं जुध कोउ जिंद न छेदै ॥
छाया माया नां मरौं नां मरौं धरनि अकास ॥
मति व्रह्मा की कहा कहै रे सोचत त्रिभवन नाथ ॥ 11 ॥
रे ऐ तौ कहा है गरब राम है गरब प्रहारे ॥
सब देव तुम से बलि हिरणाछि आदि बराहा सिंघारे ॥
सब देवन कौ देव है सब ईसन कौं ईस ॥
मो मै तो मैं षडग षंभ मैं पूरि रह्यौ जगदीस ॥ 12 ॥
कर गहि लीनौं षडग कोपि सनमुष भयौ ठाट(?)ौ ॥
देषौ जै है भगि षंभ सौं कीनौं गाढ(?)ौ ॥
बार बार तो सौं कहौं एह अंदेसौ मोहि ॥
जे षंभ मैं राम है । तौ क्यौं न छुडावै तोहि ॥ 13 ॥
असत भयौ है भांन उदौ रजनी जब कीनौं ॥
अधर बिंब कि छांह उठाय जंघन परि लीनौं ।
नष सुं उदर बिंदारियौ तिलक दीयौ प्रहलाद ॥
सप्त दीप नव षंड मैं भई तीन लोक मैं गाज ॥ 14 ॥
जहां जहां संकट परे संत के कारज सारे ।
हम से अधम उधारि कीये नरकन सौं न्यारे ॥
सुर नर मुनि गंध्रब रटैं सब कौ सुष निवास
मनसा वाचा करमना ए गावै जन रैदास ॥ 15 ॥

2

Jan Gopāl's *The Deeds of Prahlād*

Very little biographical information about Jan Gopāl has survived. The principal source for such information is Rāghavadās' *Bhaktamāl* (1969, 715–17, 777), a work probably written in about A.D. 1720. It contains three stanzas about Jan Gopāl and two about his disciples. Apart from a few brief autobiographical references in his biography of Dādū Dayāl (Jan Gopāl 1988), Jan Gopāl's works apparently contain no direct information about his own life.

Rāghavadās's first stanza notes that Jan Gopāl was a direct disciple of Dādū Dayāl and states that Jan Gopāl "spread the fame of the devotees" through his literary works including the *Dhruv charitra, Prahlād charitra, Jaḍ Bharat charitra, Datta guru chaubīs līlā,* and the *Moh vivek saṃvād*. This stanza also claims that Jan Gopāl sang Dādū's praises — a reference to his *Dādū janma līlā* — and wrote "genuine *pads*." Finally it says that Jan Gopāl followed the bhakti of love *(prem)* and rescued *(nistaryo)* the Vaishyas. The second stanza praises Jan Gopāl's compositions — without naming them — and states that he "bowed his head to the Lord of the World (Jagadīs) time and again." The third stanza says that he had first wandered about begging as a sannyasi without gaining enlightenment. Then he met Dādū in the city of (Fatehpur) Sikri. Jan Gopāl was pleased by Dādū's darshan and began to "dwell in the Name." He wrote the *Prahlād charitra, Dhruv charitra* and *Jaḍ Bharat charitra,* which pleased the devotees.

Rāghavadās's two stanzas on Jan Gopāl's disciples seem to state that there were four of them: Chain, Nārāyaṇadās, one perhaps named Haribhakta, and Nārāyaṇadās Rāṃkāvaṃś. It is possible that the two Nārāyaṇadāses are the same. The first Nārāyaṇadās had his monastic seat *(gaddī)* at Rāhorī (Jaipur). Chain had his seat at Kāṃṇotā (Jaipur) where he "composed *bhajans*" that "enchanted everyone." The third disciple is said to have stayed in Marwar where he served Paramānanda. The seat of the second Nārārayaṇadās, assuming him to be separate, is not mentioned, but he is said to be the guru of Kītāvat Paramānanda and several other sadhus.

The modern Dādū Panthī scholar Nārāyaṇadās of Ajmer (1979, 2:71–75) adds to this that Jan Gopāl met Dādū when Dādū was leaving Sikri with Rājā Bīrabal to visit the emperor Akbar. Jan Gopāl is said to have been travelling with a sadhu *(bheṣadhārī)* for twelve years (since birth?). Dādū realized that Jan Gopāl would never become enlightened if he stayed with the sadhu. Jan Gopāl read the sign in Dādū's eyes and received teaching from him. Then and there Jan Gopal decided to abandon his sadhu guru and follow Dādū. Jan Gopāl eventually made his monastic seat at Rāhorī (Jaipur).

Nārāyaṇadās of Ajmer (ibid., 76) names fifteen compositions by Jan Gopāl. In addition to those already mentioned, he includes a *Bārahamāsā, Kāyāprāṇ saṃvād, Chitāvanī grantha,* thirteen *savaiyās, Vipramatā grantha,* ninety-seven *pads* in various rāgs, various *sākhīs, Ananta līlā,* and a *Śuk saṃvād.*

The only complete work of Jan Gopāl to have been published so far is his biography of Dādū Dayāl, the *Dādū janma līlā.* It was edited by Sukh Dayāl Dādū in 1947 and has recently been critically edited and translated into English by Winand Callewaert (Jan Gopāl 1988. See also Thiel-Horstmann 1983). A number of Jan Gopāl's pads are found in Rajjab's *Sarabaṅgī* (1990) and Gopāladās' *Sarvāṅgī* (1993), two medieval anthologies that have been published recently. Manuscripts of many of Jan Gopāl's still unpublished works are found in the manuscript libraries of Jaipur and Jodhpur, principally those of the Jaipur City Palace museum, the Rājasthān Prāchyavidyā Pratiṣṭhān libraries in Jaipur and Jodhpur, and the Rājasthānī Sodh Saṃsthān library in Jodhpur.

Judging from the number of manuscripts of his compositions listed in the catalogues of these institutions, Jan Gopāl was evidently a quite popular author in Rajasthan in the seventeenth, eighteenth and nineteenth centuries. His compositions that appear most frequently in these manuscripts are the *Dhruv charitra, Prahilād caritra, Dādū janma līlā,* and *Jaḍ Bharat charitra.*

The edition and translation of Jan Gopāl's *Prahilād charitra* that follow are based on texts in twelve different manuscripts: ten found in the the above mentioned Rajasthani libraries, one from the Dādū Panthī monastery at Naraina, and one from the Hindī Sāhitya Sammelan library in Allahabad. I would like to thank the directors of all these institutions for their cooperation and help in permitting me to examine and photograph the manuscripts.

The text I prepared on the basis of these twelve manuscripts is a critical edition, which means that it is a composite text that does not consistently correspond to any given manuscript. I have adopted this procedure with some misgivings. In my previous work on Anantadās' *Kabīr parachaī* (Lorenzen 1991), I instead chose to prepare a "corrected edition" that depended primarily on one manuscript and only deviated from it when most of the other manuscripts consulted departed from the readings given in it. With texts that are so inconsistent in terms of grammatical forms and orthography as those found in manuscripts of medieval *sant* literature, this corrected edition strategy is, I think, usually the most sensible procedure to follow.

Nonetheless, in the present case no one manuscript had consistently good readings, and I was left with little choice but to create a new text based on a "consensus" of the consulted manuscripts. In cases where this consensus was difficult to establish, I preferred the readings given in the older manuscripts, especially manuscripts A, B and C. The problem with this consensus strategy is that it creates a synthetic text that eliminates the grammatical and orthographic consistencies that are likely to be found in each individual manuscript. As a result grammatical, metrical, and dialectical information of interest to linguists is inevitably lost.

In both the translation and critical edition of Jan Gopāl's text, verses and half verses that are not found in a majority of the manuscripts and that probably represent interpolations have been indented, a convention I have borrowed from W. Callewaert. The footnotes of the critical edition do not normally register minor differences in orthography. After each Hindi verse or line, the manuscripts that include the text are indicated by letter. Letters in parentheses indicate the manuscripts which probably include the text, but my photo of the page is missing.

The manuscripts used for this edition of Jan Gopāl's *Prahilād charitra* are as follows:

A. RPP (Rājasthān Prāchyavidyā Pratiṣṭhān) (Jodhpur) manuscript no. 11583, dated 1693 V.S. (1636 C.E.). This manuscript probably belongs to Dadu Panth (see Lorenzen 1991, 86–87).

B. RPP (Jaipur) manuscript no. 16 (pp. 178–80) from the Vidyā Bhūṣaṇ collection, dated 1718 V.S. (1661 C.E.). Its text of the *Prahilād charitra* is incomplete.

C. JCP (Jaipur City Palace) manuscript no. 3666 (pp. 1–24), dated 1732 V.S. (1675 C.E.).

D. JCP manuscript no. 3657 (pp. 1–14), dated 1811 V.S./ 1676 Śaka (1754 C.E.).

E. JCP manuscript no. 1334 (pp. 1–15), dated 1821 V.S./ 1686 Śaka (1764 C.E.).

F. An uncataloged extra big size manuscript kept in the monastery of the Dadu Panth at Naraina, Rajasthan. It is dated 1833 V.S. (1776 C.E.).

G. RPP (Jaipur) manuscript no. 2187 (pp. 152–68), dated 1846 V.S. (1789 C.E.).

H. RPP (Jaipur) manuscript no. 2165 (pp. 797–807), dated 1876 V.S. (1819 C.E.).

I. RPP (Jaipur) manuscript no. 74 from the Vidyā Bhūṣaṇ collection, not dated. The catalog estimates it to belong to eighteenth century V.S.

J. JCP manuscript no. 904 (pp. 83–98), not dated. It may belong to the nineteenth century V.S.

K. RPP (Jodhpur) manuscript no. 14741 (pp. 230–53), not dated. The catalog dates it in the nineteenth century V.S.

L. HSS (Hindī Sāhitya Sammelan, Allahabad) manuscript no. 1900, not dated. It belongs to the Shahapura branch of the Rām-snehī Panth (see Lorenzen 1991, 85–86).

Manuscripts H and L are closely related and contain many verses not found in other manuscripts. Manuscripts D and E are also closely related. Manuscripts C and K contain a few verses not found in other manuscripts.

The Deeds of Prahlād

translated by
David Lorenzen and Shukdeo Singh

Section One

First I bow my head to Hari and the Guru. With their permission, I will tell [Prahlād's] story. I will study it, meditate on it, and spread the fame of the Lord's devotee.

Corresponding to the four yugas, the Veda has four parts:*Rg, Yajur, Sāma,* and *Atharva.* Through the fifty-two syllables, the sound OM becomes manifest as the three worlds.

There are four *varṇas* and four *āśramas.* Their many aspects have [often] been described. One person may dedicate himself to yoga, another to the world. Another sets his mind on pilgrimages and religious vows.

Another says that charity and virtue are best. Another says that one should save the soul. The Hindus and the Turks proclaim two separate paths. If one meets the True Guru, the two become one.

Without devotion to Ram, Ram remains apart. People's everyday concerns are about this and that. No one knows the true nature of the Lord until He bestows His favor.

Is the Thought-jewel sold for money? Does the Wishing-tree grow in one's yard? Tell me, who doesn't want the Philosopher's stone? Who feeds the Wishing-cow?

One doesn't find Ram merely by proper conduct unless one dedicates oneself to Him in word, mind and deed. This is what the saints teach. This is what the gods Śaṅkar, Brahmā and Śeṣ teach.

dohā:
I cannot count all the saints that have appeared since the beginning of time, but I will describe the famous deeds of Prahlād, thinks Jan Gopāl.

Section Two

> *chaupaī:*
> When Sanak and the others gave their curse, Hiraṇyakaśipu and Hiraṇyākṣa were created. The former had four mighty sons, and Prahlād was the foremost among them.

Brahmā had four sons: Sanak and his brothers. They were born from his mind and had authority. They forever remain as if they were five years old. Naked and carefree, they sing Govinda's virtues.

In the morning Śeṣ tells them stories. At noon they go to the world of mortals. In the evening they enter the city Vaikuṇṭha. In this fashion, Sanak and his brothers move about.

As a cow loves its calf, as a child runs crying to its mother, as a thirsty persons wants to drink water, so the hope of God's darshan grew [in their hearts].

When they put their feet on the threshold, the two watchmen got up and stopped them: "Ask before entering another's house. If the Master gets angry, what excuse can we give Him?"

> Sanak and his brothers said: "We know this. But He knows us well. In God's presence we are always welcome. We can't be accused of being strangers. You have become filled with arrogance.

"Arrogance has no place here. You will become demons and move about on earth."

As soon as Sanak and his brothers gave this curse, [the watchmen] were made to do [this as the demons] Hiraṇyaka and Hiraṇyākṣa.

But the watchmen Jay and Vijay first said: "Listen, sirs. When will we meet [God and be saved]?"

"It won't be long. If you worship Him, then it will be after seven births. If you oppose Him, however, it will be after only three births.

"Often a friend forgets a friend, but an enemy sticks in one's heart. One can touch fire either knowingly or unknowingly. One may have a darshan of Brahman through either good sentiments or bad ones.

> "Go and meditate on Him with love if you like. Otherwise resolve to oppose Him."

Those two warriors were mighty and powerful. They had no equals in all the three worlds. For ten thousand years they went searching. No one could equal them in battle.

In anger [Hiraṇyākṣa] pressed down the Earth under their feet. The Earth trembled and cried out: "Save me! Save me!"

At that moment the Creator of creation, the very mighty [Vishnu], made a boar for the sake of His devotees.

[The boar] killed Hiraṇyākṣa and made the Earth firm once again. Then the evil Hiraṇyakaśipu got angry: "Hari is my enemy. Hari's servants are my enemies. I shall spread fear and wipe out the sentiment of devotion."

> The curse that Sanak and his brothers gave created Hiraṇyakaśipu and Hiraṇyākṣa. The former had four mighty sons, and Prahlād was foremost among them.
>
> Hiraṇyakaśipu overpowered the world of mortals and then went to Indra's city. Afraid of the demon, the gods ran away and arrived at Vishnu's world.
>
> The gods said: "Listen, King of the three worlds. From fear of the demon, we have come to you for refuge. Protect us and be our guardian! We have been humbled. Show us compassion!"
>
> Then Vishnu performed a trick, but no one caught on to it. Famous saints and tradition tell how he killed the demon and gave refuge to the gods.

When the gods and the demons became enemies, Hiraṇyakaśipu went to practise asceticism. At that time Indra, the king of the gods, went and attacked the demons' city. The demons' women were tied up and taken away.

Then the sage Nārad appeared before Indra, who showed him great respect. Hari's devotees are called "lovers of the downtrodden." They are pained by others' pain.

Nārad said: "O foremost king of the gods, tell me. How did you [dare to] burn the unprotected city?

"If a man does something to another man, it is considered acceptable. You, however, have done something contemptible. Have you no shame?"

Nārad said: "Listen, king of the gods. You have done something contemptible. Aren't you ashamed?"

Indra said: "Listen now, sir. I killed the children, not the women."

The sage Nārad thought about this. He understood devotion and considered what could be done to help.

Then Nārad played his *vīnā* and sang Hari's virtues. [In this way] he charmed the [unborn] Prahlād's mind. Nārad told him the words of the saving mantra. He did this kindness and no one knew it.

Nārad gave Prahlād teachings pleasing to himself. Then he spoke again to Indra.

Nārad said: "Come here, Indra, and listen. There is a devotee in this woman's womb.

"This queen is in your care. Offer her whatever service you can."

The king of the gods said: "You have said this, O devotee of Hari, but I cannot believe you."

Indra said: "How can such a devotee be born in a demon's family?"

Indra said: "There isn't any place for such a devotee in the four *varṇas*. Why would a devotee of Hari appear in a demon's family?"

When the king of gods asked this, the sage replied: "Listen, brother."

Then Nārad said: "Listen, king of the gods. No one is high or low to Hari, the Lord of the three worlds. One is called high or low according to his conduct. Hari's devotees worship Hari and become one with Him.

"If one gives poison to high and low persons, they will both die when they eat it. Likewise, if high and low persons sit together in a boat, they both will cross to the other shore.

Thus there is no special cause [to determine who is born] in Hari's family. Both Untouchables and Brahmins should worship Him as their savior. Moreover, no body is high or low. All bodies are made from the same five elements."

Nārad said: "By some mistake, he has appeared in a demon's family. The creator caused this chance of fate. His name will be Prahlād and he will become Nārāyaṇ's formost servant."

dohā:
The Brahmin and the Untouchable share a single essence. Gold is not different [no matter what shape it takes]. Jan Gopāl says: For the Lord of the universe, one's family is irrelevant.

Section Three

Nārad describes the characteristics of the saints:
chaupaī:
"They have a pacific character. They are kind and not aggressive. They possess knowledge and wisdom. They are incorporeal and without delusion. They distinguish what is essential from what is not. They regard both friends and enemies impartially.

"They give happiness to cows, Brahmins, and saints. They join the individual soul to the Supreme soul. Other's sadness makes them sad and others' happiness makes them happy. It is for these reasons they are called Hari's devotees.

"Offer them service in whatever way you can. The gods will be your protectors."

Then Nārad bid fairwell to Indra and made a circumambulation. [Before he left] Indra made a big request.

Indra said: "Don't return her. Take her away with you. For the sake of devotion, protect her at your place.

I am well disposed to devotion. You take her away. I am your servant. Do me this favor."

Then Prahlād's mother stayed at the sage's place while her dear son developed in her womb.

There, Nārad gave many sermons. For Prahlād's sake, he preached to the mother. No awareness entered the mother's heart, but the son memorized what he heard.

Too much water makes a plant wither. Similarly, she became ashamed because of having to give birth in another's house.

"What stroke of fate has caused this chance? Has some sin of mine come to fruition?"

Nārad said: "Listen, my dear daughter. After your son is born, you can return to your own house."

The sage was pleased and gave her his blessing. The mother accepted his blessing.

Elsewhere, Hiraṇyakaśipu strengthened his asceticism. He crushed his senses, his body, his mind, and his egoism. He began a great *uradh* penance in which he supported himself on his toes.

All the gods became terrified. Then they went and spoke to Brahmā.

The demon performed fierce penance and desiccated his body. Then the troop of gods spoke [to Brahmā]:

"Give us our own place, o Brahmā, or else we will have to do whatever Hiraṇyakaśipu says.

"This foremost [demon] has accumulated great ascetic power. The whole city of the gods is trembling."

Then Brahmā considered the problem. He and the gods went the the demon's door. Brahmā set out from heaven and went directly to earth to give a boon [to the demon].

Pleased [with the demon's penance], Brahmā thought: "I will give the demon any boon he requests. Brahmā went and poured a pitcher of water over the demon's body. He broke the demon's trance and spoke.

The demon did penance for a hundred years. Brahmā was pleased and gave him a boon.

Brahmā said: "What do you want, demon? For what boon are you burning your body?"

When Brahmā said this, the demon was overjoyed.

Hiraṇyakaśipu said: "Make me invincible by fire, water, and poison, invincible at night and during the day, invincible both inside and outside any house.

"No enemy will ever be a threat to me. Give me this boon with no conditions.

"Make my death impossible in any such situation: not by man nor lion, not in heaven, nor hell, nor on earth, not by magic nor by any warrior in battle.

"I must never die anywhere in Brahmā's creation." Then Brahmā said: "So be it."

The demon did penance for a hundred years of the gods. Brahmā became pleased and gave him a boon. Hiraṇyakaśipu was overjoyed. He wasn't aware of his future fate.

Then Hiraṇyakaśipu went home. Meanwhile the sage set off for there with Prahlād's mother. She arrived just when the baby was due. Prahlād was born [then and there].

As he was born, drums sounded in heaven. Gods and men all prepared *āratī*. All the saints were filled with bliss. Govinda was the Inner-controller.

Prahlād's devotion was kept [hidden] for one year, then two, three, four, and five years.

> Then he remembered the wisdom he had learned while still in the womb. His mind was opened, and he began to worship Ram. He gained courage and took to the great code of conduct. He thought about dharma, compassion, and knowledge.
>
> The karma he earned in the past became manifest. The heap of bliss that is God's Name appeared. He swung in joy, absorbed in love. From head to foot, he forgot his body's woes.

With the help of the saints, everything is possible. Through the grace of the guru, everyone can cross to the other shore.

dohā:
At the age of five, Prahlād, the demon's son, became a saint. Jan Gopāl says: Hiraṇyakaśipu did not understand [what had happened]. He was absorbed in enjoying the child's play.

Section Four

Hiraṇyakaśipu summoned the sage Śukra: "Prahlād's success or failure [to be educated] is in your hands. Teach him about all about politics. Tell him about the special dharma of our family."

Śukra determined the best day and moment to begin. Then he properly informed the king. At the appointed moment, musical instruments were played. In every house an auspicious *kalaś* pot was displayed.

The boys came to school for their education. They worshipped Sarasvatī and Gaṇeś and made all sorts of offerings. Prahlād, however, paid no attention to any of this.

Then Śukra[1] said: "Listen, prince. Study, think about, and understand proper conduct." He gave Prahlād a slate on which he wrote: *Oṃ namaḥ siddhāya*. Hand in hand with Prahlād, Śukra taught the lesson.

Prahlād said: "I only know how to write *ra rau ma mau*.[2] I won't accept anything else told or heard."

The [demon teachers] Śaṇḍa and Marka said: "Read, boy, so that the king will be happy."

Prahlād said: "I know the only King. Why should I speak lies? It is He who created the sound *Oṃ*, and He who drew out the whole universe from the five elements.

"It is He who created the four forms and the 84 *[lakhs]* of births; He who created heaven, hell, and the living souls that dwell in the three worlds; He who created men, women, poison, and immortal nectar. Without the true Guru, no one can know this.

"It is He who created the universe and its many worlds and parts. Look at the deeds of that King. Recite only the texts that please that King. There is no point to recite other texts."

> This is what Prahlād told them. Then the Brahmins *[vipra]* grew wary: "What other tactic can we use [to make him obey]?"

The Brahmins went off to eat and bathe. Then the other children urged [Prahlād to speak].

> His classmates said: "We want to ask you something since our gurus have gone for their baths.

"Tell us, Prahlād, what you have to say. We are all your friends.

"Which text do you think is best? Tell us what you feel in your heart.

> "We are asking you what you have to say. Tell us, master, we are poor and have no guide.
>
> "Brother, to deceive a friend is the worst fault possible. The Vedas and the Purāṇas tell us this. Be kind to us and tell us words of wisdom. Explain how our thoughts can become good."

Prahlād said: "Listen, children. Living souls spend much time in the cycle of birth and death. I know the great device by which birth and death are overcome.

> "Resort to the device of worshipping Ram. Free yourself from the snare of time. Time is the snare that traps the world. Without the eye of knowledge you will get trapped like a blind man.

"If you bring fire and blow air on it, the living soul will get burned and not be happy.

"If you fall into a dark well, how will you be able to cross the ocean of existence?

"You are trying to get immortal fruit from a poison vine. You eat the poison fruit and expect to win immortality. How can you cross the ocean in an iron boat loaded with the stones of sin?

"How can you happily sleep in a house that's on fire? How can you find coolness there? How can you arrive in the west by going east? How can you find the path if you have no eyes?

"You are getting trapped by the flavor of sexual play with lusty women. Why do you suffer in a world filled with sins? Sons and families are traps of sin. Your body, wealth and youth won't endure. They will go.

"Shouldn't you take medicine, brothers, before you get sick? When your house is already burning, you decide to dig a well. Superior persons are laughing at you, brothers.

"If you don't let your feet get muddy, why will you need to wash them? Pain and pleasure enter the world together with the material elements like earth and water. Without the water of knowledge they cannot be removed.

[. . .][3]
"If you can avoid falling in love with the first taste of this world, then you won't get tied to it, nor involve others in it.

"As long as your feet are not shackled, you should search for the path. You should flee, young princes, while the guards are not present.[4]

"Leave everything and go off to the forest. Join the saints and sing Hari's virtues. Don't be frightened by the [king's] warriors. Worship the Name Ram without fear.

"Think about knowledge, devotion, and detachment. This is how you can save yourselves. You won't get this body again. Why not find your proper place in this birth?"

dohā:

> The devotee Prahlād gave all these good teachings for their welfare.
> The was the foremost saint and seeker. He told them well.

"I will not abandon the Name Ram even if our gurus get the blame."

Jan Gopāl says: Prahlād spoke these thoughtful words to his companions.

Section Five

chaupaī:

Sometimes Prahlād went to his father's house. The king sat him in his lap. He kissed his face and embraced him: "Tell me, son, about what you've been doing.

"Tell me about the good wisdom you have learned. Don't keep anything from me. I will immediately give you anything you ask for. There is no limit to what you can demand from me."

Prahlād said: "One should listen, do *kīrtan,* and remember Him. One should serve His feet and offer Him your mind and body. One should praise Him and consider oneself His slave. Through firm faith, one will be called His friend.

"One should offer one's Soul to Him. One should offer Him one's love through the nine types of devotion. Wisdom is that by which one recognizes Brahman. All other things are simply ignorance and material illusions.

"As long as one doesn't forget the concepts of 'I' and 'mine,' how can a corporeal being find happiness? The whole world is trapped by 'I' and 'mine.' The saints abandon all else and move about in Ram alone.

> "Oblations, sacrifices, vows, offerings, charity: you should leave aside these sorts of things, O mighty king. Why, father, do you act in this way? Leave all this and worship Ram's company.
>
> "Without the Lord, there can be no joy in this house. All living souls have got lost in error. Fallen into error, they have forgotten the Lord. They waste their birth believing what is false to be true.

"Iron and gold are both a snare. Whoever does what is good sees this. Gods, men and demons all regard poison as if it were bliss. But only animals and birds get bliss in this way.

"The rope that one imagines to be a snake has swallowed the whole world. The world has been fooled by a dream. Everyone is running after the water of a mirage. In this way living souls are tied to esteem for their bodies.

"Take the example of the parrot and the [tasty-looking but inedible] pods of the silk-cotton tree. Like the parrot, living souls are trapped without really being trapped. If you abandon all attachments, what can trap you? Consider ignorance to be a sin and offer devotion.

"In the hundred years of a person's life, fifty are lost in sleep. Twelve years are lost in childhood [and most of the rest are lost] in household affairs and sensual amusements. It is through worshipping Ram that the temporal world is forgotten.

> "You are the best scholar of the Vedas and Agamas. But why are you studying these other things without [offering worship] to Hari? True wisdom is worshipping Ram with devotion. Leave aside all other actions.
>
> "If one dives into vile and petty actions, how can one expect this to lead to good consequences? This will never produce good consequences. One makes a lot of effort and falls into error.
>
> "One should abandon all else and worship Ram. Then one's work will always get completed. When one lets poison defects enter the body, the means to worship Ram will never be acquired.
>
> "One will not get a body like this again and again. When the chance is lost, one will be forced to repent. For this reason the opportunity is now. The guru has been kind and explained this [all to me].

"When doubts are resolved, wisdom appears. Then who will chase after ignorance? I believe that wisdom *is* devotion. Without devotion one knows only lies.

"One will get wisdom only after looking and understanding. No one will cross to the other shore without meditating on Hari.

"I express these thoughts to you after hearing the testimony of the sage Nārad. No other teachings can satisfy me." Having heard Prahlād's words, the demon was filled with remorse [at what had happened to his son].

dohā:
The temporal world is like falling into a dream. As long as one stays asleep it is true. Jan Gopāl says: Worship Hari and wake up. Save yourself from the errors of your dreams.

Section Six

chaupaī:
When he heard what Prahlād had to say, the demon was shocked. He summoned all his ministers and demanded: "Who taught Prahlād this doctrine?

"Prahlād is steadfastly meditating on my enemy, the enemy who killed my brother Hiraṇyākṣa. Prahlād is offering service to cows, Brahmins, sages, the Vedas, the gods, and Vishnu.

"I placed my confidence in his teachers, but you have ruined my son and done me an injustice. Take him right now and teach him properly. Otherwise you will not be allowed to live."

The enraged demon then spoke these words: "Know it to be true [that I will live] without Prahlād [if nothing can be done]."[5]

The Brahmins took Prahlād and taught him [the political strategies of] pacification, aggression, and creating dissension.

Then the teachers wrote the letters *"ka, kha, ga, gha, ṅa."* They said: "Recite these other syllables, brother."

Prahlād said: "This sort of false learning is not pleasing to me. My knowledge was acquired in the womb.[6]

"Listen, pandits. I recite only two letters. I reject all the fifty letters except for those of Hari's Name."

The Brahmins said: "Your father has conquered the whole universe. The Vedas, Brahmins, and the gods all fear his injustice. Why are you causing us so much trouble. A good person does what he is supposed to do."

Prahlād said: "No one is causing you trouble. Vishnu protects us in the fire of the womb. He gives you milk to drink when you raise your mouth in the womb. After, you come out and are born.

"If Ram saves you, who can kill you? If Ram kills you, who can save you? Life and death are in his hands. You and I, the whole universe, is under his control.

> "Think about God in this way. Be pure and offer Him your whole mind and body.

"Who will talk to you time and again? Who will give up nectar to taste poison?"

All the children made a request: "How can we be saved?"

> In this way they offered praise to Prahlād. Then Prahlād showed them compassion.

Prahlād said: "Listen to my words, O demon princes. Nārad's discourse has the authority of the Vedas. [Ideas like] "I," "you," and "mine" [are the things that create] the temporal world. Thoughts about Brahman are devoid of such ideas."

"Lust, anger, confusion, frenzy, and envy: if you conquer these, you will find the supreme, indestructible [Brahman].

> "O friends, abandon all [the things of this world] and consider; keep your minds fixed on the supreme Brahman, the sole stream."

The children said: "Listen, Prahlād. Where did you have a dialogue with the sage Nārad?

"You didn't go to him, and he didn't come here. Resolve our doubts about this.

"We have no protector. We are asking you, dear sir. Tell us about devotion to Hari so that our doubts flee from us and our minds become fixed on His lotus feet.

Prahlād showed kindness to them and taught them, saying things that drove away all his companions' worries.

Then he told them an ancient story: "Once my father went away to practice asceticism.

"While he was gone, the king of the gods attacked and destroyed the demon's city, burning it to the ground. My mother became a prisoner of the king of the gods. I was with her as an embryo embodied in her womb.

"[In this condition], I managed to have a darshan of the sage Nārad, who gave much advice to the king of the gods.

"Nārad said: 'Listen, Indra. Don't bear enmity against this child.

"'This child is Hari's servant. He has the light of knowledge of Brahman.'

"The king of the gods said: 'I will have nothing to do with this. Take her away, O sage, to your own place.'

"Then the sage took my mother away with him and imparted knowledge to me while I was still in the womb.

"Treating her as a daughter, Nārad protected her while he gave instruction to the child she nourished.

"Without further ado, he gave her initiation. Within the womb I listened. That is the teaching I have given to you. It is not easy to get body such as this.

"I am putting this body on the path to Hari. I will not abandon Hari and waste this birth.

"Ram is the Name that gives salvation. Saying it, hearing it, remembering it, it is beautiful. Skill in reciting it, praising it, singing it: this is everyone's opportunity, brothers.

"Nothing is needed to serve Hari. When one offers service to Him one obtains food, money and cloth. Material offerings are not needed. Love of devotion alone is what gives sustenance.

"No other god has any authority. He has nothing to do with [social distinctions such as] Kshatriya, Vaishya and Shudra. Everyone has a right to practice devotion to Ram, from Brahmin to Untouchable. You should consider this well.

"When one sings the virtues of Hari with love, one gets that most difficult to obtain goal."

By then the demon princes' hearts were filled with devotion. They made Prahlād their guru and began to meditate.

> Śukra's sons became poisoned against him. Very agitated, they went to the king.

Śaṇḍa and Marka went and called the king of demons, who wears a cloth turban: "Your son is speaking in the way that things are understood in the Vedas and Puranas.

"He has created problems with the other students. They have strayed from the path of royal conduct. Don't accuse us of being at fault. You should do whatever you like with him.

> "He has taken away our life's vocation. He has turned his mind in another direction.
>
> "We are not at fault, O king. Your son Prahlād is absorbed in devotion to Hari."
>
> This is what the Brahmins told the king. Then the demon became very angry.

dohā:

> Śaṇḍa and Marka complained aloud to the demon. Then Hiraṇyakaśipu got enraged and decided to kill Prahlād.

A drummer went round the town [spreading the news]: "Everyone should go kill Prahlād."

Jan Gopāl says: Ram alone was Prahlād's helper.

Section Seven

Dūhā [?] in motīdām meter:

They tied Prahlād, the great sage and saint.
He gets lashes and blows from all four sides.

The sage stays firm, no fear for his body.
Venomous snakes are sent to bite him.

The deadly *halāhal,* time and again.
An elephant attacks, but breaks its tusks.

Absorbed in Hari, he never flinches
while muskets and arrows rain like water.

Clubs and lances fly in profusion.
Bricks and rocks and countless darts.

Discuses and missiles wend crooked paths,

The jagged swords. With resolve he endures it.[7]

So many weapons, so many blows.

They all got exhausted but couldn't break in.[8]

Ram is true. He did the work.

dohā:
They tortured him for twelve hours, but the demons couldn't accomplish their task. Jan Gopāl says: Ram and only Ram can touch Prahlād.

Section Eight

chaupaī:
Then Prahlād stood there [so still that he looked] like a lamp in a painting. His life-breath stayed with God. Hot air had no effect on his body.[9]

The fire itself became cool, as it does when a truthful person undergoes an ordeal. When god protects a truthful person, what can the ignorant say [to cause him harm].

> *sākhī:*
> Dādū says: Neither the blade of a sword nor poison can kill him. Nothing has any effect. The devotee remains as long as Ram remains, even in the water of the storms of time.

The messenger said to the demon: "Not one strategy is left for us to try. We have tried elephants, snakes, and all sorts of weapons. We also gave him the deadly *halāhal* to drink.

"I don't know who has protected him. Perhaps his body has become divine after tasting some immortal nectar. To the demon, the night seemed to last six whole months. He thought: "Isn't there anyone who can kill Prahlād?"

In the morning he said: "Drown him in the water. Tie him in chains and let him loose in the current. That way, when you throw him in the crocodiles will take him."

As soon as the order was given, Prahlād was taken away. They sent for a heavy iron anchor. The demons tied him to the anchor and began to drown him, but a miracle occurred that seemed to startle them awake.

The chains loosened and it was the brother [demons] who sank.[10] Prahlād floated like a lotus leaf.

> What God does can't be explained. No one knows the movement of the Unknown.
>
> O Ram, life of the devotees, you are blessed. Everywhere you make good their work.
>
> By the power of the Name, he is saved from drowning. Lord Ram protects his devotees.
>
> When Ram saves, no one kills. The world learned that even a rock can float.[11] Meeting together, the demons decided to go and call the king.

dohā:
Even tied by chains that would keep an elephant bound, [Prahlād] manages to run away.[12] Jan Gopāl says: In this way Hari gave help to Prahlād.

Section Nine

chaupaī:

The messenger called and said: "We caught Prahlād as [sure as] Rāhu catches the body of the moon. We bound him with chains and threw him in the water. We didn't see how the chains could be broken.

"When he came out of the water and stood before us, all we demons fell into a state of deep shock."

Then Hiraṇyakaśipu called all the demons together: "Bring him to me and we will kill him.

"He is fixed liked a wound in my heart. Tell me how you think he can be killed. Tell me whatever ideas you have about it. You should kill him now.

"I the king will protect whoever becomes his killer."

The messenger said: "Listen, Prahlād. Don't try to use false arguments against us."

Prahlād said:

dohā:

"How can I give up the worship of Vishnu once I have got it? The saints tell us that in this world devotion is foremost."

chaupaī:

Then Hiraṇyakaśipu, furious, rose and said: "Throw him in a deep, dark well. Will he dare to reject my words? Respect for elders has been broken. Pay attention to what I have said.[13]

"It would be better to be without a son than to have one who doesn't follow his family duty."

They grabbed Prahlād and threw him in a well. Then they covered him with earth and stones.

Everyone said: "Save him! Save him!. How can Ram protect him at every moment?"

The Protector is always aware of everything. He never experiences any ignorance or lack of awareness.

dohā:
Everyone got worried, but nothing happened to the devotee. When Prahlād recites the Name of Ram, he looses all consciousness of his body.

Birah in motīdām meter:

His mother weeps. She withers and falls.
His nursemaid weeps, crying "haaii, haaii."

His sisters weep. They feel like they're dying.
The warriors weep, their courage lost.

His friends all weep, more and more worried.
The children all weep and beat their heads.

The saints all weep, saying "Where is Prahlād?"
The gurus weep, saying "Who will serve us?"

Great sages weep, saying "Where is our joy?"
The townsfolk weep and search for Prahlād.

The village folk weep, his name on their lips.
Even animals weep and search with their eyes.

The gods all weep, saying "Who will serve Hari?"
But no breath was drawn, for fear of the demon.

Everyone grieved and couldn't speak.
Ram was Prahlād's companion and his joy.

dohā:
The whole world was in pain. Nothing could be done against the demon.
There was no way that Govinda's unknown movement could be seen.

Hiraṇyakaśipu was delighted, for the moment in bliss. Jan Gopāl says:
In the house Prahlād shone like the full moon.

Section Ten

chaupaī:

Then Prahlād was put back on the surface via some hidden path. Everyone shouted "Victory! Victory!" When he saw this, the demon was amazed. No one can fully know Hari's deeds.

> Like water in water, like earth in earth, O brother, like air meeting with fire, Prahlād was absorbed in Brahman. He felt no fear from the weapons, fire or poison. God gave his devotee fame and made him stand without flinching.

Hiraṇyakaśipu said: "Tell me, Prahlād. Who is your chosen deity who thwarts my purpose?[14] Which medicine and which mantra has saved you? I have tried many ways to kill you."

Prahlād said: "Hear, O king, the identity of my chosen god. It is He who has created all this, and in Him all this gets absorbed again. It is also He who pervades the whole of creation. Only the ignorant believe that He is distant.

"My mantra is Ram's Name. This is the medicine of life that I always keep in my heart. [You have] thought about death from sword blades, poison and fire, in water, on earth, and on mountains.

"No one need worry about fearing Death's fever. Even the fire of universal destruction can't burn God's devotees.

> "When I heard the mantra [of Ram's Name], I accepted devotion. Because of your ignorance, you fought and lost."

The demon said: "Listen. Anyone can say 'Ram.' What more is there in you [that makes it so powerful]?"

> When the king asked this question, then Prahlād explained it to him.

Prahlād said: "[It is true that] everyone can sing Ram's Name, but without faith how will they obtain Its fruit? He who says 'Ram' after offering his own head will get the fruit. One's work doesn't get done just looking at it.

"If someone goes into battle just to look, when the enemy crowd advances he will show his back.

"[One can compare] the person who merely looks and says `Ram' while at home with the *satī* who say Ram in her agony. The *satī* doesn't flinch her body even a little. She burns herself together with her beloved dead husband.

"Someone may carry a pot of nectar on his head, but he will die if he does not drink it with his mouth.

"Cooked food may be placed in many ways in front of someone's mouth, but his hunger won't go away unless he eats it.

"If the bread is kept behind someone, his hunger won't go away. Thirst is not quenched unless one drinks some water.

"Even if there is a medicinal tree in front of someone's door, the fool will die unless he applies the medicine."

Prahlād explained [the power of] Ram's Name. He gave pain to the evil-doers and joy to the saints.

The *chintāmaṇi* jewel has not a single flaw. With it one's wishes come true.

That *chintāmaṇi* is Hari's Name. As is one's wish, just so is the result.

dohā:
Hope has nothing to do with the body. Know that all bodily pleasures are false. Jan Gopāl says: Keep your mind fixed on Sārańgapāṇi like Prahlād did.

Section Eleven

Prahlād, the very incarnation of devotion, calls out: "Let the whole world hear Ram's Name."

One moment he weeps; one moment he sings and dances; one moment he plays the cymbals.

Shameless, he is drunk on Ram's nectar. All his relations with his body and the world are broken. He and his companions are shouting Hari's Name. He thinks only about knowledge, meditation and asceticism.

He speaks the truth and the people run to kill him. Does light please a thief? In this way the people become the enemies of the devotee. Blessed is Ram who protects my honor.

The demon thinks about [the possibilities of using] deceit, force, and trickery: "Isn't there anyone who can kill Prahlād? Tie him up now and throw him from a mountain peak. O demons, carry out this task for me."

> When the king has said this, the messengers get up and bow their heads.

The demon has him tied up in a bundle and taken away, but Prahlād has no fear. The demon says: "Listen, prince. What will Vishnu do to protect you now?

> The messengers give him a warning: "Accept our advice."

Prahlād says: "Vishnu is found in the water, on land, on the mountains, and in fire. I have lost all fear of sword blades and poison. Go ahead and throw me. The sin is not yours. [If you don't do it,] the demon will get angry with you.

As soon as they threw him, his bonds broke. Saying "Ram, Ram," the devotee escaped. Prahlād happily came flying down singing Ram's virtues like a bird in the sky.

> The messengers arrived there quite pleased with themselves. Then they saw on the earth, the saint they had thrown down. The earth supported the true devotee. The power of Ram drove away the evil doers.

In the water, on land, and on the mountain, Prahlād was protected from having to fear sword blades and poison. Jan Gopāl says: Prahlād has the full light of Brahman.

Section Twelve

chaupaī:
Hiraṇyakaśipu says: "Listen, Prahlād. Why don't you give up Vishnu's doctrine. I am your father and you are my son. All the glory of the royal throne is yours."

Prahlād says: "Vishnu is my father and mother both. He is my kinsman, lover, beloved, and brother. All other relationships are worthless. We come and go through 8,400,000 births.

"[These relationships] arise from Maya. Forget them.[15] It's wrong to waste one's life on sense objects. Only in one's dreams is the royal capital truly real. When one awakes, one sees that it's worthless.

> "In this way, when one thinks and gets absorbed in meditation, one's body and kingdom all vanish.

"Why should I go to my own death? Father, how can I abandon Vishnu?

> Mother, father, wife, kinsmen: in every birth one meets these relations. Even birds and mammals get a chance for bliss, wealth, and the enjoyment of sense objects.
>
> But it is evident that these [lives] are in no way stable. They are soaked in the effects of deeds done in former lives. For this reason, nowhere is there real bliss without Hari. Stay with him always and drink His love.

When Prahlād spoke the word "Vishnu," his father got up in anger and said: "Kill him quickly. Don't let him get away.

> "Prahlād's heart is fixed on someone else, and this is causing me great pain.

"A bamboo has taken root in a forest of sandal trees. At any moment he will destroy our family. It's almost as if a snake had bitten our toe, and the *halāhal* poison was spreading in waves from foot to head.

"In such a case one should cut off the toe and throw it away. If it causes poisoning, then it destroys everything.[16] Bodily pain is pleasing to no one, but the pain goes away if one applies medicinal herbs.

"My enemy has taken the disguise of my own son. No one likes a hot coal [that burns up one's] family."

Then the demon sent snakes, lions and dogs against Prahlād. [By the grace of] the Inner controller, they couldn't even get close to him.[17]

Then Prahlād was tied with a rope of snakes. The demon prayed that he be drowned in the ocean. Then they took him and squashed his body under a mountain. The earth swayed and Śeṣ's head trembled.

The mountain became like a flower on Prahlād's head. The rope of snakes fell away, and the water became as [solid as] the earth. Ram pervades and protects everything and everyone. Ram speaks the truth through His devotee Prahlād.[18]

dohā:
If the Almighty is your protector, then no one can destroy you. Jan Gopāl says: All of them try their best, but don't touch a hair.

Section Thirteen

Sister Horī[19] said: "Listen, king. I will finish your work for you. I have done all sorts of ascetic penance. For this, Shiva has given me a fearless character.

"When I burn, I myself don't get burnt. When I'm extinguished, I don't die. I will do the task at hand for you. I will take Prahlād and mount the pyre. Then you should light the fire.

> "My body is made from a thunderbolt. No fear can pervade it. There is no other way to kill Prahlād. I accept the task in front of the whole assembly."
>
> This made the king quite happy. He said: "When my sister takes on a task it's sure to get done. I will get no rest until Prahlād is out of my sight for good."

They collected wood with enthusiasm. None of them liked the sentiment of devotion. Then they constructed a house-sized pile of wood. A veritable mountain [of wood] was piled up in all directions.

Horī took Prahlād in her lap. She was forever the foremost of evil sinners. One look at her and one can really see the true character of the demons who oppose Hari.

The king constructed a great marvel. The men and women of the city went to see. Horī took Prahlād and mounted onto the pyre. Putting him in the center of it, she sat crosswise over him.

> After he had prepared this marvel, the demon lit the fire. The inconceivable Brahman is beyond all thought. May he support Prahlād now.

Anyone whom Ram protects has nothing to fear. Those whom he abandons will be taken away even in their own homes.

Jauhar in motīdām meter:[20]

When the king arrived, one heard "hai, hai."
"Light the fire, so he can't get away."

. . . ,[21] he got up and shouted:
"Kill him right here, right where he is.

"Pick up a weapon and kill him before me."
They joined together in millions and millions.

The warriors happily milled about.
They sprayed on the oil, a carnival of fire.

They filled up the pile with cotton seeds.
The demon's sons brought bundles of hemp.

The fires light lit up earth and sky.
The demon said: "Our worries are over."

The fools don't know that ocean of mercy.
If Ram protects you, you'll never fail.

> Prahlād felt joy beyond all bounds.
> The fire kept away, for him it was cool.

dohā:
In twelve hours the fire burned itself out. Horī was turned into ashes. The sparkle of gold increased and millions of *ghuṅghachī* seeds were burned.[22]

> The fire became like cool water. The heat of the fire had no effect. Jan Gopāl says: Ram gave help to Prahlād.

Hatred against a devotee is the worst thing possible. Never let it happen. Jan Gopāl says: Horī burned up in the fire.

Section Fourteen

The demon's heart was filled with pain. Outwardly he revealed nothing by what he said. He couldn't tolerate Hari's glory. His sinner's heart felt sorrow and torment.

He thought: "This kingdom here will not be mine while my son Prahlād is in the wrong. He has sought out the side of my enemy. He hasn't done a single thing for royal duty and the family.

"Even while I am alive, he is doing this evil thing. What will he do after I'm dead?

"O Prahlād, do what I want you to do. You have cruelly tortured me in this world.

> "The gods, men and demons all obey me. I don't know what you think [you're doing].

"If you don't [obey me,] I will grab you and kill you right now. Afterwards no one will blame me."

Prahlād says: "Listen, O king. You are blind and ignorant and speak worthless nonsense.

"Even now you have no faith in Him who protected me in the water, on land, and in the fire. If the moon [were to rise] in the east and the sun in the west,[23] if the Ganges and the Yamuna were to disappear,

if the fire were ever to become cool, even then I wouldn't abandon Ram's Name."

Then the demon ran and caught Prahlād and tied him to a pillar. He said: "If anyone speaks [to interfere], I will kill and eat him."

He pulled out his sword and ran to kill Prahlād. Prahlād felt no fear.

The demon said: "Tell me. Where is the Ram who does your work now?"

> The cruel demon said these words, but the devotee Prahlād felt no doubts.

Prahlād said: "The saints understand that He is in everything. How can He be seen [by those who are lost] in anger and desire?

"O king, you have become a fool. Without Hari's favor, no one can acquire knowledge.

"He is in the sword, in the pillar, in me, in you. Regard perfect Brahman as the True reality. Brahman roams about in every body. When *rajas* and *tamas* come into existence, Brahman is no longer perceived.

"Egoism and pride have made you blind. You have forgotten that the Inner controller is always near.

"He is in me, in you, in the sword, in the pillar. The Merciful one is in everything. Death will have no power over him who thinks about the Ram who roams about [in every body]."

Hiraṇyakaśipu raised his hand [to strike Prahlād]. The sound "hai, hai" filled the three worlds.

The whole of creation — gods, men, saints, *siddhas,* even the five elements — got angry at that moment.

In the worlds of the gods, men, and snakes, everyone cried out "Hai, hai."

Hari always helps his devotees. He gave sustenance to the behavior of His devotee Prahlād. The Lord created a unique form. He became a Man-lion and tortured the demon sinner.

sākhī:
Dādū says: When a saint is tortured, then everything turns topsy-turvy. The sky is ruined and the earth is destroyed. The three worlds sink [into chaos].

dohā:
Hiraṇyakaśipu's hatred was turned back upon itself and became a lion. Such was Prahlād's faith. [God and he were] like cow and calf.

It was like the case when one looks in the mirror and sees the image of one's own face. Jan Gopāl says: He's here as soon as you think of him.

Section Fifteen

Affection in devotion, in motīdām meter:

The Man-lion appeared in front of Prahlād.
He split the pillar, he performed a marvel.

He roared aloud and the enemy cringed,
But the ignorant fool decided to fight.

The Man-lion responded and threw him down.

Not on earth nor in air, he sat him in his lap.

At the door of the house he began to kill.

Not daytime nor night, with claws and teeth.
Neither male nor female, it was like Brahman.

Even the gods and Śeṣ were afraid at the sight.
The amazing form had no compare.

Man-lion and Prahlād were like cow and calf.
Whoever comes near, she runs to attack.

His blood-red eyes, his terrifying roar,
His huge big teeth, shining down his throat.

His mighty arms all red with blood.
Mercy, mercy! Mercy, mercy!

The eternal Protector, he is death to death.

dohā:

Affection in devotion was made manifest. He displayed the form of the Man-lion. Jan Gopāl says: Prahlād was made the king of devotion.

Section Sixteen

Praise of Brahman, in motīdām meter:

O mighty Lord, you hold the world.
You destroyed in a flash, and created again.

> You strengthened devotion, and bestowed your grace.
> The army of the gods is at your command.[24]

No bottom no constraint, say all the saints.
No limit no defeat, say all traditions.

No end no number, say all the saints.
Unplumbed and unfathomed, they call you unreachable.[25]

Unseen and invisible, say the gods and Śeṣ.
Undivided and uncut, say all the Vedas.

No boundary no support, they call you formless.
no movement no weight, they call you priceless.

No duality no fear, say the songs of praise.
No chant no image, they call you measureless.

No body no opening, they call you homeless.
No limbs no companion, unbroken, unbroken.

dohā:
Even Śeṣ cannot reach His further shore. The Vedas sing His praises as "not this and not that." Śiva invokes the sound *"ra, ra."* [But even this] does not end His praises.

He treats all creatures equally. He is [all-pervading] like water. If anyone torments the saints, then He becomes harsh.

Pleased, the Man-lion said: "Ask me for anything, Prahlād. I will keep nothing from you." Jan Gopāl says: [The Man-lion considered Prahlād to be] "my foremost devotee."

Section Seventeen

Prahlād said:
chaupaī:
"I ask for nothing else except you, O Lord. Give me firm devotion. I belong to You. Grant me an inner character of loving devotion. Let me drink the nectar of Your lotus feet.

"Let Your Name be on my tongue; let Your darshan be in my eyes; let Your story be in my ears; let Your feet be in my touch. Let my speech be pure; let me sing Your virtues. With mind and heart I offer myself to You.

"And, O Lord, grant me the company of the saints. Grant me this grace without reserve.

> "When I was deep in my mother's womb, Your incomparable devotee Nārad came there and met me.
>
> "He gave me his wise teachings. By his own force and power he became my teacher. He taught me Ram's saving Name. He brought me, a demon, to Your company.
>
> "How can I forget, O Lord, the fruit of my association with Your saint Nārad. Your devotees bring salvation to everyone. By their own power, they rescue living beings.
>
> "In addition to Your Name, the devotees bring wisdom and asceticism, and release from egoism and delusion. They also bring faith, compassion, good conduct, contentment, and other noble virtues that lead to salvation.
>
> "Such are the virtues found in the company of the saints. All this is by Your favor alone, not anyone else's. The favor of the saints is in fact Your favor. In this world there is no other refuge.
>
> "Devotion is obtained in the company of the saints. Those who obtain devotion come to Your feet. For this reason, grant me the company of the saints. I will serve them unbrokenly with mind, deed, and speech.

"I will not seek the eight *siddhis* or the nine *nidhis*. I will forever serve Your feet.

"Give me all the troubles of this world and make happy all living creatures. The cities of Indra, Brahmā and Shiva are not pleasing to me. Who wants to manage mundane affairs?

"Kingdoms, wealth, and even life as a god are small things. One who gives up devotion and asks for these other things is a fool. It is as if one were to prefer a cowrie shell over a *chintāmaṇi* jewel; as if one were to collect poor-quality grain instead of [the fruit of] a wishing-tree.

"A true servant requests nothing. For instance, a mother does everything possible to protect her child. She keeps him away from snakes, fire, and dirt. If the child feels pain, the mother feels pain.

"One who asks for things cannot be called a true devotee. At the end of time, he'll become a beggar. It's like the behavior of the dog and the lion. The dog goes running after his boss.

> "He performs labor and not love, like someone who does something and expects to get paid for it.
>
> "Someone who takes something for serving you, is not a true servant. He is called a laborer. No one is more a fool than he is. He bathes first and then gets dirty.

"Those who seek salvation want salvation, but the devotee wants only to serve.[26] This is what is pleasing to You, O Inner controller. I am like a child. I don't know what to ask for. What can be hidden from You, O Lord.

> "I have no liking for the city of the gods nor the cities of men and snakes. My mind is set on worshipping Your lotus feet. Wherever I take birth, O Lord, grant me firm devotion and Your company.

dohā:

> "I have no liking for anything except You: not the city of the gods nor the cities of men and snakes."
>
> In this way, the blessed devotee Prahlād made his request.

The Man-lion put both hands on Prahlād's head and said: "My good saint Prahlād!"

Jan Gopāl says: Like me, all the saints sing his praises.

Section Eighteen

Praise of Unmoving Brahman in motīdām meter:

In It no sin, in It no merit,
In It no substance, in It no void.

In It no head, in It no feet,
In It no parts, in It no emotion.

In It no ear, in It no eye,
In It no mouth, in It no voice.

In It no nose, in It no breath,
In It no body, in It no smell.

In It no hand, nothing hidden,
In It no life, no thought, no matter.

In It no back, in It no belly,
In It no blood, in It no semen.

No mundane world, no transmigration,
In It no sound, in It no silence.

In It no movement, in It no state.

Unborn, Unborn, Unborn, Unborn!

dohā:
It knows Its own movement, that no one else knows. How can the fruit be latent in the seed and the seed in the fruit.

Even Śāradā could not write down everything about It, even if the whole earth were the paper. How can anyone describe the greatness of the devotees and the Lord?

Even Śāradā could not write down everything about It, but anyone can speak and hear about It. Worship It and obtain Its own abode. You will find out how to reach the further shore.

Prahlād's fame is like immortal nectar. Anyone who speaks and hears about it will obtain the immortal abode free from fear. Through devotion he will get the fruit of salvation.

The glory of Hari and Hari's devotees should be heard and told with love. Jan Gopāl says: "Bear this story in your heard and perform devotion to Ram with love.

> By the grace of the Guru and Govinda, sing the virtues of the saints. The speaker and the hearer get the fruit. They spontaneously get absorbed in Hari's abode."

Jan Gopāl says: The matter may be less or it may be more, but I have told the story as I see it. The father understands what is good for the child.

Here ends "The Deeds of Prahlād"

The Deeds of Prahlād

प्रहिलाद चरित्र -- 1

प्रथम सीस हरि [1] गुर कूं नांऊं ।
कहूं कथा जौ आग्या पांऊं ॥
भगवंत भगत सुजस [2] बिसतारूं ।
करि आलोकन ध्यांन [3] बिचारूं [4] ॥ **1** ॥ **ABCF-L**

च्यारि जुगनि के चार्यों भेदू [5] ।
रुग जुग स्यांम अथरबन बेदू ॥
बांवन अषिर वोऊं [6] कारा ।
तीनि लोक बहु बिधि बिसतारा ॥ **2** ॥ **A-L**

च्यारि बरण च्यार्यों आश्रमां ।
तिनि के कहिऐ नाना धरमां ॥
इक त [7] जोग इक [8] जगि दिढावैं ।
इक [9] तीरथ ब्रत सौं चित लावैं [10] ॥ **3** ॥ **A-L**

---

1. C सत .
2. A कौ सुजस ; HL कौ जस .
3. F हिरदै ; K ग्यांन .
4. This verse not in DE.
5. BHL बेदू ; D बेद ; E बेदु .
6. Texts BDEGJ omit the syllable वो .
7. BDEK omit त ; CF तौ .
8. ACF omit इक .
9. DE add त .
10. D लगावै ; E लगांवैं .

ऐक त [11] कहैं दांन पुनि नीकौ ।
येक त [12] कहैं उधार करि जी [13] कौ ॥
हीदू तुरक कहैं रह [14] दोई ।
सतगुर मिलै त येकै [15] होई ॥ **4** ॥ A-L

रांम भगति बिन रांम नियारा [16] ।
ये वै ले [17] जग के ब्यौहारा ॥
भगवंत धरम न जांनैं [18] कोई ।
जब लग क्रिपा [19] करै नही सोई ॥ **5** ॥ A-L

चिंतामनि क्यूं [20] मोलि बिकाई ।
कलपबृछ का कै घरि जाई ॥
पारस कहौ कौंन कौं चाहै ।
कांमधेन कौं को निरबाहै ॥ **6** ॥ A-L

करम धरम करि रांम न पावै ।
जौ मन बच क्रम मन न [21] लगावै ॥

---

11. BCI omit त .
12. BCIJK omit त .
13. A होइ जीय ; C है जी ; DEJL करि जीव ; F करि जीय ; H करि जाव .
14. G हरि .
15. D कारिज ; E कारज ; J ववेक .
16. AFGIJK निनारा ; L निराया .
17. A उ ले ; C वै ला ; GH वो ले ; J वै ते ; L बो ले .
18. A मानैं .
19. DE क्रिया .
20. B जब ; D पैं ; E पै .
21. B बच क्रंम न मन ; C बच करि मन न ; D बच क्रम नम न ; E बच क्रम नम ; HL बच क्रम करि मन न ; J बचन क्रमन न ; K बच क्रम नांम मन न .

इहि बिधि साध कहै उपदेसु ।
संकर ब्रह्मादिक अरू सेसु ॥ **7** ॥ A-L

दोहा ॥
आदि अंति जेते भये [22] । साध न पाऊं पार ॥
जस बरनौं प्रहिलाद कौ । जन गोपाल बिचार ॥ **8** ॥ A-L

प्रहिलाद चरित्र -- 2

चौपई ॥
सनकादिक सराप जब दीनौ ।
हरनकसिब हरनाषि जु कीनौ ॥
ता कै च्यारि पुत्र भए भारी ।
तिन मांहीं प्रहलाद अधिकारी ॥ **a** ॥ HL

ब्रह्म पुत्र सनकादिक चारी ।
मनसा तैं उपजे अधिकारी ॥
पंच बरस के रहैं सदाई [1] ।
नगन मगन गब्यंद गुन गाई ॥ **1** ॥ A-L

प्रात सेष मुष कथा सुनाई ।
अरू [2] मध्यांन [3] मृत मंडल जाई [4] ॥

22. B गऐ .
1. C सदा रहावै .
2. CK omit अरू .
3. DE धध्यांन .
4. A माही ; C मै जाही .

संध्या पुर [5] बैकुंठ प्रवेसा ।
सनकादिक बिचरै इहि भेसा ॥ **2** ॥ A-L

जैसै गऊ बछ कौं भावै ।
मात मात करि बालक [6] धावै ॥
त्रिषावंत ज्यूं नीर पियासा ।
यौं बाढी दरसन की आसा [7] ॥ **3** ॥ A-L

जबही पाव पौरि मैं [8] दीनौं ।
उठे पारषत अंतर [9] कीनौं ॥
पर घर गवन पूछि कैं [10] कीजै ।
प्रभू रिसाइ उतर कहा दीजै ॥ **4** ॥ A-L

सनकादिक उबाच ॥ A-L

हम जानै ऐह [11] हम ही पिछांनैं [12] ।
प्रभु कै निकटि सदा सनमांनैं [13] ॥
अनपरचै कौ औगुन नांहीं ।
अहंबुधि आई मन मांहीं ॥ **a** ॥ CDEHJKL

---

5. HL समै .

6. HL omit बालक .

7. A दरसन कारनि बाढी आसा .

8. K परि .

9. D रेकन ; E रोकन .

10. A करि .

11. DE ये ; K जे ; L ऐक .

12. J हंम जाह हंम ही पहिचानै .

13. C सदाई जानै ; K सहाई जांनैं .

अहंग्रब [14] कौं ठाहर नांहीं ।
होइ असुर बिचरौ जग मांहीं ॥ A-L
सनकादिक निश्राप यूं [15] दीनौं ।
हरनकसिब हरनाछि जु कीनौं ॥ **5** ॥ A-GIJK

जै र बिजै कहैं सुनौं गुसांई ।
बहुरि मिलैं कब अंतर नांहीं [16] ॥
सपत जनम आराध कराहू ।
कै बिरोध तीसरै मिलाहू [17] ॥ **6** ॥ A-L

मिंत्र हि मिंत्र [18] बिसरि पुनि जाई ।
बैरी हिरदै रहै समाई ॥
जांनि अजांनि अगनि कौं [19] परसै ।
भाइ कुभाइ ब्रह्म यौं [20] दरसै [21] ॥ **7** ॥ A-L

भावै प्रीति सूं जाबौ ध्याई ।
नतर बिरोधै ठांनौ जाई ॥ **a** ॥ HL

---

14. DE अहुबुधि ; L अहंबुधि .

15. A जब .

16. C कब ईह ठाई ; G कछु अंतर नांही ; H कहूं अतर पांहीं ; K कब इहि ठांई ; L कभूं अंतर पांहीं . CK preface verse with जै बिजै उबाच ।।.

17. C दस जनम आराधे आऊ । तीजै जनम बिरोधे पाऊ ।। ; K सप्त जन्म आराधे आंऊं । तीजे जन्म बिरौधे पांऊं ।। .

18. HL add कूं .

19. F मैं .

20. BI कूं ; FGJ कौं .

21. HL invert *padas* c and d.

प्रबल बली बलिवंत [22] सु जोधा [23] ।
नही समांन कोउ त्रिभवन सोधा [24] ॥
बरष सहंस दस [25] दूढत जाही ।
जुध हों स पुजवै को नाही [26] ॥ **8** ॥ A-L

षिजि [27] पृथी पाव तलि [28] चांपी ।
त्राहि त्राहि करि पृथी कांपी ॥
करतम करता [29] अनथा [30] सम्रथ ।
कीयौ [31] बराहु तत छिन [32] जन कै रथ ॥ **9** ॥ A-L

हति हरनाछि धरनि [33] थिर थापी ।
हरनाकुस तब कोप्यौ पापी ॥

---

22. HL अप्रबली बलबंत .

23. C बि सुधां .

24. C जुधा .

25. B-E omit दस ; K सौ .

26. HL जुध ह् सूं कहूं पं जै नांहीं ।। .

27. BFGIJ तब षिजि .

28. I पावन ; J पाव तन .

29. B क्रतम करम ; C करतम करन ; F करतमे करता ; GIJ करतम करत ; K कृत्म क्रप्त.

30. A अन्याथा ; B अनथ ; CK अनिथा ; D अनाथ ; E अनाथ् ; FG अनथा ; HL है ; I अनंथ ; J अनाथा .

31. A दीयो .

32. For तत छिन , C reads चरित ; DEHK चिरत ; L बपु .

33. A धनि ; K पृथी .

हरि बैरी बैरी [34] हरि दासा ।

भाव भगति मेटौं करि [35] त्रासा ॥ **10** ॥ A-L

सनकादिक निस्राप यौ दीनौ ।
हिरणकसिब हिरणांषि जु कीनौ ॥
ता कौ चारी पुत्र भये भारी ।
तिन माही प्रहलाद अधिकारी ॥ **a** ॥ CK

म्रति लोक सब बसि करि लयौ ।
तब हरनकसिब इंद्र पुर गयौ ॥
असुर त्रास सुर चले [36] पलाई ।
बिसन लोक ते पहुचे जाई ॥ **b** ॥ CK

देव कहै सुनि [37] त्रभवन राया ।
दैतनि भैं तुम सरनै आया ॥
राषौ हम हि करौ प्रतिपाला ।
दीन जानि अब होह दयाला ॥ **c** ॥ CK

तब तैं बिस्न कला ईक कीनी ।
काहू पै गति जाई न चीनी ॥
प्रसिध साध सुम्रति ही भाषै ।
मारी असुर सुर सरनै राषै ॥ **d** ॥ CK

---

34. AJ omit the second बैरी ; HL substitute कै .

35. HL मैं करूं ज .

36. K गऐ .

37. K सद .

सुर [38] असुर बैर जब [39] भयौ ।
हरनकसिब [40] तपस्या [41] गयौ ॥
तब सुरपति सो [42] पुरी लगाई [43] ।
असुर त्रिया बंदि ले जाई ॥ **11** ॥ A-L

सनमुष [44] नारद दरसन दीनौ ।
तब हि इंद्र बहु आदर कीनौ [45] ॥
दीन बछल हरि दास [46] कहावै ।
पर पीरा तैं अतिदुष पावै ॥ **12** ॥ A-L(E)

> नारद उबाच ॥ AHL
> देव राज अधिकारी कहिये ।
> सूंनी पुरी कवन बिधि दहिये ॥ **a** ॥ BFGIJ

पुरष पुरष [47] स्यूं करै सु छाजै ।
न्यंद करम करि होई न [48] लाजै ॥ ABC

---

38. BGIJL सुर अरू ; DE सुर गुर .

39. BDEFGIJ have variants of यौं .

40. BFGIJ add जु .

41. HL add कूं ; K adds तब .

42. HL जाइ .

43. AC परी लराई .

44. HL तब सनमुष .

45. HL जब हीं इंद्र सनमांन सु कीन्हौ ।। .

46. K भगत .

47. A पुरषु र पुरषु र ; B पुरष पुरिष .

48. C कीये प्रभु ता .

नारद कह्यो सुनौं [49] सुर राई ।
निंद [50] करम करि लाज न आई [51] ॥ **a** ॥ D(E)HKL

इंद्र कहै अब [52] सुनौ गुसांई ।
बालक हतौं त्रिया कौं नांहीं ॥ **13** ॥ A-L(E)

जब नारद मुनि कियौ बिचारा ।
भगति जानि गिनेयौ उपगारा ॥ **b** ॥ HL

तब हरि गुन सहित बजाई बीना ।
प्रहिलाद कौ मन [53] हरि लीना ॥
तारुक मंत्र [54] सुनायौ बांनी [55] ।
क्रिपा करी काहू नही जांनी ॥ **14** ॥ A-L(E)

करि उपदेस आपणूं भायौ ।
बहुरि इंद्र कूं बचन सुनायौ ॥ **a** ॥ HL

नारद कह्यौ इंद्र सुनि आई [56] ।
या कै उद्र भगत है भाई ॥ A-L(E)

---

49. HL कूंन बुधि करी ; K नारद इंद्र कहैं सुनौं .

50. HL नीच .

51. These two *padas* are evidently variants of the previous two.

52. H omits अब ; L substitutes तुम .

53. B चित .

54. BF-JL रांम .

55. D(E) कांनि .

56. HL सुनौ सुर राई .

तुम रांणी कौ करि अधिकारा ।
कीज्यौ सेवा बहुत प्रकारा ॥ **a** ॥ **HL**

सुरपति उबाच ॥
तुम इह बचन कहे हरि दासा ।
परि मेरै नहीं आवत बिसवासा ॥
इंद्र कहै ऐसौ काहा भगत ।
दैतन कुल आयौ अनुसकत ॥ **b** ॥ **HL**

इंद्र उबाच ॥ **BFGJ**
चारि बरन मैं [57] ठाहर नांही ।
क्यूं हरि भगत [58] असुर कुल [59] जांहीं ॥ **15** ॥ **ABD-L(E)**

ऐसी पूछ करी सुर राई ।
जब ही रिष कही सुन भाई ॥ **a** ॥ **HL**

नारद उबाच ॥
तब नारद बोल्यौ सुनि सुरपति ।
ऊंच नींच हरि नांही त्रिपति ॥
ऊंच नीच सो क्रंम कहावै ।
हरि जन हरि भजि हरि ही समावै ॥ **b** ॥ **HL**

ऊंच नीच कूं ज्यौ बिष देवै ।
षाइ दोन्यूं म्रिति ही लेवै ॥

---

57. D(E) कहौं .

58. BG भगति ; HK भक्ति .

59. D(E)K घर ; F घरि .

फुनि ज्यूं नौका बैठै कोई ।
ऊंच रु नीच तिरै सोई सोई ॥ **c** ॥ HL

ज्यूं [60] हरि कै कुल कौ नहीं कारन ।
अंतिज विप्र भजै ता तारण ॥
जदिप ऊंच लघु तन हूं नांहीं ।
पंच तत करि सबै बनांहीं ॥ **d** ॥ HL

नारद उबाच ॥ BFGJ
कौंन हूं [61] चूक असुर घरि आयौ ।
बिधिना बिधि संजोग बनायौ ॥
अजात सुत्र नांव प्रहिलादू ।
नाराइण कौ सेवग आदू ॥ **16** ॥ A-L(E)

दोहा ॥
ब्रह्मा अंतिजु [62] ऐक रस । कनक भिन नही होइ [63] ॥
जन गोपाल जगदीस कै । कुल कारण नहीं कोइ [64] ॥ **17** ॥ ABD(E)-L

---

60. H तूं .
61. A किंन ही ; HL कोऊ .
62. D(E) आदिजो ; F अंतिसु .
63. D(E)GIJ कोइ .
64. L होइ .

प्रहिलाद चरित्र -- 3

नार्दोवाच साद्ध लछिंन ॥ ABD(E)GHJL

चौपई ॥

सांति सील [1] क्रिपाल अद्रोही ।
ग्यान बिग्यान बिदेह बिमोही ॥
सारासार बिबेक बिचारै ।
सत्र मिंत्र समदिष्टी सारै ॥ **1** ॥ A-L(E)

गो ब्रह्मण संतनि सुष दाई ।
परआत्म [2] आत्म समाई ॥
पर दुष दुषी सुषी सुष पावै ।
ता ही तैं हरि भगत कहावै ॥ **2** ॥ A-L(E)

बहुत भांति करि कीज्यौ सेवा ।
तुम कौं रछिक ह्वैहै [3] देवा ॥
तब नमसकार परदछिना दीनी ।
तब हि इंद्र बहु बीनती कीनी ॥ **3** ॥ A-L(E)

---

1. D(E) सील संतोष .

2. HL परमातम .

3. A है यहु .

इंद्र उबाच [4] ॥ BFGHJL
फेरि [5] न दै उंन हूं ले जांऊं ।
भगति हेत राषौ तुम ठांऊं [6] ॥ BD(E)-L

भगति भांऊं तुम ही लै जांठ [7] ।
ह्व सेवग तुम क्रिपा करांउं [8] ॥ **a** ॥ AB

रिषि असथांन रही तब माता ।
ग्रभ सहत जब आयौ ताता ॥ **4** ॥ A-L(E)

तांहां नारद बहु दीयौ प्रमोधा ।
हित प्रहलाद मात सै बोधा ॥
परि माता कूं उरि सुधि नांहीं ।
सुत श्रोता धार्यौ मन मांहीं ॥ **b** ॥ HL

बहुत भांति सीचत कुमिलाई [9] ।
पर घर जनम लाज यहु आई [10] ॥ BD(E)-HJKL

---

4. HL सुरपति उबाच ; ACD(E)IK omit this.

5. D(E)HKL छाडि .

6. A स्वामी आ हि न फेरि पठाउं । आग्या भंग होइ लै जांऊं ।। ;
C नारद यों हि तुम्ह ले जाहु । बहुत भाती करि सेवक राहु ।। .

7. Read जांउं .

8. C तब नारद माता ले आयौ । जन प्रहलाद कौं ग्यान सुनायौ ।। .
For the verbs B reads भाइ ; जांहीं ; हौ ; कराई .

9. A सोच करै मन मैं पछितावै .

10. BFGJ पुत्र न होइ बडाई ; D(E) जान लाज यह आई ; HL जनम लाज यूं आई .

कूं दई संजोग बनायौ ।
मेरौ पाप प्रगट है आयौ ॥ **a** ॥ HL

नारद उबाच ॥ BFGHJL
बेटी बहन सुनहु री बाई [11] ।
होइ पुत्र [12] अपनैं घरि जाई ॥ **5** ॥ ABD(E)-HJKL

है प्रसन रिष आशिषा [13] दीनी । ABD(E)-HJKL
माता तब ही सीस घरि लीनी [14] ॥ AD(E)HKL

वांहां हरणकसिब तपस्या मांडी ।
इंद्री तन मन ममता [15] षांडी ॥
असुर उरध तप ठांनौ भारी ।
चरण अगुष्ट [16] देह आधारी ॥ **a** ॥ HL

सकल देव गण भऐ दुराषे ।
तब सुर जाइ बीरंच [17] ही भाषे ॥ **b** ॥ HL

---

11. D(E) सुनि हरिष राई . For बाई , J has छाई and K माई .

12. A पुत्र जनम .

13. A रिक्षि आग्या ; BFGJ नारद बर ; HKL रिष आसिका .

14. BFGJ जै जै कार भयौ पुर तीनूं । . Texts AD(E)HKL all seem to read घरि , but धरि would be a better reading.

15. L समता .

16. H अंसुष्ट .

17. L बीच .

कीयौ उग्र तप देह सुकांनी ।
तब हि [18] देव गन बोले बांनी ॥ **6** ॥ ABD(E)-HJKL

देव गन उबाच ॥ BFGHJL
कै बिधि [19] हंम कौं ठाहर दीजै ।
कै हरनाकुस कहै सु कीजै ॥ ABD-HJL

तपस्या बौहौत करी अधिकारी ।
देव पुरी कंपत है सारी ॥ **a** ॥ HL

तब ब्रह्मा मन कीयौ बिचारा ।
सुरन सहित चाल्यौ तिहि बारा ॥
सुरग लोक तै ब्रह्मा सिधाऐ ।
बर दैण कौ तत छिन भू आऐ ॥ **b** ॥ HL

ब्रह्मा हुलसि बिचारत सोई ।
बर द्यौ असुर मागत है जोई ॥
आइ असुर तन छिरक्यौ झारी ।
करि चेतन फुनि बचन उचारी ॥ **c** ॥ HL

दिब सत बरष तप तिन कीनौ ।
होइ प्रसन ब्रह्मा बर दीनौ ॥ **d** ॥ CK

ब्रह्मा ऐसी गिरा उचारी ।
जब ही असुर मन हरष्यौ भारी ॥ **e** ॥ HL

---

18. HL भौ मानि .

19. BFGJ प्रभू ; HL ब्रह्मा .

ब्रह्मा कहै असुर का चाहै ।
कूंन कांमनां तन कूं दाहै [20] ॥ **7** ॥ BCFGHJKL

हरनाकुस उबाच ॥ FGHJL
सस्त्र अगनि जल बिष भै [21] नांही ।
रैनि द्यौस बाहरि घर मांही ॥ ABD-HJKL

> सत्र संकट कबहूं नही होई ।
> मन क्रम बचन दैहु बर सोई ॥ **a** ॥ HL
>
> नर नाहर अरु आलौ सूकैं ।
> सुरग पताल अरु ऊपरि भू कैं ॥
> जंत्र मंत्र जोधा रण मांहीं ।
> अती ठौर मम मृत्यु जु नांहीं ॥ **b** ॥ HL

ब्रह्म सिष्टि पैं [22] मरौं न कबहू ।
हो हो [23] ब्रह्मा कह्यौ [24] तबहू ॥ **8** ॥ A-L

---

20. HL ब्रह्मा उबाच ।। उठि बछ क्यूं तन कूं दाहै ।। मागि हू बर जो मन मैं चाहै
In C *padas* 7cd are preceded by *padas* 9ab.

21. F डर .

22. DEHKL मैं .

23. B होह हो ; CFGJ होह होह ; DE होहो होहो ; IK होहु होहु .

24. D कह्यौ है ; E कह्यौ हे ; HL कह्यौ यूं .

दिब्य [25] बरष सत तप जिन [26] कीनौ ।
है प्रसन ब्रह्मा बर दीनौ [27] ॥ B-L
हरनाकुस हरष्यौ मन मांहीं ।
होणहार गति संमझी नांहीं [28] ॥ **9** ॥ BFGHJKL

तब हि हरनकसिब [29] घरि आयौ ।
माता ले रिष तहां सिधायौ ॥
ग्रभ समौं पूरौ भयौ आई ।
प्रहिलाद सुत [30] जनम्यौ जाई ॥ **10** ॥ A-L

जनम भये दिबि दूंदभी बाजी [31] ।
सुर नर सकल आरती साजी [32] ॥
सब संतनि कै मनि आंनंदू ।
अंतरजांमी है गोब्यंदू ॥ **11** ॥ A-L

---

25. DE द्वादश .

26. B तिन ; HL तांहां ; K जब . All others have जिन or जिनि .

27. In C these two *padas* precede *padas* 7cd. In I these two *padas* come before 8cd.

28. HL बर ले असुर हरषि हीय मांहीं । सब मैं हरि गति जानै नांहीं ।।. In B these two *padas* appear after 7cd.

29. HL add अपणै .

30. BD-L तब .

31. DE देव दुंदभी बजावै ; K तब दुदभि बागी .

32. DE करावै .

एक बरष द्वै तीन र चारी ।
पंच बरस कै भगति संभारी ॥ A-L

ग्रभ ग्यांन सुमरत सो आई ।
रांम भजन लाग्यौ सुधि पाई ॥
धीरजवंत नीति लीयां भारी ।
धरम दया अरू ग्यांन बिचारी ॥ **a** ॥ HL

प्रगट कुमाई आगली भ्यासी ।
ले उकसे नांव सुष रासी ॥ HL
प्रेम मगन आनंद मैं झूलै ।
देह दसा नष सष तैं [33] भूलै ॥ **b** ॥ DEHKL

संत कृपा तैं कहा न होई ।
गुर प्रसादि तिरै सब कोई ॥ **12** ॥ BFGJ

दोहा ॥
पंच बरस कौं जब भयौ । साध पुत्र प्रहिलाद ॥
जन गोपाल समझै नही । बाल केलि रस स्वाद ॥ **13** ॥ A-L

प्रहिलाद चरित्र -- 4

चौपई ॥
हरनकसिब लीयौ सुक्र बुलाई ।
या की तुम कौ लाज बडाई ॥

---

33. HL लूं .

राज नीति सब जाई पढाऊ ।
मम कुल धर्म बसेष [1] सुनाऊ ॥ **1** ॥ A-L

सुदिन महूरत सुक्र हि [2] सोध्यौ ।
नीकै करि राजा [3] परमोध्यौ ॥
भलै महूरत बाजा बाजे ।
घरि घरि मंगल कलस बिराजे ॥ **2** ॥ A-L

ग्यांन करत चटसाल जु आऐ ।
सरसती और गनेस पुजाऐ [4] ॥
बहु बिधि [5] बालनि [6] पूजा कीनी ।
प्रहिलाद [7] सो ऐक न चीनी ॥ **3** ॥ A-L

तब तिनि [8] कह्यौ सु [9] राजा कंवारू ।
पढौ गुनौ समझौ ब्यौहारू ॥

---

1. A सबै .
2. A स ; C ज ; DE त ; HKL जु ; GIJ omit word.
3. A यो कौ (for राजा).
4. A सरसुति आनि गऐ . For last word, HL have मनाऐ .
5. A स पुजा ये बहु बिधि .
6. B कलनि ; C बालकनि ; L बालक .
7. CK जन प्रहिलाद .
8. HL सुक्र ; K उन .
9. B omits सु ; DEH-L सुनि .

वो [10] नम सिध पटी लिषि दीनी ।
कर सौं कर [11] सिषावनि [12] कीनी ॥ **4** ॥ A-L

र रौ म मौ आपनु लिषि [13] जांनौं ।
कही सुनी न और की मांनौं ॥
संडा मुरका कह्यौ पढि [14] बाला ।
जैसैं षुसी होइ भुवाला ॥ **5** ॥ A-L

कहि प्रहिलाद भुवाल हि जानू ।
तौ कत मिथ्या बाद बषांनू ॥
जिहि कीयौ उतपति वोऊं [15] कारा ।
पंच तत थैं [16] सकल पसारा ॥ **6** ॥ A-L

चार षांनि जोनि चौरासी ।
सरग नरक जीव [17] तिहूं पुर बासी ॥
पुरिष नारि बिष अंमृत कीनां ।
सत गुर बिना न जाई [18] चीनां ॥ **7** ॥ A-L(E)

---

10. A उ ; BGK ॐ ; HL वोऊं ; I ओ ; J ऊ .

11. B omits the last *pada*. After कर C adds गहि ; D-GJK add जु ; HL add जोडि .

12. FGJ लिषावनि .

13. DE पढि .

14. K सुनि .

15. A उं ; B ओ ॐ ; C वोवं ; D वोऊ ; F वो ॐ ; G ॐ ; H वौ ॐ ; I ओऊं ; J ऊ ; K वौऊं ; L वों .

16. C अर ; K लौं .

17. HL नाग .

18. For न जाई , D(E) read जाय कौं ; HL जाइ नहीं .

षंड ब्रह्मंड रची बहु धरणी ।
देषौ वा राजा [19] की करणी ॥
पाढ पढौ जिहि रीझै राजा ।
और पढन सौं नाही काजा ॥ **8** ॥ **A-L(E)**

ऐसी कथा प्रहलाद सुनाई ।
तब ही बिप्र कै आसंक्या आई ॥
कूंन उपाइ करैयौहौ आंनां । **a** ॥ **HL**

बिप्र गये भोजन असनांनां ।
तब बालनि हठ कीयौ निदांनां [20] ॥ **A-L(E)**

हम पूछै बिप्र गऐ असनांनां । **a** ॥ **HL**

कहि प्रहिलाद आपनी गाथा [21] ।
हम सब सषा तुम्हारै साथा ॥ **9** ॥ **A-L(E)**

कौंन पाढ तोहि लागै नीकौ ।
हम [22] स्यौ कहौ भाव तौ जी कौ ॥ **A-L(E)**

हम तुम सुं पूछी ऐह गाथा ।
कहौ प्रभू हम दींन अनाथा ॥ **a** ॥ **HL**

---

19. A साहिब .

20. HL preface to this *pada* चटड़ा उबाच ।। .

21. C prefaces to this *pada* बालक उबाच ।। .

22. B तुम .

मिंत्र कपट सम दोष न भाई ।
बेद पुरांन कहैं समझाई ॥ D(E)HKL
तुम क्रपा करि ग्यांन जु भाषौ ।
भली बुधि होइ सो दाषौ ॥ **b** ॥ HL

कहि प्रहिलाद सुनहु रे बाला ।
जनम मरण जीव कौं बहु काला ॥ **10** ॥ A-L(E)

जा तैं जनम मरण मिटि [23] जाई ।
हूं जांनौं सो बडौ उपाई ॥ A-L(E)

करौ उपाय रांम कौ भजनौं ।
जगत जाल काल कौ तजनौं ॥
जगत जाल काल कौ फंदा ।
ग्यांन नैन बिन उलझै अंधा ॥ **a** ॥ HL

अगनि लाइ जो बाहिर [24] दिषाई ।
सुष नहीं पावै [25] जीव जरि बरि जाई ॥ **b** ॥ D(E)HL

अंध कूप ग्रह मैं जो परिये ।
तौ भव सागर कैसैं तिरिये ॥ **11** ॥ A-L(E)

बिष बन बेलि अमृत फल चाहै ।
बिष फल षाइ र अमर उमाहै [26] ॥

---

23. B मरम मिलि .
24. H बारि ; L बाइ .
25. D(E) omit पावै .
26. For these two *padas*, B reads: बिष बंन बेलि । अमर उमाहै ।.

लोह नाव कैसैं निस्तरिये ।
अर जे पाप पषांननि भरिये ॥ **12** ॥ **A-L(E)**

अगनि ग्रेह [27] कैसैं सुष सोई [28] ।
कौन भांति सीतलता होई ॥
पूरब जात पछिम कत [29] आवै ।
नैंन बिना मघ कैसैं पावै ॥ **13** ॥ **A-L(E)**

कांम केलि कांमनि रस बीझै [30] ।
पाप पसारे मैं क्यूं सीझै ॥
सुत [31] परिवार पाप [32] की पासी ।
तन धन जोबन रहै न जासी ॥ **14** ॥ **A-L(E)**

जब लग रोग ग्रसित [33] नही भईऐ ।
तब लग वोषदि काहे न षईऐ ॥
जब घर जरै अरू [34] कूप षनाई ।
उदिम लोग हसै रे भाई ॥ **15** ॥ **A-L(E)**

पहली पांव कांप नहीं भरीऐ ।
तौ पीछैं कांइ पषालन परीऐ ॥

---

27. C लगाई .
28. CHL सोवै .
29. B कति ; D(E)GJ कैसै ; HL कित .
30. A रीझै ; CD(E) भीझै .
31. G सुर .
32. BGIJK पाव ; C पावक .
33. D(E) रिसक .
34. F तब .

षित जल संगि दुष सुष जग मांहीं ।
ग्यांन उदक बिन छूटै नांहीं ॥ **a** ॥ HL

अजरीक लै मिष्ट कैं मांहीं ।
कर मीडै पनि [35] सुलझै नांहीं ॥
प्रथन स्वाद सनेह न लावै ।
तौ बंधन परै न पर लिपटावै ॥ **b** ॥ HL

जब लग पाई परै नही बेरी ।
तब लग मारग [36] लीजे हेरी ॥
जब लग रहै नही रषवारू ।
तब लग भजिये बाल कंवारू ॥ **16** ॥ A-L(E)

ता तैं सब तजि बन मैं जईये ।
साध संगति मिलि हरि गुन गईये ॥ A-L(E)
सूरातन स्यौं संक न कीजै ।
रांम नांम निरभै भजि [37] लीजै ॥ **17** ॥ BFGIJ

ग्यांन भगति बैराग बिचारै ।
इहि बिधि आप आपनपौ त्यारै ॥ D(E)HKL
बार बार यह तन नही पावै ।
ऐसौ जनम ठौड किन लावौ ॥ **a** ॥ CK

---

35. H पर . 36. H हरि मघ ; L हरि मग .

37. B only भजि . F जपि ; GI पद ; J पद त .

दोहा ॥

सकल प्रबोध नीकां दीयौ । जन प्रहलाद हित लाइ ॥
प्रथम संत परमारथी । नीकै कही बनाइ ॥ **b** ॥ HL

रांम नांम छाडौं नही । गुर कूं आवै गारि ॥
जन गोपाल सषांनि सौं । कहै प्रहिलाद बिचारि ॥ **18** ॥ A-L(E)

प्रहिलाद चरित्र -- 5

चौपई ॥

कबहू ग्रह प्रहिलाद पधारे [1] ।
राजा ले उछंग [2] बैठारे ॥
मुष चूंबन करि हिरदै धारे ।
कहौ पुत्र ब्यौहार तुम्हारे ॥ **1** ॥ A-L

नीकी विद्या पढी सु भाषौ ।
सो तुम हम [3] सौं कछू न रषौ ॥
जो मांगै सो देउं तुरंतू ।
मेरै कौ न बोल [4] कौ अंतू ॥ **2** ॥ A-L(J)

---

1. C सिधारे .
2. BDE उचै . HL omit ले and add गोद after उछंग .
3. BCFGI मो ; DE मौ .
4. H कोई न बस्त ; L नही कोई बसत .

प्रहिलाद उबाच ॥ **A-HKL**
श्रवन [5] कीरतन सुमिरन कीजै [6] ।
चरन सेइ अरू तन मन दीजै ॥
बंदन करि दासातन भावै [7] ।
दिढि बिसवास तैं सषा कहावै ॥ **3** ॥ **A-L(J)**

अरू आतमा समरपन कीजै ।
नौधा भगति प्रेम मन दीजै [8] ॥
बिद्या सो जिहि ब्रह्म पिछांनैं ।
और अबिद्या परपंच [9] हि जानैं ॥ **4** ॥ **A-L(J)**

जब लग [10] मै मेरी नही भूलै ।
तौ तन पाइ कौन बिधि [11] फूलै ॥
सब जग [12] बंध्यौ अहं अर ममिता ।
साधू सब तजि रांम ही रमिता ॥ **5** ॥ **AC-L(J)**

होम जग्य ब्रत पूजा दांनां ।
बलदेव तजे जग बिधि नांनां ॥
काहे तात करै बिधि ऐती ।
सब तजि भजीऐ रांम संगेती ॥ **a** ॥ **HL**

---

5. DE अवन .
6. L हरि कौ श्रबन कीरतन कीजै .
7. DE कीजै .
8. AK रस पीजै .
9. C झुठी .
10. In B the text ends here.
11. D पैं ; E पै .
12. A जीव ; D युग ; EF जुग .

भगवत बिनां सदन सुष नांहीं ।
सकल जीव भूले भ्रम मांहीं ॥
पर्यौ भरम भूल्यौ भगवांनां ।
षोवै जनम ब्रथां सति मांनां ॥ **b** ॥ **HL**

लौहै कंचन [13] एक ही बेरी ।
जो नीकैं करि देषौ हेरी [14] ॥
सुर नर असुर बिषै सुष जैसें ।
पसु पंषी सुष पावै तैसें [15] ॥ **6** ॥ **AC-L(J)**

रज कै स्नप सकल जुग षायौ ।
सुपिनैं [16] जगत बिसु डहकायौ ॥
धावत म्रिग त्रिसना कै पांनी ।
यूं जीव बंधे देह अभिमांनी ॥ **7** ॥ **AC-L(J)**

सुक नलनी दिष्टांत दिषायौ ।
इहि बिधि जीव अबंध बंधायौ ॥
छाडि देइ तौ कौनै बांध्यौ ।
यौ अग्यान करि दुष आराध्यौ ॥ **8** ॥ **AC-L(J)**

सौ मैं सोवत गई पचासा ।
बारा बरस बालापन नासा [17] ॥

---

13. F-IKL कनक .

14. K तौ नीकै करि देहु हेरी ।।.

15. पर पंषी सुष मांनै जैसें ।।.

16. H यू सुपनै ; L यूं सर्पने .

17. DE बारा बाल ब्रिध पुन्या नास्यौ ।।.

कांम केलि कै ग्रिह ब्यौहारा ।
रांम भगति बिसर्यौ [18] संसारा ॥ **9** ॥ AC-L(J)

बेदागम बर बिद्याबांनां ।
हरि बिनि काहि पढै ऐ आंनां ॥
बिद्या भगति रांम कौ भजनौं ।
आंन सकल करमन कौ तजनौं ॥ **a** ॥ HL

जे षल तुछि क्रंमन अबगाहै ।
ता ही मै सद फल कूं चाहैं ॥
सो सद फल नही पावै क्यूं हीं ।
करि करि श्रम भरमै ते यूं हीं ॥ **b** ॥ HL

ता तै सब तजि भजीयै रांम ।
सदा नरंतर ह्वैन्ह कांम ॥
बिष बिकार सब देह जु आवै ।
रांम भजन बिधि कभूं न [19] पावै ॥ **c** ॥ HL

बार बार नर देह न पईऐ ।
औसर गऐ बहुरि पिछतईऐ ॥ HL, DE at 10.cd
ता तै ओसर [20] अब कै आयौ ।
किरपा करि गुर कहि समझायौ ॥ **d** ॥

---

18. HL बिनि मर्यौ .

19. H क .

20. L और .

संश्रति मिटै सु बिद्या भावै [21] ।
और अबिद्या कौ को धावै ॥ AC-L(J)
बिद्या भगति ताहि हूं मांनौं ।
भगति बिनां झूठ करि जांनौं [22] ॥ **10** ॥ FG

समझि देषि हू दैयहै ग्यांनां ।
कौ निसतर्या बिन हरि ध्यांनां ॥ **a** ॥ K

ऐह बिचार हम तुम सूं भाषी ।
मुनि नारद की सुनि कै साषी ॥
और पाठ सो नांहीं भावै ।
सुनि करि असुर बौहौत पिछतावै ॥ **b** ॥ HL

दोहा ॥
सुपन पाइ [23] संसार है । सोवत ही [24] लौं साच ॥
जन गोपाल हरि भजि जगे । तिनि निद्रा भ्रम बाच ॥ **11** ॥ AC-L(J)

---

21. K पावै .

22. A बार बार बाद नही कीजै । रांम नांम बिण कैसै जीजै ।।; CK बिद्या राम नाम निज बांनी । और अबिद्या झूठी जांनी ।।; DE is roughly the same as 9d.ab; HL ऐसा बिद्या तात मैं जांनूं । और सकल अबिद्या मांनूं ।।.

23. DE प्राइय ; HL परि .

24. E तब .

प्रहिलाद चरित्र -- 6

चौपई ॥

इतनी बात सुनी है जब ही ।
असुर हि भयौ अचंभौ तब ही ॥
सब मंत्री मिलि [1] लीये बुलाई ।
या बिद्या कौनै समझाई ॥ **1** ॥ AC-L(J)

मम द्रोही कौ ध्यान [2] दिढायौ ।
तौ हरिनाछि मुवो हम भायौ [3] ॥
गाइ बिप्र रिष बेद र देवा ।
ये तौ करै बिसन की सेवा ॥ **2** ॥ AC-L(J)

हम इन की कीनी परतीती ।
पुत्र बिगार्यौ करी अनीती ॥
अब लै जाइ याहि [4] समझावो ।
नांतर जीवत [5] रहन न पावो ॥ **3** ॥ AC-L(J)

असुर रिसाइ कही यहु बांनी ।
बिन [6] प्रहिलाद सति करि जांनी [7] ॥ AC-L(J)

---

1. HL जब मंत्री सब .
2. DE नाव .
3. DEHK ही भायौ ; L ही आयौ .
4. K याह जाइ .
5. A नहि तौ [-]य सैं .
6. HL जन .
7. A मांनो .

तब हि बिप्र प्रहिलाद हि ल्याये ।
स्यांम डंड [8] अरू भेद बताये [9] ॥ **4** ॥ AC-L

क ष ग घ नां जु लिष्यौ तब आई [10] ।
औरै अषिर पढि रे भाई [11] ॥ AC-L

प्रहलाद उबाच ॥ CHL
झूठी बिद्या मोहि नही भावै ।
तेरी अकलि ग्रभ मैं आवै ॥ **a** ॥ HL

द्वै अषिर पढि हौं सुनि पांडे ।
हरि [12] बिन और पचासौ छाडे ॥ **5** ॥ AC-L

बिप्र उबाच ॥ CFHL
तेरे पिता दिसा सब [13] जीती ।
बेद बिप्र सुर डरै [14] अनीती ॥

---

8. D सामौ डंड ; E साभौ डंड ; HL सांडा मुरगा .

9. F सुनाये .

10. A जु लिषि दीयौ आई ; HL पाटी लिषि दीन्हीं .

11. HL modify these two *padas* and add two as follows: क ष ग घ ण पाटी लिषि दीन्हीं । बिप्र बिद्या सिषावन कीन्हीं ।। और अषिर पढि रे भाई । जा सूं षुसी होइ है राई ।।.

12. HL ता .

13. D जब .

14. A बेद पुरान नि सौ जरै ; C बेद बिप्र सुर करौ ; DE बेद बिप्र सब डरै .

बिना म्रित [15] हम कौं कत [16] मारै ।
साध सोई पर कारिज सारै ॥ **6** ॥ AC-L

कहि प्रहिलाद न मारै कोई ।
जठर अगनि मैं राषै सोई ॥
उदर [17] उरध मुष षीर पीवायौ ।
प्रगट भयौ तब बाहरि आयौ ॥ **7** ॥ AC-L

तारै रांम कहौ को मारै ।
मारै रांम तबै [18] को तारै ॥
जीवन मरन [19] हाथि है जा कै ।
हम तुम बिसु सरन है [20] ता कै ॥ **8** ॥ AC-L

ऐसा प्रभु कौ सुमिरन कीजै ।
होइ सुधा ता तन मन दीजै ॥ **a** ॥ HL

बार बार तुम सौं को भाषै ।
अमृत छाडि बिषै को चाषै ॥

15. A मिंत्र ; C म्रति ; DE म्रत्य ; F म्रिति ; G मृत क ; K मृत ; L मृत्यु .

16. C क्या ; DE कोई ; HL क्यूं ; K यह .

17. DE जिहि उदर ; HL जिहि उद्र .

18. A omits मारै and for तबै has कहौ ; for तबै DEK have तब ही and L has कहै .

19. H म्रित ; L मृत्यु .

20. A कल है ; DE मरन सब ; FGJ सकल बसि ; HIL सरन सब .

बालक सबै [21] जु बीनती करही ।
कौन भांति करि हंम निसतरही ॥ **9** ॥ AC-L

ऐसी भांति अस्तुति कराई ।
तब ही प्रहलाद कै करूंनां आई ॥ **a** ॥ HL

प्रहलाद उबाच ॥ CHL
असुर कवार सुनौ मम [22] बांनी ।
नारद उकति बेद परवांनी [23] ॥
मै तै [24] मेरी यहु संसारू ।
या तै रहित सु [25] ब्रह्म बिचारू ॥ **10** ॥ AC-L

कांम क्रोध मोह मद मछर ।
जीतौ इनै मिलै पर [26] अछिर ॥ AC-L

सषा सबै तजि करौ बिचारा ।
पार ब्रह्म सुमरौ इक धारा ॥ **a** ॥ HL

बालक [27] कहै सुनौ प्रहिलादू ।
रिष सौं कहां भयौ संबादू ॥ **11** ॥ AC-L

---

21. FGIJ असुर कवार and minor variants.

22. F यहु .

23. DL परमांनी .

24. DE मै .

25. H सो ही ; I सो ; K जु ; L सोई .

26. CDEHKL परम and variants.

27. DE तब बालक . Prefaced to this *pada*, C has बालक उबाच ।।; H has सिषा उबाच ।।; L has सषा उबाच ।।.

तुम न गये वै इहां न आये ।
यहु संदेह [28] कहौ समझाये ॥ AC-L

हम अनाथ तुम पूछहि गुसांई ।
तुम हरि भक्ति [29] कहौ समझाई [30] ॥
ता तै हमरौ सांसौ भागै ।
चरण कमल मन दिढ करि लागै ॥ **a** ॥ HL

प्रहलाद उबाच ।
तब क्रिपावंत है कियौ उपदेसु ।
सब सिषांन कौ गयौ अंदेसु ॥ **b** ॥ HL

तब कथा पुरातन कहि समझाई ।
मेरौ पिता तपस्या जाई ॥ **12** ॥ AC-L

ता पीछै सुर पति चढि आयौ ।
नग्र बिधूस्यौ पावक लायौ ॥ CFGHJKL
सुर पति बंदि परी मम माता ।
उद्र ग्रभि हौ रह्यौ [31] संगाता [32] ॥ **13** ॥ AC-L

रिषि नारद कौ दरसन पायौ ।
बहुत भांति सुर पति [33] समझायौ ॥ AC-L

---

28. F अंदेस .

29. L भगत .

30. H सुनांई .

31. A omits रह्यौ ; CK हुतौ .

32. DEG समाता ; I संघाता .

33. AC सुर पति बहुत भांति .

नारद कह्यौ इंद्र सुनि लीजै ।
या बालक स्यौ बैर न कीजै ॥ **a** ॥ CFGJK

यहु बालक है हरि कौ दासा ।
या कै ब्रह्म ग्यांन प्रकासा ॥
सुर पति कह्यौ [34] नही मम कामा ।
रिषि ले जाहु आपनैं धामा ॥ **b** ॥ CFGJK

तब माता कौं रिषि [35] ले आयौ ।
ग्रभ वास मोहि ग्यांन सुनायौ ॥ **c** ॥ CFGJK

पुत्री जांनि करी प्रतिपाला ।
हित उपदेस पुष्ट [36] है बाला ॥ **14** ॥ AC-L

बीन [37] बाट है दछ्या दीनी ।
ग्रभ स्थान क [38] मैं सुनि लीनी ॥ CFGHJKL
सो हौं तुम स्यौ [39] कहूं समझाई ।
दुर्लभ देह कष्ट करि पाई ॥ **15** ॥ AC-L

सो देही हरि मारग लांऊं । FGJ
हरि कौं छाडि ब्रिथा न गमांऊं ॥ **a** ॥ FG

रांम एति ऐ तारग नांम ।
कहत सुनत सुमिरत अभिरांम ॥

34. K adds रिष after कह्यौ .

35. K has ह्रं for कौं रिषि .

36. E पुछ .

37. C प्रान ; H बैं नि ; L वै नि .

38. H जू ; L सु .

39. DEI तुम हि ; K तुम्हैं .

पढन गुणन गान चतुराई ।
ऐ सब जगत जोग है भाई ॥ **b** ॥ HL

हरि सेवा कौं कछू न चहिये ।
अन [40] धन बस्त्र समर्प्यौं लहिये ॥
सेवा सामग्री नही चाहै ।
एकै [41] भगति प्रेम [42] निरबाहै ॥ **16** ॥ AC-L

देवा दुजा [43] नही अधिकारी । AC-L
छत्री बैस सुद्र तै न्यारी [44] ॥
रांम भगति कौ सब अधिकारी । ACF-L
ब्रह्मा अंतिजु लेहु [45] बिचारी ॥ **17** ॥ AC-L

प्रेम सहत हरि के गुन गावै ।
सब तैं दुर्लभ सो पद पावै ॥
असुर कुवार भगति मन [46] लावै ।
जन प्रहिलाद हि [47] गुर करि ध्यावै ॥ **18** ॥ AC-L

सुक्र पुत्र अतिबिस मैं [48] भयौ ।
अति आतुरि राजा पै गयौ ॥ **a** ॥ ADEHL

---

40. HL तन .
41. DE ये .
42. A मुगति पेम ; CDE प्रेम भगति .
43. C पुजा ; K धिजां .
44. C तौ नारी ; GIJ त्रिय न्यारा ; HL त्रीऐ नारी ; K त्रिय नारी .
45. C देव .
46. C ल्या .
47. C कौ .
48. DE भौ ; H भै .

सांडा मुर्क पुकारे जाई ।
पट की पाघ असुर के राई [49] ॥
तेरौ पुत्र कहै बिधि ऐसी ।
बेद पुरानन समझै तैसी ॥ **19** ॥ AC-L

औरै सषा संग के भांडे ।
राज नीति के मारग छाडे ॥
ता तै हम कौं दोस न दीजै ।
जो भावै सो या [50] कौ कीजै ॥ **20** ॥ AC-L

जीवनि ब्रिति जु हरी हमारी ।
ओर दिसा जै है जु [51] बिचारी ॥ **a** ॥ DEHL

अब हम दोस नही है राई ।
पुत्र प्रहलाद हरि भक्ति समाई ॥
ऐसी बात द्विज जाइ सुनाई ।
जब ही असुर रिसायौ भाई ॥ **b** ॥ HL

दोहा ॥

सांडा अर मृक असुर पै । ऐसै करी पुकार ॥
तब हरणांकुस कोपि कैं । मारण कियौ बिचार ॥ **c** ॥ HL

नगरि ढंढोरौ फेरियौ । सब कोई मारण जाई [52] ॥
जन गोपाल प्रहिलाद कै । एकै रांम सहाई ॥ **21** ॥ AC-L

---

49. HL पाई .

50. CFH-L वा ; G हम .

51. H दिसा चाहै सु ; L दसा चाहै सु .

52. FGJ धाइ .

प्रहिलाद चरित्र -- 7

दूहा ॥ *मोतीदांम छंद* [1] ॥

बांध्यौ प्रहिलाद । महा मुनि साध ॥
सु साट [2] प्रहार । करै दिस [3] चार ॥ **1** ॥ AC-L

महा मुनि [4] धीर । डरै न सरीर ॥
लगावै भुजंग । रहै बिष संग ॥ **2** ॥ AC-L

हलाहल घोरि । ते [5] देहि बहोरि ।
झुकावै मैमंत । टुटै तिहि दंत ॥ **3** ॥ AC-L

न मोरै सु अंग । लग्यौ हरि रंग ॥
तुपक र तीर । बरषै [6] नीर ॥ **4** ॥ AC-L

---

1. This is text of F. Only K also identifies the meter as मोतीदांम . Other manuscripts identify it as follows: C दुहे ; DE दूहा ; G टोहा ; HL दुहा ; and J दोहा . This meter recurs in several later sections. It is syllabic and rhymed, but the syllable length is not always exact. The syllables are ordered ।ऽ। ।ऽ। .

2. For सु साट (CHK) , A has सटा ; DEFGIJ साट ; L सु माट .

3. K दिन .

4. CG मनि ; DEJK मन ; I मनिं ; L मुनी .

5. ADEG omit ते ; F कि ; HL सो ; J ति .

6. DE परष ही ; HL ब्रषै ज्यूं .

गुरज र सेल । बहै मुह मेल [7] ॥ AC-L
सु [8] ईट पषाण । बहै बहु बाण ॥ **5** ॥ ACF-L

गोला अर चक्र । चलै अतिबक्र [9] ॥ AC-L

षदरा तरवारि । सुहै हि बिचारि [10] ॥ **a** ॥ DEHL

जिते हथियार । करै परहार ॥ **6** ॥ AC-L

रहे पचि हारि । सरी नही [11] द्वारि ॥ **7** ॥ AC-L

स हीं सति रांम । कीयौ जन कांम ॥ **a** ॥ FGJ

दोहा ॥
च्यारि जाम करि जातना [12] । असुर सर्यौ नही कांम ॥
जन गोपाल प्रहिलाद कौं । छुवै सु रांम हि [13] रांम ॥ **8** ॥ AC-L

---

7. DE omit this and next three *padas* ; H बजै मूहुं मेल ; L बजै बहु मेल .

8. AFGHIJL omit सु .

9. A बहु बक्र ; DE बह् बह् बक्र .

10. HL षपवा तरबार । सो देह बिचार ।।.

11. CK सरीर हि ; DEJ सरीर नही ; HL सरी न .

12. GHKL सासनां .

13. For सु रांम हि , D reads एक ही ; E स रांम की .

प्रहिलाद चरित्र -- 8

चौपई ॥

जन प्रहिलाद रहे तब [1] ऐसै ।
मनहु चित्र कौ दीपक जैसै ॥
प्राण रह्यौ परमेसुर संगा ।
ताती बाव न लागी अंगा ॥ **1** ॥ AC-L

साचौ दिब [2] देत है जैसै ।
सीतल बहनि होत है तैसै [3] ॥
यौं [4] साचे कौं परमेस्वर राषै ।
कहा जगत अग्यांनी [5] भाषै ॥ **2** ॥ AC-L

साषी ॥
दादू षडग धार बिष नां मरै ।
कोई गुण ब्यापै नांहिं ॥
रांम रहै त्यूं [6] जन रहै ।
काल झाल जल मांहिं ॥ **a** ॥ FGIJ

दूतनि [7] कही असुर सौं बाता ।
हम सौं बची न एकै घाता ॥

1. A बिधि ; HL जब ; K जु .
2. K तौंबौ बिधि .
3. A जैसै ; FGIJ कैसै .
4. ADEHL omit यौं .
5. HL अग्यांन हि .
6. G स्यूं .
7. DE ईतनी .

सब आवध [8] गज श्रप लगाये ।
बिचि बिचि बांटि [9] हलाहल पाये [10] ॥ **3** ॥ AC-L

ना जानौ यहु [11] कौनै राष्यौ ।
दिबि देह अमृत सौ चाष्यौ ॥
असुर हि [12] रैणि छ मासी होई [13] ।
है प्रहिलाद हि मारै कोई ॥ **4** ॥ AC-L

भोर भये कह्यौ जल मै बोरौ ।
मेलि [14] जंजीर धार मै छोरौ [15] ॥
ऐसी भांति [16] डारि हौ जब ही ।
मगरमंछ लै जैहै तब ही ॥ **5** ॥ AC-L

हुकम करत प्रहिलाद ही ल्याये ।
भारे लंगर लोह मगाये [17] ॥
बांधि असुर [18] जब बोरन लागे ।
भयौ अचंभौ सोवत से [19] जागे ॥ **6** ॥ AC-L

---

8. K आजुधन .
9. A घोरि ; C घोलि ; D बांधि .
10. CHKL पाऐ ; D पावै ; E पाइ ; G पाए ; I प्याऐ ; J प्याये .
11. DF-J वो ; E वौ ; KL वह .
12. DE omit हि .
13. DE जाई .
14. C बाधि ; J मेति .
15. J कोरौ .
16. A ऐसैं पकरि .
17. C पहराऐ .
18. DE जंजीर .
19. ADEGK omit से .

छूटि जंजीर बूडि गये भाई [20] ।
पदम पत्र प्रहिलाद तिराई ॥ **7** ॥ **AC-L**

संमर्थ करै सु कहे न होई ।
आविगति गति जांनै नही कोई ॥ **a** ॥ **A**

धनि तुम जन की जीवनि रांमां ।
जहां तहां संवारै कांमां ॥ **b** ॥ **FGJ**

नांव प्रताप बूडि नहीं जाई ।
जन कूं राषै रांम गुसांई ॥ **c** ॥ **HL**

तारै [21] रांम न मारै [22] कोई ।
सिला तिरी जानैं जगु सोई [23] ॥ **DEHKL**
माहो मांहि मिलि करै बिचारा ।
जाइ राइ पै करो पुकारा ॥ **d** ॥ **HL**

दोहा ॥
जिन के बांधे गज रहै । तिन सूं बांध्यौ धाइ [24] ॥
जन गोपाल प्रहिलाद की । यौं हरि करी सहाइ ॥ **8** ॥ **AC-L**

---

20. K नांही .
21. HL राषै .
22. K बौरै ; L बोरै .
23. K सब कोई ; for whole *pada* HL read: देषै दूत अचंभो होई ॥.
24. C जाइ .

प्रहिलाद चरित्र -- 9

दूत उबाच ॥ चौपई ॥
दूत पुकारत कीन्हीं बाता ।
हम पकर्यौ ज्यूं राहा चंद कौ गाता ॥
बांधि जजीर नाष्यौ जल मांहीं ।
तूटत जंजीर हम देषे नांहीं ॥ **a** ॥ HL

जल तै निकसि भऐ जब ठाढे ।
सब असुरनि अचरज परे गाढे ॥
या कौं मारै मा [1] पै लाई ।
सकल दैत मिलि लीऐ बुलाई ॥ **b** ॥ HL

करौ मतौ जैसै जो [2] मरही ।
हिरदै साल मेरै यौ बसही ॥
ता तैं सब तुम कहौ सु बाता ।
अब तुम करौ सु या कौ घाता ॥ **c** ॥ HL

या कूं है कोई मारणहारू ।
ता की नृपति करै प्रतिपारू ॥
दूतन कहौ सुनौ प्रहलादू ।
अब मति झूंठौ करौ बिबादू ॥ **d** ॥ HL

1. H मो .

2. H एह .

प्रहलाद उबाच ॥ *दोहा* ॥
बिस्न उपास जु हम लीयौ । सो क्यूं छोड्यौ जाइ ॥
जगत भगति [3] यूं आदि है । साध कहै समझाइ ॥ **e** ॥ HL

चौपई ॥
हरिणकसिब तब उठ्यौ रिसाई ।
अंध कूप मै डारौ जाई [4] ॥
मेरी बात न मानै कौ नौं ।
तूटै कांन कहा सो [5] सौनौं ॥ **1** ॥ AC-L

पुत्र चाहि तैं भलौ अऊत् [6] ।
जौ कुल धरम न चालै पूत् ॥
गहि प्रहिलाद कुवा [7] मै दीनौ ।
माटी [8] सिला पाटि तिहि [9] लीनौ ॥ **2** ॥ AC-L

त्राहि त्राहि सब कोई भाषै ।
छिन छिन रांम कहौ क्यूं राषै ॥
राषणहारौ सदा [10] सचेत् ।
जानै नही अज्ञान अचेत् ॥ **3** ॥ AC-L

---

3. L भगत .

4. CFGIJK डारौ भाई ; DE गाडो भाई .

5. A करै ; HL जो .

6. A बुतु .

7. C कुप ; HL कूप .

8. HKL मोटी .

9. C तिन ; D-GIJ तब ; HKL जब .

10. FGIJ सु सदा .

दोहा ॥
सकल विस्व चिता भई । जन कैं कछू न होइ ॥
रांम कहै [11] प्रहलाद यूं । तन की सुधि न कोइ ॥ **a** ॥ HL

बिरह ॥ *मोतीदांम छंद* [12] ॥
रोवै ता की माइ । परै मुरझाइ ॥
रोवै ता की धाई । करै हाइ हाइ ॥ **4** ॥ AC-L

रोवै पित धीय [13] । नही तिहि [14] जीय ॥
रोवै सब बीर । कहां मति धीर ॥ **5** ॥ AC-L

रोवै सब मिंत । परे बहु चिंत ॥
रोवै सब बाल । पटकहि भाल ॥ **6** ॥ AC-L

रोवै सब साध । कहां प्रहिलाद ॥
रोवै गुर देव । करै कौंन सेव ॥ **7** ॥ AC-L

रोवै रिष राइ । कहां सुष दाइ ॥
रोवै पुर [15] ठाट । निहारि हि बाट ॥ **8** ॥ AC-L

रोवै सब गांव । लिये मुष नांव ॥
रोवै पसु पंषि । निहारै हि अंषि ॥ **9** ॥ AC-L

---

11. H पुकारै .

12. ADEG बिरह कौं छंद ; C छंद जौहर कौ गिद उछल ; HL छंद ब्रिह कौ ; IJ बिरह; K छंद मौतीदांम बृह कौ .

13. C पति धीय ; K पति धीह ; L पति धीर .

14. DE मानैं ; HL मांनू .

15. DE सब .

रोवै सुर [16] देव । कहां हरि सेव ॥
न काढ हि सास । दयंत [17] की त्रास ॥ **10** ॥ AC-L

सबै दुष पावै । बोल्यौ नहीं जावै ॥
प्रहलाद कै रांम । संगी सुष धांम ॥ **a** ॥ HL

दोहा ॥
सकल बिसु दुष पाईयौ । दैत सौं न [18] बसाई ॥
अबिगति गति गोब्यंद की । क्यूं ही लषी न जाई ॥ **11** ॥ AC-L

हरिणकसिब कौं सुष [19] भयौ । मान्यौ छिन आनंद ॥
जन गोपाल प्रहिलाद गृह । प्रगट्यौ पूरण चंद ॥ **12** ॥ AC-L

प्रहिलाद चरित्र -- 10

चौपई ॥
मारग गोपि धरनि तब दीनौ ।
जै जै कार सकल जग कीनौ [1] ॥
देषि असुर मनि अचिरज होई [2] ।
हरि को चरित न जानै कोई [3] ॥ **1** ॥ AD(E)GHJKL

---

16. C गुर .

17. L दैपूत .

18. For न DEHKL have कछु न .

19. DE दुष .

1. D(E) भयो पुर तीनों ; HL सकल पुर कीन्हौ .

2. HL असुर कै मन अचंभौ होई ।.

3. D(E)K अबगति गति जानैं नही कोई ।।; HL अबगति की गति लषै न कोई ।।. Manuscripts GJ put this verse before the final *dohā* of section 9.

जल मैं जल धर मै धर [4] भाई ।
अगनि पवन मिलि ब्रह्म समाइ ॥
सस्त्र अग्नि बिष भै नही [5] व्यापै ।
जन कौ जस दे निहचल थापै [6] ॥ **a** ॥ AGJ

हरणकसिब उबाच [7] ॥
कहि प्रहिलाद इष्ट को तेरौ ।
जा तैं परहस सरै न [8] मेरौ ॥
कौंन जरी किहि मंत्र [9] उबार्यौ ।
हम [10] तू बहुत भांति करि मार्यौ ॥ **2** ॥ AC-L(E)

प्रहिलाद उबाच ॥ CFGHJKL
मेरौ इष्ट सुनौ हो राई ॥
जिहि सब कीयौ र मंझि [11] समाई ॥
स चराचर मै ब्यापक [12] सारै ।
अग्यांनी ताहि [13] दूरि बिचारै ॥ **3** ॥ AC-L(E)

---

4. A omits the second धर ; G घर में घर .

5. A सस्त्र अग्नि जल बिष नही ; J सह अगनी बिष भै नही .

6. Manuscripts GJ put this verse, like previous one, before the final *dohā* of section 9.

7. D(E)I omit this line. HL असुर उबाच ।।; K राजा उबाच ।।.

8. A परिहंस चलै न ; C परहस लगत न ; D(E) परहरै संग .

9. D(E) मित्र ; L मिंत्र .

10. D(E) मै .

11. D(E) रूप मुझि ; L र मंडि .

12. C बर तौ .

13. A ते ; F सो जो ; GIJ सो .

रांम नांम निज मंत्र हमारै ।
जीवनि जरी सदा उर धारै ॥
षडग धार बिष अगनि मंझारी [14] ।
जल थल परबत मौति बिचारी [15] ॥ **4** ॥ AC-L(E)

जम जौरा भै कौंन [16] बिचारै ।
परलै अग्नि जन कौं नही जारै ॥ AC-L(E)

ऐसी सुणि हम भगति सम्हाई ।
तुम अग्यांन हीं लडत गुमाई ॥ **a** ॥ HL

असुर उबाच [17] ॥ HKL
सब कोई रांम कहै रे भाई ।
तोहि माहि कहा अधिकाई [18] ॥ **5** ॥ AC-L(E)

ऐसी पूछ करी तब राई ।
जब प्रहलाद कहै समझाई ॥ **a** ॥ HL

प्रहिलाद उबाच ॥ GHJKL
रांम नांम सब कोई गावै ।
बिन बिसवास कहा फल पावै ॥ AC-L(E)
सीस उतारि कहै सो [19] रांमा ।
देषा देषी सरै न कांमा ॥ **6** ॥ CFGHJKL

---

14. D(E) उबारी .
15. HL निवारी .
16. FGIJ जौरा की कौंन ; HL जूरा कौ भै न .
17. K राजा उबाच .
18. D(E) संकलाई .
19. C को ; F जो ; K जे .

देषा देषी जो रण मैं जावै ।
भीड पड्या सै पूठि बतावै ॥ **a** ॥ **HL**

मरि करि रांम सती कहै जैसै ।
देषनहार [20] कहै घरि बैसै ॥ **AC-L(E)**
सती नैंक नही मोर्यों अंगा ।
आपौ जारि रही पीव संगा ॥ **7** ॥ **CFGKJ**

अमृत [21] कलस सीस परि लीजे [22] ।
मरि जईये जौ [23] मुषा न पीजे ॥ **AC-L(E)**

बहु बिधि पाक धर्यो मुष आगै ।
बिन षाऐ भूष नहि [24] भागै ॥ **a** ॥ **CK**

रोटी पूठि भूष [25] नहि जाई । **AC-L(E)**
बिन जल पीये त्रिषा न बुझाई [26] ॥ **8** ॥ **AC-I(E)KL**

वोषदि रूंष आहि [27] घर बारा [28] ।
बिन घसि लाये मरै गंवारा ॥
रांम नांम कौ ब्यौरौ कीनौ ।
दुष्टनि दुष संतनि सुष दीनौ ॥ **9** ॥ **AC-L(E)**

---

20. D(E) कोतिगहार .
21. D(E) ज्यों अम्रत .
22. A परि धरिये ; D(E)FGIJ भरि लीजे ; K धरि लीजे .
23. A तौ ; K सौ .
24. K षाऐ तैं भूष न .
25. HL षुध्या .
26. D(E) जाई .
27. D(E) इहि .
28. K द्वारा .

चिंतामनि कौ दोस न कोई ।
जो बांछै सो प्रगट होई [29] ॥ **10** ॥ CFGHJKL

चिंतामनि हरि जी कौ [30] नांमां ।
जैसी मनसा तैसै कांमां ॥ **a** ॥ FGHJL

दोहा ॥
नही आस सरीर की । सब सुष झूठे [31] जांनि ॥
जन गोपाल प्रहिलाद यूं [32] । सुमिरै सारंगपानि ॥ **11** ॥ AC-L(E)

प्रहिलाद चरित्र -- 11

चौपई ॥
प्रगट भगति [1] प्रहिलाद पुकारै ।
रांम नांम सुनिये [2] जग सारै ॥
षिन रोवै षिन नाचै गावै ।
षिन ही मै करताल बजावै ॥ **1** ॥ AC-L(E)

लज्या रहित रांम रसि मातौ [3] ।
टुटौ देह जगत कौ [4] नातौ ॥

---

29. HL प्रापति होई ; K प्रगटै सौई .

30. HL है हरि कौ .

31. D(E) बूझे .

32. D(E) कै .

1. IK भगत .

2. K कहीयौ .

3. D(E) रातो .

4. D(E)GIJK सौं and variants.

सषानि सहित हरि नांव उचारै ।
ग्यान ध्यान बैराग [5] बिचारै ॥ **2** ॥ AC-L(E)

सांच कहै जगत मारन धावै ।
चोर हि क्यूं उजियारौ [6] भावै ॥
इहि बिधि जगत भगत कौ बैरी ।
धनि रांम राषै पति मेरी [7] ॥ **3** ॥ AC-L(E)

दयंत छल बल दाव [8] बिचारै ।
है कोई प्रहिलाद हि मारै ॥
अब कै बांधि सिषर [9] तैं डारौ ।
अहो असुर मम कारिज [10] सारौ ॥ **4** ॥ AC-L(E)

इतनौ जाब कह्यौ है राई ।
दूत उठे अर सीस नबाई ॥ **a** ॥ HL

मोट [11] बांधि असुर लै जांहीं ।
प्रहिलाद [12] कै भै कछु नांहीं [13] ॥ AC-L(E)

---

5. D(E) मन मांहि .

6. D(E) कौं अंधियारौ .

7. C राषै पन मेरी ; D(E) राषै पुनि नेरी ; FGIJ राषै पुर नैरी ; H पण राषै मेरी ;L पति राषै मेरी .

8. CF डाव .

9. K बरत .

10. J कीजै .

11. HIKL पोट .

12. CHKL जन प्रहलाद .

13. A भै काही ; D(E) भय को नांहि ; H कहूं भै नांहीं ; K भै कहूं नांही ; L कहूं भय नांहीं .

असुर [14] कहै सुनि राज कवारा ।
कहा बिश्न अब करै संभारा [15] ॥ **5** ॥ AC-L

दूत प्रमोध देत है ऐसै ।
मानौ सीष हमारी जैसै ॥ **a** ॥ HL

प्रहलाद उबाच ॥ CGHJKL
जल थल बिश्न अरू परबत आगी ।
षडग धार बिष तैं भै भागी ॥
डारौ बेगि तुमैं नही दोसू ।
तुम सौं असुर करैगो रोसू ॥ **6** ॥ AC-L

डारत ही बंधन सब [16] टूटे ।
यूं जन रांम रांम कहि छूटे ॥
ज्यूं पंषी आकास तै आवै [17] ।
यूं प्रहिलाद मगन गुन गावै ॥ **7** ॥ AC-L

यांहां दूत मन मोद हि आयौ ।
प्रथ्वी देष्यौ साध गुडायौ ॥
सांचा जन कूं अबनी झेलै ।
रांम प्रताप दुष्ट सब पेलै ॥ **a** ॥ HL

दोहा ॥
जल थल परबत राषीयौ । षडग धार बिष त्रास ॥
जन गोपाल प्रहिलाद कै । पूरण ब्रह्म प्रकास ॥ **8** ॥ AC-L

---

14 HL दूत .

15. DE राषै इहि बारू .

16. FGIJ से .

17. K धावैं .

प्रहिलाद चरित्र -- 12

हरणकसिब उबाच [1] ॥ चौपई ॥ CDEHKL

हरणकसिब कहै सुनि [2] प्रहिलादु ।
छाडै क्यूं न बिसन कौ बादु ॥
तौ हूं पिता पुत्र तू मेरौ ।
राज पाट बिभौ सब तेरौ ॥ **1** ॥ AC-L

कहै प्रहिलाद बिसन पित [3] माता ।
सगौ [4] सनेही प्रीतम भ्राता ॥
ता बिन [5] सब थोथरी सगाई ।
लष चौरासी आवै जाई ॥ **2** ॥ AC-L

माया सौं रचि ताहि बिसारै ।
मिथ्या जनम बिषै सौं [6] हारै ॥
सुपिनै मै रजधांनी सांची ।
जागि परै तब दीसै [7] काची ॥ **3** ॥ AC-L

> इहि बिधि देह राज सब जांहीं ।
> करि बिचार अरु ध्यांन समांहीं ॥ **a** ॥ HL

---

1. HL असुर उबाच .
2. EK omit सुनि .
3. For बिसन पित , K has पिता अरु . HKL preface to this *pada* प्रहलाद उबाच .
4. G सजन .
5. E ता हिन ; K जा बिन .
6. F लगि ; HL संगि .
7. A जागि देषौं तौ सब ही .

कै सो [8] जाइ कै आपुन मरिये ।
पिता [9] बिसन कैसैं परहरिये ॥ AC-L

माता पिता कलत्र कुल बंधू ।
देह देह प्रति मिलै समंधू ॥
सुष संपति रु बिषै रस भोगा ।
पसू पंषी हू लेह ऐह जोगा ॥ **a** ॥ HL

परि ऐही देष्या थरि नांहीं ।
पूरब जनम के क्रत अबगाही [10] ॥
ता तैं हरि बिन कहूं न सुष ।
सदा संगांती [11] प्रेम पिवष ॥ **b** ॥ HL

बिसन कहत सो [12] उठ्यौ रिसाई ।
मारौ बेगि भागि नही [13] जाई ॥ **4** ॥ AC-L

जा कै तौ मन और ही रहा [14] ।
जा तै मैं दुष पांऊं माहा [15] ।। **c** ।। HL

चंदन कै बनि [16] उपज्यौ बांसू ।
जब तब [17] करै कटुंब कौ नासू ॥

---

8. AB सोई ; EK सौ ; H वौ ; L बौ .

9. DEHL तौ पिता .

10. H अब आंहीं .

11. H संगती .

12. A तब .

13. A भाजि जिनि ; C भागि जिन .

14. H आंहीं .

15. H मांहीं .

16. A विडै ; K कै संग .

17. AF जदि तदि .

जैसें श्रप अंगूठा लागै ।
नष सष लहरि हलाहल जागै ॥ **5** ॥ AC-L

ता तैं काटि अंगूठा डारै ।
मोह करै तौ स्रब सहारै ॥
तन कौ दुष न काहि सुहाई [18] ।
बन [19] बूंटी तैं बेदन जाई ॥ **6** ॥ AC-L

सत्र पुत्र [20] कौ भेष बनायौ ।
कुल अंगार न काहू भायौ ॥
श्रप [21] स्यंघ अरु स्वांन लगाये ।
अंतरजांमी निकटि न आये ॥ **7** ॥ AC-L

बहुर्यों [22] नाग पासि स्यौं बांधे ।
समद बोरि दयंत [23] आराधे ॥
तब तिन ले परबत तन [24] चांपे ।
डोली धरणि सेस सिर कांपे ॥ **8** ॥ AC-L

परबत भये मनहु सिर [25] फूला ।
छूटी पासि जल थल सम तूला ॥

---

18. DEK सुनाई .

19. H बिनि ; KL बिन .

20. C मित्र .

21. DEL तब सरप ; HK तब श्रप .

22. DE तब तिहि ; J बहु सौं .

23. A बोरि रु दैंत ; K बौरि अरु दैंत .

24. A तिहि गहि परबत से ; C तिन ले परबत से ; DE omit ले ; HL have गहै/गहि for ले .

25. A सिर परि .

सकल बियापी सब मैं राषै [26] ।
जन प्रहिलाद [27] रांम सति भाषै [28] ॥ **9** ॥ AC-L

दोहा ॥
संम्रथ राषणहार है । तौ मारणहार न [29] कोई ॥
जन गोपाल जग झषि मरै [30] । बाल न बांकौ [31] होई ॥ **10** ॥ AC-L

प्रहिलाद चरित्र -- 13

चौपई ॥
होरी बहन कहै सुनि राजा ।
मो तैं सरै तुम्हारौ काजा ॥
मैं [1] बहु भांति तपस्या कीनी ।
तब स्यौं [2] मोहि अभै गति दीनी ॥ **1** ॥ AC-L

जारी जरौ न मारी मरौं ।
अब कै काज तुम्हारौ करौं ॥

---

26. For मैं राषै , K has ही भाषै .

27. For प्रहिलाद , J has प्रहिलाद मैं .

28. K राषै .

29. DE मारि न सकै ; J मारन संहार न .

30. HIKL रहै .

31. A बार न बंकौ ; DE बार न कब कौ ; FGIJ बांकौ बाल न .

1. A य्यैं .

2. C सीव ; D शिव ; EHL सिव ; FI स्यौ ; K सेव .

बहुत भांति करि काठ मगावो ।
ले पैठों [3] तुम अगनि लगावो [4] ॥ **2** ॥ AC-L

मेरी बजर मइ देह है सोई ।
जा कूं भै नहीं ब्यापै कोई ॥
और उपाइ या कूं कोई नांहीं ।
सकल सभा मिलि मानूं या ही ॥ **a** ॥ HL

तब राजा मन हरष्यौ भयौ ।
बहन हमारौ कारज करिलयौ ॥
जदि प्रहलाद हि देष्यौ नैंनां ।
तब लग नांहि न मो कूं चैनां ॥ **b** ॥ HL

काठ सकेलै करै उछाहू ।
भगति भाव [5] भावै नही काहू ॥
तब घर रच्यौ काठ बिसतारे ।
दसौ दिसा [6] परबत से डारे ॥ **3** ॥ AC-L

होरी गोद लीयौ प्रहिलादू ।
नित [7] की अधम दुष्टनी [8] आदू ॥

---

3. CDEGK बैठौं .

4. C पावक लावो ; J अगनि लऊ .

5. H भगति वांन ; L भगत वांन .

6. HKL दसा .

7. CKL तिन .

8. C दुसट अर मणि ; D अधरम नि दुष्टनी ; E अध्रम दूस्टनी ; G अधरमि न दुष्टनी ; K दुष्ट अधर्म नी .

जौ कोई वा कौ दरसन [9] देषै ।
हरि [10] तै बिमुष असुर गति लेषै ॥ **4** ॥ AC-L

राजा रच्यौ अचंभौ भारी ।
देषन गये नगर [11] नर नारी ॥
लै प्रहिलाद तत छिन पैठी [12] ।
भीतरि दे [13] आडी होइ बैठी ॥ **5** ॥ AC-L

दोहा ॥ CHKL
असुर अचंभौ मांडि कैं । दीन्ही अगनि प्रजारि ।
अचिंत ब्रह्म चिंता रहत । सो अब लेह सम्हारि ॥ **a** ॥ HL

जिन कौं राषै रांम जी । तिन कौं कहूं भै [14] नांहि ।
जिन कौं छाडै हाथ तैं । ते लीजै घर [15] मांहि ॥ **6** ॥ CF-L

मोतीदांम छंद [16] ॥
आयौ तब राइ । भई हाइ हाइ ॥
लगावहु [17] आगि । न जाइ सु [18] भागि ॥ **7** ॥ AC-L

---

9. C मुष .

10. DEHKL तौ हरि .

11. A आये नग्र ; DE गये सकल .

12. C बैठी .

13. C बारि अहोइ ; DE भीतरि तैं .

14. C कोई भै ; F भै कहूं ; K भै कंहू .

15. HL ते बचै नहीं घर .

16. A छंद जौंहर कौं ; C छंद गीद उछाल ; D छंद ; EGIJ omit the phrase; HL जहुर कौ छंद ; only FK call meter मोतीदांम .

17. HL लगावै सो .

18. For जाइ सु , K has जाहु .

करी गज [19] बारि । उठै ते पुकारि [20] ॥
मारौ इहि [21] ताइ । जहां है [22] जाइ ॥ **8** ॥ AC-L

गहौ हथियार । सनमुष मार [23] ॥
कर सौं कर जोरि । ते [24] लाष करोरि ॥ **9** ॥ AC-L

फिरैं [25] बहु जोध । करै परमोध ॥
सीचैं घ्रित [26] तेल । अगनि कै [27] मेल ॥ **10** ॥ AC-L

रुई र कपास । भरे जु [28] अवास ॥
लावै सन सूत । दयंत [29] के पूत [30] ॥ **11** ॥ AC-L

धरनि अकास । अगनि प्रकास ॥
कहै जु [31] दयंत । भागै सब [32] चिंत ॥ **12** ॥ AC-L

---

19. I राज .

20. A उठि जु पुकारि ; C उठ्यै ते ल गारि ; DE उठै तिहि पुकारि ; HL उठत पुकारि ; K उठे लल कार .

21. DEK तिहि ; HL ताहि .

22. DE तब ; FGIJ अब ; HL होइ .

23. F शार .

24. FGJ ति ; H सो ; L सु .

25. DE किरै .

26. A मेलै घृत ; DE सीचै तित .

27. DE मुह .

28. CFIJ ई .

29. HL सो दैंत .

30. FGI दूत ; J दुत .

31. FGIJ सब .

32. DEHL अब .

न जानहि [33] अंध । क्रिपा निधि सिंध [34] ॥ AC-L
राषै जाहि [35] रांम । न होइ अकांम [36] ॥ **13** ॥ DEGHJKL

माहा सुष सार । प्रहलाद अपार ॥ HL
रही बहणी दूरि । सुसीत हजूरि [37] ॥ **a** ॥ CHL

दोहा ॥
चारि पहर मैं जरि [38] बुझी । होरी ह्वै गई राष ॥
कंचन कौं बांनी चढी [39] । जरी घुंघची लाष ॥ **14** ॥ AC-L

अगनि नीर समि ह्वै गई । ताती लगी न बाइ [40] ॥
जन गोपाल प्रहलाद की । कीन्ही रांम सहाइ [41] ॥ **a** ॥ CHIKL

भगत [42] द्रोह सब तै बुरौ । कबहू कीजे नाहि ॥
होरी अगनि जु जरि गई [43] । जन गोपाल ता माहि ॥ **15** ॥ AD-HJKL

---

33. DE जानै नही .

34. A क्रिपाल न्रिरे सिधा ; CFIK क्रिपा निधि सिंध ; DEGHL क्रिपा सुष सिंध ; J किपा निधि मिंत .

35. HL ताहि . For GJ see following note.

36. GJ अनंत अपार । रहै जन लार ।।.

37. C न जांय सु दुरि । सदा ही हजुरि ।।.

38. D ब?लि ; E जलि ; K झल .

39. D-GIJK षरी .

40. C बाव ; K बावै .

41. CK सहाव .

42. AH भगति .

43. A जु बलि गई ; DE जु ह्वै गई ; G मैं बरि गई ; J जु बरि गई ; K जु जरि बुझी .

प्रहिलाद चरित्र -- **14**

चौपई ।
मन ही माहि [1] असुर दुष पावै ।
बाहरि तौ कछू कहि न जनावै ॥
सहि न सकै हरि कौ परतापू ।
पापी कै जीय [2] सोग संतापू ॥ **1** ॥ AC-L

जब लग सुत प्रहिलाद अनेरौ ।
तब लग राज नही इहां [3] मेरौ ॥
बैरी पछि [4] सोधि इहि लीनौ ।
राज धरम कुल ऐक न कीनौ [5] ॥ **2** ॥ AC-L

मो जीवत ही करै अनैसी [6] ।
मूवा पीछैं करि है कैसी ॥
करि प्रहिलाद हमारौ भायौ ।
बिस्व मांहि [7] तैं षरौ संतायौ [8] ॥ **3** ॥ AC-L

> सुर नर असुर जु आग्या कारी ।
> ना जांनौं तै कहा बिचारी ॥ **a** ॥ ADEHKL

---

1. L मन ही मन .
2. CDEHL मन .
3. DE यहु ; AHL omit इहां .
4. L पढि .
5. HL चीनौ .
6. HKL है ऐसी (for अनैसी).
7. DE नांनांव .
8. DEHL षिजायौ ; FK दुषायौ .

नातर अब गहि मारौ तोही ।
पीछै दोस न दीजै मोही ॥
कहै प्रहिलाद सुनौ हो राजा ।
अंध अग्यान बकै बेकाजा ॥ **4** ॥ AC-L

जिहि राष्यौ जल थल [9] ज्वाला मांही ।
अजहूं तोहि भरोसौ नाही ॥
जौ ससि पूरब पछिम भांनां [10] ।
गंग जमुन जौ लोपै [11] आंनां ॥ **5** ॥ AC-L

सीतल बहनी होई जौ कबहू ।
रांम नांम नही छाडौं तबहू ॥
तब पकरि षंभ सौं बांध्यौ ध्याई [12] ।
जो बोलै ताहि घालौ षाई [13] ॥ **6** ॥ AC-L

काढि षडग मारन कौं [14] धायौ ।
प्रहिलाद [15] कै भै [16] नही आयौ ॥
मोहि बताइ कहा रांमू ।
सारै सकल तुम्हारौ कांमू ॥ **7** ॥ AC-L

> होइ करूर कही इह बांनीं ।
> जन प्रहलाद संक नहीं आंनीं ॥ **a** ॥ HL

---

9. H जल थल परबत ; L परवत .
10. L पछि मांजां .
11. AC मेटै .
12. K भाई .
13. HKL घाई .
14. CF जब मारन .
15. CHKL जन प्रहलाद .
16. A डर .

प्रहलाद उबाच ॥
है सब माहि संत जन बूझै [17] ।
कांम क्रोध मै कैसै [18] सुझै ॥ AC-L

तुम तौ राजा भया अयांनां ।
हरि किरपा बिन लहै न ग्यांनां ॥ **a** ॥ HL

षडग षंभ मो तो मैं सोई ।
पूरण ब्रह्म सति करि जोई [19] ॥ ADEHKL
रमता घट घट रह्या समाई ।
रज तम अहं दिसटि नही आई ॥ **b** ॥ HL

तूं अहं ग्रब आंधौ करि डार्यौ ।
अंतरजांमी निकटि बिसार्यौ ॥ **c** ॥ FGJ

मो मैं तो मैं षदग [20] षंभ मैं ।
सब हीं मांहिं दयाल ॥
रमिता रांम बिचारि ले ।
ताहि न लागै काल ॥ **d** ॥ FGIJ

हरणकसिब कर उचौ कीनौ ।
है है [21] कार भयौ पुर तीनौं ॥ **8** ॥ AC-L

---

17. DE सब सूझै .
18. DE मैं ते नही .
19. A बाहरि भीतरि और न कोई .
20. GI omit षडग .
21. DE जै जै .

सुर नर साध सिध संसारा ।
पंचौं तत कोपे तिहि बारा ॥ **e** ॥ FGJ

सुर नर नाग लोक मधि सोई ।
है है कार करै सब कोई ॥ **f** ॥ HL

हरि भगतां कूं सदा सहाई
जन प्रहलाद की टेक निवाही [22] ॥
एसौ प्रभू ऐक रूप बनायौ ।
भयौ नर सिंह दुष्ट सतायौ ॥ **g** ॥ HL

साषी ॥
दादू जबही साध संताईये । तबही ऊंध पलट ॥
आकास धसै धरती षिसै । तीनों लोक गरक [23] ॥ **h** ॥ FGJ

दोहा ॥
हरणकसिब की बैरता । पलटि र नाहर होइ ॥
त्यूं ही भाव प्रहिलाद कौ । गऊ बछ समि [24] सोइ ॥ **9** ॥ AC-L

यहु दरपन कौ देषिबौ [25] । सूझै [26] मुष उनहारि ॥ AC-L
जन गोपाल जैसौ इहां । तैसौ उहां बिचारि [27] ॥ **10** ॥ AC-HJKL

---

22. H निभाई .

23. J गरट .

24. DEK बछलौं (for बछ समि).

25. G पेषनो .

26. DEF दीसै .

27. I बैरी कौं बैरी सदा । म्यंत्र हि म्यंत्र बिचारि ।।.

प्रहिलाद चरित्र -- 15

भगति बछलता ॥ *मोतीदांम छंद* ॥ **F**

प्रगट्यौ नरस्यंघ । जहां निज अंग ॥
फार्यौ तिहि षंभ । कीयौ सु अचंभ ॥ **1** ॥ **AC-L**

उठ्यौ गल गाजि । रह्यौ रिप [1] लाजि ॥
अग्यांनी अबुध । कीयौ तिहि जुध ॥ **2** ॥ **AC-L**

गह्यौ ललकारि । धरनि पछारि ॥ **AC-L**

न भूंमि अकास । उछंग बठास ॥ **a** ॥ **HL**

जहां घर बार । तहां मची मार ॥ **3** ॥ **AC-L**

दिवस न राति । हत्यौ नष दांति ॥
पुरिष न नारि । सु ब्रह्म बिचारि ॥ **4** ॥ **AC-L**

भयांनक भेस । डरे सुर सेस ॥
अदभुत रूप । न देष्यौ [2] अनूप ॥ **5** ॥ **AC-L**

प्रहिलाद कै अंग । गऊ बछ संग ॥
मारै ताहि धाइ । निकटि जु जाइ ॥ **6** ॥ **AC-L**

रगत्र से नैन । भयांनक बैन ॥
बडे बडे दंत । सोहै गलि अंत ॥ **7** ॥ **AC-L**

---

1. G रिषि .

2. CHL देष्यौ जु .

श्रोनित लाल । ते [3] बाहु [4] बिसाल ॥
दयाल दयाल । दयाल दयाल [5] ॥ **8** ॥ AC-L

सदा प्रतिपाल । सो काल कौ काल ॥ **a** ॥ HL

दोहा ॥
भगति बछलता प्रगटी । देष्यौ नरस्यंघ रूप [6] ॥
जन गोपाल प्रहिलाद तब । कीयौ भगति के भूप ॥ **9** ॥ AC-L

प्रहिलाद चरित्र -- 16

ब्रह्म अस्तुति ॥ *मोतीदांम छंद* ॥ F

प्रभू समरथ । सबै तुम हाथ ॥
प्रलै छिन मांहि । श्रीज्यौ सब ताहि ॥ **a** ॥ DEHKL

भगत [1] दिढाव । कीयौ जु पसाव ॥
ठाढे सुर सैंन । देषै मन नैंन [2] ॥ **b** ॥ DEHKL

अगाध अबाध । कहै सब साध ॥
अतीत अजीत । कहै सब रीत [3] ॥ **1** ॥ AC-L

---

3. C दो.
4. GL बहुत .
5. HL भगति किरपाल .
6. A अदभूत रूप ; CHL अरूपारूप ; DE देषि अरु रूप ; K अरूपी रूप .
1. HKL भगति .
2. DE मन मैंन ; K सुन नैंन .
3. AC गुन गीत ; DEJ सब संत .

अनंत अगनंत [4] । कहै सब संत ॥ **ACF-IKL**
अगाहु अथाहु । कहै जु अलाहु [5] ॥ **2** ॥ **AC-L**

अलेष अदेष । कहै सुर सेष ॥
अभेद अछेद । कहै सब बेद ॥ **3** ॥ **AC-L**

अपार अधार [6] । कहै निरकार [7] ॥
अडोल अतोल । कहै जु अमोल ॥ **4** ॥ **AC-L**

अद्वीत अभीत [8] । कहै गुन गीत ॥
अजाप अथाप । कहै जु अमाप ॥ **5** ॥ **AC-L**

अदेह अछेह । कहै जु अग्रेह ॥
अनंग असंग । अभंग [9] अभंग ॥ **6** ॥ **AC-L**

दोहा ॥
सेस पार पावै नही । निगम नेति जस गाइ ॥
ररं कार कौं स्यौ जपै । अस्तुति करी [10] न जाइ ॥ **7** ॥ **AC-L**

---

4. GHL अनंत .
5. HL जग लाह .
6. K अषार .
7. DE निरधार .
8. C अजीत ; GI अतीत .
9. DEK कहै जु .
10. F कहीं .

सम द्रिष्टि [11] सब जीव सौं । जल समांन है [12] सोइ ॥
जे कोई सतावै [13] संत [14] कौं । तबही बिषम [15] सौ [16] होइ ॥ **8** ॥ AD-L

बिगसि कह्यौ नरस्यंघ तब । मांगि मांगि प्रहिलाद ॥
तुम तैं कछू न राषि हूं । जन [17] गोपाल मम [18] आदि ॥ **9** ॥ AC-L

प्रहिलाद चरित्र -- 17

प्रहलाद उबाच ॥ चौपई ॥ [1]

तुम बिन नाथ [2] कछू नही मागौं ।
देहु भगति दिढ [3] तुम सौं लागौं ॥
प्रेम भगति अंतर गति [4] दीजै ।
तुम्हारे चरन कवल रस पीजै ॥ **1** ॥ AC-L

---

11. A समष्टि ; DE हरि सम द्रिष्टि .

12. F-L रहै .

13. K दुषवै .

14. DEFK साध .

15. DE तहां बिमष .

16. L सिर .

17. CDEGIJ कहै .

18. FGIJ हरि .

1. Before these verses, manuscripts D and E add a कबित्त of several verses.

2. FGIJ हरि बिन और .

3. F भगति दिढ हरि .

4. HL अपनी प्रेम भगति मोहि .

रसना नाम [5] नैन निज [6] दरसन ।
श्रवननि कथा चरन कर परसन ।।
बांनी बिमल होई गुन [7] गांऊं ।
मन मनसा ले तुम सौं [8] लांऊं [9] ।। **2** ।। AC-L

अरू प्रभु साध संगति मोहि दीजै ।
यहु प्रसाद [10] अवसि करि कीजै ।। AC-L

जब मै हुतौ मात ग्रभ कूपा ।
वांहां तुम जन आइ मिले अनूपा ।। **a** ।। HL

तिन मो कूं ग्यांन दीयौ उपदेसा ।
अपनी सकति संम्रथ धरि भेसा ।।
तारिग रांम नांम समझायौ ।
मो असुर हि तुम संग लगायौ ।। **b** ।। HL

सो तुम साध संगति फल ऐसैं ।
जो मैं प्रभू बीसरौ कैसैं ।।
तुम्हरे जन सब लेह उधारै ।
अपनी सक्ति जीव निसतारै ।। **c** ।। HL

---

5. L रांम .
6. CDHKL तुम .
7. C जस .
8. A ले तुम हि ; DEHKL तुम सूं ल्यौ ; FIJ हरि तुम सौं .
9. A लगांहु ; G नांऊं .
10. F पसावा .

नांम सहत ग्यांन बैराग ।
अहंबुधि अरू मोह कौ त्याग ॥
सरधा दया सील संतोष ।
उतिम गुन दे करै जु मोषि ॥ **d** ॥ HL

ऐसे गुण सत संगति मांहीं ।
कै तुम क्रपा और कूं नांहीं ॥
साधू क्रपा क्रपा तुम होई ।
या भव सरणि और नहीं कोई ॥ **e** ॥ HL

संतनि संग भगति कूं पावै ।
भगति पाइ तुम चरणां आवै ॥
ता तैं मोहि दीजै सत संगा ।
सेऊं मन क्रम बचन अभंगा ॥ **f** ॥ HL

अठ सिधि नौ निधि मुकति न लेऊं ।
तुम्हारे चरन निरंतरि सेऊं ॥ **3** ॥ AC-L

सकल बिस्व कौ दुष मोहि दीजै ।
प्राणी जंत सुषी सब कीजै ॥
इंद्र ब्रह्म स्यौ पुरी न भावै ।
अरथ दरब [11] की कौण चलावै ॥ **4** ॥ AC-L

राज रिधि अमर पद थोरौ ।
भगति छाडि मांगै सो भोरौ [12] ॥

11. HKL धरम .

12. A बौरौ .

ज्यूं चितामनि पै [13] कौडी बांछै ।
कलप ब्रिछ पै [14] कोदौ साचै [15] ॥ **5** ॥ AC-L

इहि बिधि सेवग कछू न चाहै [16] ।
माता मन ले पुत्र नबाहै [17] ॥
श्रप अगनि माटी जु [18] छुडावै ।
बालक दुषी माता दुष पावै ॥ **6** ॥ AC-L

मागनहार न भगत [19] कहावै । ACF-L
अंत कालि जाचिग पद पावै ॥ CF-L
स्यंघ स्वांन की ब्रति कहावै । C-L
वहु डेलै वहु [20] षसम हि [21] धावै ॥ **7** ॥ AC-L

ज्यूं भाडैती भाडिस रीति ।
मसकति करै और नहीं प्रीति ॥ **a** ॥ HL

जो [22] तुम सेइ लेइ कुछि आंनां ।
दास नहीं वे मजूर [23] बषांनां ॥

---

13. G में .

14. CDE तजि .

15. HL जाचै .

16. L मांगै .

17. AC माता मन ले पुत्र हि बाहै ।; HL माता मन ले पुत्र निभावै/है ।; K माटी दे माता नही बाहै ।.

18. DE माई ; FGIJK हि .

19. GHK भक्ति .

20. DE ऊह लै उह ; G वहु डोलै वहु ; HL दूंका हेत .

21. HL संग .

22. H ज्यूं .

23. L ब मजूर .

ता पर मूरष और न कोई ।
करि सनांन अरू कांम [24] लगाई ॥ **b** ॥ HL

मुक्ति ममुछ भगत [25] सह कांमी ।
तुम कौं भावै अंतरजांमी ॥
हूं बालक कछू मागि न जांनौं ।
तुम तैं नाथ कहा है छांनौं ॥ **8** ॥ AC-L

सुर पुर नर पुर नाग न भावै ।
चरन कवल भजिबो जिय [26] आवै [27] ॥ DEHL
जांहां जांहां जनम मोहि द्यो नाथा ।
अबचल भजन तुम्हारौ साथा ॥ **a** ॥ HL

दोहा ॥
तुम बिन कछू न भाई [28] । सुर पुर नर पुर नाग ॥
इहि बिधि कीनी बीनती । जन [29] प्रहलाद बड भाग ॥ **b** ॥ ACHKL

दोऊ [30] कर माथै दीये [31] । साध साध प्रहिलाद ॥
मम [32] समांन गुन गाइ है । कहै [33] गोपाल सब [34] साध ॥ **9** ॥ AC-L

---

24. H कांप .

25. DE मुकत ममुछु भगति ; G मुक्त ममुछ भगत ; H मांगै मुकति भगति ; IJ मुकत ममुछ भगत ; K मुक्ति मोक्ष भक्ति ; L मांगै भगति मुकति .

26. E भजिबौ जीय ; HL भजि मांहि .

27. HL समावै .

28. HL चाहीयै .

29. AK omit जन .

30. DEHL तब दोऊ .

31. A धरै .

32. CFGIJ हरि .

33. CK जन .

34. A मम .

प्रहिलाद चरित्र -- 18

अथ निहकरमी ब्रह्म की असतुति छंद मोतीदांम ॥ **K**

नही तिहि पाप । नही तिहि पुन्य ॥
नही तिहि थूल । नही तिहि सुन्य ॥ **1** ॥ **AC-L**

नही तिहि सीस । नही तिहि पाव ॥
नही तिहि भेद । नही तिहि भाव ॥ **2** ॥ **AC-L**

नही तिहि कांन । नही तिहि नैन ॥
नही तिहि मुष । नही तिहि बैंन ॥ **3** ॥ **AC-L**

नही तिहि नास [1] । नही तिहि सास [2] ॥ **AC-L**
नही तिहि प्यंड । नही तिहि बास ॥ **4** ॥ **ACF-L**

नही तिहि हस्त [3] । नही तिहि अस्त ॥
नही तिहि जीव [4] । बिचार न बस्त ॥ **5** ॥ **AC-L**

नही तिहि पीठि [5] । नही तिहि पेट ॥ **AC-L**
नही तिहि श्रोनित । बीज सहेट ॥ **6** ॥ **AC-FH-L**

नही तिहि संश्रिति [6] । आवागवन ॥ **AC-FH-L**
नही तिहि बोल । नही तिहि मौनि ॥ **7** ॥ **AC-L**

---

1. K सास .
2. DE पास ; K आस .
3. H स्त ; L बसत .
4. G जात .
5. DE पीव .
6. C असति ; K श्रुति न

नहीं तहं चाल । नहीं तहं हाल ॥ **a** ॥ HL

अजोनि अजोनि । अजोनि अजोनि ॥ **8** ॥ AC-L

दोहा ।
अपनी जांनै आप गति । और न जांनै कोइ ॥
कौंन भांति [7] फल बीज मैं । फल मैं [8] बीजक होइ ॥ **9** ॥ AC-L

सारद लिषत न अंत कहूं [9] । बसुधा [10] कागद होइ ॥
महिमा भगत [11] भगवंत की । क्यूं करि बरनैं कोइ [12] ॥ **10** ॥ AC-L(J)

सारद लिषत न अंत हु । कहै सुनै जौ कोइ ॥ HL
तहि भज निज पद पाईऐ । पार काहां सुं होइ ॥ **a** ॥ H

अमृत रस प्रहलाद जस । कहै सुनैं जे कोइ ॥ DEHK
अभै अमर पद पाईऐ । भगति मुकति फल होइ ॥ **b** ॥ DEHKL

सुनै सुनावै प्रीति जुत । हरि जन हरि जस ऐह ॥
कहै गोपाल उर धारि कैं । रांम भगति सुं नेह ॥ **c** ॥ HL

---

7. FGI कहै गोपाल and variants; HKL जन गोपाल .

8. DEHL थैं/तैं .

9. Manuscripts H and L here substitute the *pada*: सात समद की मसिकरूं.

10. CFGI जे बसुधा .

11. AHL भगति .

12. K सोइ .

गुर गोब्यंद प्रसाद तैं । संतनि के गुण गाई ॥
बक्त श्रोता मुक्ति पल[?] । हरि पद सहज स्माई ॥ **d** ॥ A

मैं मति सारू आपनी । कही जु घटि बधि बात ॥
कहि [13] गोपाल सुत हेत कौं । नीकैं समझै तात [14] ॥ **11** ॥ AC-L(J)

इति श्री प्रहिलाद चरित्र संपूर्ण स्मासिव ॥ A

13. CHL जन .

14. AGHIK मात .

– II –
Kabīr
and Friends

3

Singing about Saints

In the bhakti tradition of North India, particularly *nirguṇī* bhakti, early poet-saints such as Nāmadev, Kabīr, Raidās, Gurū Amar Dās, Mīrābāī, Dādū Dayāl, and Palaṭū Sāhab dedicated many of their songs to singing the praises of earlier saints. The saints listed in these songs include both mythological devotees from earlier yugas like Prahlād and more historical persons of our own Kali Yuga. Although such songs often allude to well-known events in the lives of these saints, they rarely attempt to present connected narratives, even of single episodes of their lives. The poets take for granted that the listeners already know the stories. The songs are hagiographic, but not hagiographies.[1]

In this chapter I will propose and discuss a classification of the themes of these hagiographic songs into three categories: songs with a *eulogistic* theme, songs with a *testimonial* theme, and songs with an *egalitarian* theme. Although more than one these themes may be present in a single song, usually one clearly dominates.

The examples chosen to illustrate the three types of hagiographic songs have been culled from a variety of sources including W. Callewaert and B. Op de Beeck's 1991 anthology of Hindi songs by Dādū, Kabīr, Nāmadev, Raidās, Haradās, Gorakhanāth, and Sundaradās; Maṅgaladās' 1962 anthology of the songs of Haridās and other Nirañjanī Panthī saints; Gaṅgāśaraṇ Śāstrī's 1988 collection of Kabīr bhajans from various manuscripts in the Kabīr Chaurā Maṭh library, an anthology of songs by the poet-saints Yārī Sāhab, Bullā Sāhab, Gulāl Sāhab, Bhīkhā Sāhab, and others of the Bhuṛakuṛā monastery near Gazipur *(Mahātmāoṃ kī vāṇī,* 1933); an anthology of songs by many different saints edited by Khemadās of the Nirañjanī Panth (1989); Nārāyaṇadās of Ajmer's collection of the songs of Rajjab (1967) and Sundaradās (1989); Rajjab's *Sarabaṅgī* anthology of songs by various poets (1990); Gopāladās' similar *Sarvāṅgī* (1993); several anthologies of songs by Mīrābāī (1966; 1972; 1988); the Sikh *Gurū Granth Sāhib* (n.d.); and the recently republished Belvedere Press series of volumes of songs and poems by various saints including Dharmadās (1985), Dharanīdās (1976), Dūlanadās (1985), Garībadās (1985), Jagajīvan Sāhab (1983–90), Kabīr (1987–89), Malūkadās (1988), Palaṭū Sāhab (1987–90), the Bhuṛakuṛā poets, and others. I have paid less attention to Tulasīdās, Sūradās, and the poets of the Vallabh Sampradāy — all of whom apparently composed very few hagiographic songs — and have not attempted to include songs in Marathi or in languages normally written in scripts other than Devanāgarī and Gurmukhī.

As far as I know, the only significant academic study of this sort of hagiographic song is an essay by J. S. Hawley on "Creative Enumeration in the *Vinaya* Poetry of Sūrdās" (1992). Hawley's essay is a fine analysis of three poems by Sūradās that contain lists of mythological devotees who lived in earlier yugas. The main focus of the essay is literary. Hawley shows how Sūradās first presents apparently "objective" enumerations of saints and then adds to them counterposed references to his own person that evoke, with artistic skill, a deeply personal religious experience.

Several of the hagiographic songs I want to present here display considerable artistic merit. Others, however, are of more interest for their contents than their art. My aim here is not to evaluate them as literature, but to discuss their basic themes and to offer some suggestions about why such songs became popular among the followers of the bhakti movement.

One notable feature of these songs is that their authors mix together references to what academic scholars normally would distinguish as either mythical or historical saints. For the authors of the songs, all the famous saints and sages of Hindu tradition were historical figures in the sense that they are thought to have really existed. Nonetheless, we do find a traditional distinction that is functionally equivalent to that now drawn between history (or legend) and myth: the distintion between the saints and sages who lived in previous yugas and those of our own Kali Yuga. The saints and sages of previous yugas correspond to those that academic scholars would classify as mythical figures and those of the Kali Yuga to historical (or legendary) persons.

Many of the saints and sages of previous yugas mentioned in these songs are the heroes of stories narrated in the *Bhāgavata-purāṇa*. It is very likely that, directly or indirectly, this text was the principal source from which their names were taken. Other names are taken from the stories of the *Rāmāyaṇa* and the *Mahābhārata*. Although only a few of the authors of the songs knew Sanskrit, all must have heard vernacular retellings of the stories either as oral commentaries to Sanskrit recitations or as independent texts.

The saints and devotees of earlier yugas often mentioned in these songs include Dhruv and Prahlād, Vibhīṣaṇ and Rāvaṇ, Ajāmil, Nārad, Śukadev, Ambarīṣ, the mind-born Sanak and his three brothers, Dattātreya, Jaḍ Bharat, the Bhīl woman Śavarī, the prostitute Jīvantī, Vidur, Sudāmā, Draupadī, the crocodile Hūhū, the elephant king, and the vulture Jaṭāyu. Most of these beings have some major innate or behavioral "defect." They include demons, animals, women, sinners, and paupers. All, however, are devotees of some form of the god Vishnu, even those like Rāvaṇ who practise a "devotion of hate" and those like the prostitute Jīvantī and the evil Brahmin Ajāmil whose devotion is unintentional. In the end, all the devotees — good, evil, and unintended — are favored and/or saved by this god.

Sometimes it is an avatar of Vishnu who favors the devotee. The Man-lion rescues Prahlād. Rāmachandra favors Vibhīṣaṇ, Śavarī, Jaṭāyu, and even, by killing him, Rāvaṇ.[2] Sometimes it is simply Vishnu himself — under names such as Hari, Ram, and Nārāyaṇ — who favors the saint. In many cases, particularly in *saguṇī* songs about Rāmachandra and Krishna, the story of an avatar becomes the main subject of the songs. Such songs are biographic, but they cannot be said to be hagiographic since their subject is God himself and not his saintly devotees. In so far as saints like Kabīr and Nānak are sometimes considered to be virtual avatars of the divine Satguru, however, the distinction between the two sorts of songs often becomes somewhat problematic. In any case, this chapter will not discuss songs about traditional avatars of Vishnu such as Rāmachandra and Krishna.

Of more interest to me here are the songs that include, in their lists of saints and devotees, the more or less historical personalities of our own Kali Yuga. The vast majority of these songs come from nirguṇī rather than *saguṇī* tradition.[3] Many of the saints mentioned in them belong to the same sectarian traditions as their authors. For example, Dādū Panthī authors often mention Dādū Panthī poet-saints, and Bhuṛakuṛā authors often mention Bhuṛakuṛā poet-saints.

Some saints and devotees, however, are named in songs belonging to many different sectarian traditions. These include Jayadev, Gorakh, Nāmadev, Kabīr, Raidās, Dhanā, Sen, Sadanā, Pīpā, Nānak, and, with somewhat less frequency, Rāmānanda, Dādū, Mīrā, Sūr, Narasī Mehatā, Rāṅkā and Bāṅkā, Trilochan, Gopīchanda, Matsyendra, Bharatharī, and others. For basic information about all these saints and devotees, pre– and post–Kali Yuga, the reader can consult the glossary at the end of this book.

An interesting question is why appeals to the personal religious authority of famous saints and devotees are so prominent in bhakti tradition, particularly *nirguṇī* bhakti, and mostly absent in the literature of *śāstrik* and Vedic Hinduism. The basic reason for this seems to be a deep bias against the historical legitimation of religious authority in Brahminical Hinduism. Mīmāṃsā thinkers in particular insist that the Vedas and *śāstras* have no creators, neither humans nor gods. These texts are eternal and were revealed to the Vedic *ṛṣis* long before the Kali Yuga.[4] The only proper role for the historical authors of religious texts is as commentators on these eternal, ahistorical revelations.

In bhakti tradition, on the other hand, famous historical saints like Kabīr, Nānak, Mīrā, and Dādū were thought to have discovered the Truth by their own efforts. Indeed, their words *(bānī, śabda)* are considered to be direct embodiments of religious Truth. When the authors of hagiographical songs make an appeal to the examples of these and other saints, they are grounding their texts on the historical authority and witness of those who discovered the Truth for themselves. The lesser prominence of such songs in *saguṇī* tradition probably reflects the fact that Vedic and *śāstrik* authority is still accepted in that tradition, whereas in *nirguṇī* tradition it is largely rejected.[5]

One somewhat unexpected feature of the lists of sages and poet-saints in *nirguṇī* songs is the absence of any mention of Muslim saints, with the exception of occasional references to Sheikh Farīd and Ibrāhīm bin Adham. This absence is unexpected since many *nirguṇī* saints such as Kabīr, Dādū, Rajjab, Yārī Sāhab, Bullā Sāhab, Bājīd, and Ratanabāī were probably born and raised in Muslim families. In addition, it is likely that the Sufi movement had an important influence on *nirguṇī* tradition, despite the fact that this influence is rarely acknowledged by *nirguṇī* poets.[6] Most *nirguṇī* devotees were undoubtedly familiar with the devotional songs and verses of many Muslim Sufi poet-saints. Songs by the Sufi poets Sheikh Farīd, Kazi Mahamūd, and Sheikh Bahāvadī are included in Rajjab's *Sarabaṅgī* and Gopāladās' *Sarvāṅgī.* Farīd's songs are also found in the Sikh *Guru Granth Sāhib.*

As might be expected, the references to Kali Yuga saints and devotees become much more frequent in the songs of the later poets of *nirguṇī* tradition. The *nirguṇī* poet-saints of the late fifteenth and early sixteenth century like Rāmānanda, Kabīr, Raidās, Nānak, Pīpā, and Dhanā were in fact the founders of a new tradition, both religious and linguistic, who had few direct historical predecessors in North India. The poet-saints who come closest to filling this role are Nāmadev, Gorakh, and perhaps Jayadev. Kabīr does mention these three earlier saints in several of his songs, along with several mythical saints of previous yugas. It is curious, however, that Kabīr almost never mentions his guru Rāmānanda, his contemporaries like Raidās, Pīpā, or Dhanā, or any Sufi poets.[7] Songs attributed to Kabīr's reputed contemporaries Raidās, Pīpā, and Dhanā do mention Kabīr as well as Nāmadev and Gorakh. Later *nirguṇī* poets of the later sixteenth and the seventeenth and eighteenth centuries, on the other hand, introduce ever longer lists of Kali Yuga saints and devotees in their songs.

The hagiographic songs with a *eulogistic* theme are those that are wholly dedicated to telling one or more episodes in the legendary life of one particular saint. As we have seen in chapter one, some eulogistic songs tell about events in the lives of mythical heroes such as Prahlād and Dhruv. Other eulogistic songs are autobiographical and tell about events in the legendary lives of their supposed authors. Many songs attributed to Nāmadev, Kabīr, and Mīrābāī, for instance, are of this type.[8] Still other eulogistic songs relate events in the legendary lives of famous saints who are historical persons and are not identified as the authors of the songs. It is mostly this last sort of song that I want to discuss here.

All these songs are too short to contain sustained narratives and mostly simply allude to, rather than tell, the stories. Nonetheless, there do exist fuller hagiographical narratives that were apparently meant to be sung. Anantadās's *parachaīs* of Nāmadev, Kabīr, and others are good examples.[9] Such texts are much longer than the eulogistic songs considered here, however, and are generally divided into a series of "chapters," each dedicated to just one or two episodes in the saint's life.[10]

Several of the earliest eulogistic songs in North Indian vernacular languages are about Nāmadev. Three are found in the Sikh *Gurū Granth Sāhib* (1604 C.E.), all attributed to Nāmadev himself.[11] Two others, also by Nāmadev, are included in the collection of his songs edited by Callewaert and Lath.[12] The song translated below, however, is attributed to Harirām Vyās, a *saguṇī* poet who died about the end of the sixteenth century:[13]

Nāmadev found true devotion.
The world and the Vedas offer praise
    to him who Krishna favored.
The Lord knew his love and drank his milk,
    then beautifully thatched his hut.
He grabbed Hari's feet and like a rogue
    insisted until He spoke.
For his sake Hari turned the temple
    and made a dead cow live.
For Śyām[14] he buttered a piece of bread
    and handed it over to eat.

His caste and family was Viṭṭhal alone.
All the saints were his brothers.
Vyās announces the greatness of him
to whom even Kanhāī submitted.

Two important eulogistic songs about Kabīr are found among those sung during the *chaukā* ritual of the Kabīr Panth. One is used during the Dharmadāsī version of the rite and the other during the Kabīr Chaurā version.[15] The latter has been translated here in the chapter on the rites of the Panth (below, pp. 250–51). Roughly the same song is attributed to Dharmadās in the Belvedere Press collection of Dharmadās' songs (Dharmadās 1985, 3–4). The fact that these two eulogistic hagiographic songs are included in the *chaukā* ritual is a clear reflection of the importance of Kabīr's life to the followers of the Panth.

Another eulogistic song about Kabīr is attributed to Malūkadās (1574–1682). It alludes to the well-known legends of Kabīr's death at Magahar, his saving the priest of Jagannāth from being burnt, and his saving the temple of Jagannāth from the ocean (Lorenzen 1991), as well as one or two legends that are not so easily identified:[16]

Chant only Kabīr's name, O mind.
In the city of Kashi the guru appeared,
with wisdom so profound.
From Kashi he came to Magahar,
the *pīr* of both religions.
Some want to bury him, some to burn him,
no one keeps his temper.
The True guru has no blemish,
his body neither ages nor dies.
The guru once used to play the flute
on the Jamuna's quiet bank.
Gods, men and sages were all content,
as the Jamuna's water swirled.
The Nine Nāths, the eighty-four Siddhas,
and the fifty-two heroes all fled.[17]
He poured water on his own two feet
and saved Hari's priest from burns.
He kept Jagannāth's temple from harm,
and ocean's water retreated.
Malūkadās recites these verses.
Search for the master Kabīr.

One final eulogistic song about Kabīr that I want to cite is by the Rajasthani saint-poet Haridās Nirañjanī. It refers to the popular legend about Kabīr's ordeals at the hands of the Muslim sultan, Sikandar Lodī:[18]

The devotee Haridās says: This is bliss,
 to enlighten your own mind.
Kabīr's path is hard. I have searched it.
I have turned away from *saṃsār,*
 my love is for the Lord God.
The devotee Haridās says: Kabīr's style
 is somewhat topsy-turvy.
Bliss is on this topsy-turvy road,
 on it the supreme saint.
The devotee Haridās says: Without the guru
 not even one can reach it.
Fire does not burn him, water does not drown him.
 His chains simply fall away.
The devotee Haridās says: Kabīr worships Govinda,
 and his mind becomes free of fear.
The *kāzī* calls out: Kill him, kill him.
 Tie him under the elephant's feet.
The devotee Haridās says: Heat won't burn him.
You are the savior, the killers are countless.
The devotee Haridās says: No one was able
 to weaken Kabīr's resolve.

A eulogistic song about the sultan of Balkh Bukhara is attributed to Kabīr. In fact, it is almost certainly a more recent composition. Kabīr Panthī legends claim that it was Kabīr who turned the sultan's mind to religion, but the sultan is none other than the much earlier Sufi saint Ibrāhīm bin Adham (c. 730–778 C.E.):[19]

The sultan of Balkh Bukhara,
Who once wore exquisite shawls
 with gold and silver threads,
Has begun to hoist the load
 of a ten ton beggar's quilt.
He once ate sweets and dates.
Now he eats only some crumbs
 at morning and evening times.
His army and nine-hundred horse
 were like the clouds in the sky.

Now he has become a monk,
  and walks on rustic paths.
They used to strew his bed
  with rare and delicate flowers.
Now he has put this aside,
  but look at the wisdom he got.
He has left all his concubines
  for the Name of your Lord.
Kabīr says: Listen, monk,
  he has joined the holy order.

The hagiographic songs with a *testimonial* theme are quite numerous. Their basic structure is generally quite simple. The names of a large number of former saints are invoked as testimony to the power of God's grace or the benefits of religious devotion. The choice of saints tends to be quite eclectic. The names of various mythical sages and historical *saguṇī* and *nirguṇī* saints are often jumbled together in the same song. The following anonymous, rather artless, but pleasing bhajan about the boat of *satsaṅga* ("association with the saints") is fairly typical:[20]

Hari has built the boat of satsaṅga.
In it sat Dhruv and Prahlād,
  and also Hariśchandra.
In this boat sat Moradhvaj
  and the butcher Sadanā.
In it sat Nāmadev and Dhanā,
  and the carpinter Parasā.
In this boat sat Narasī
  and also Sain the barber.
In it sat Sūradās and Tulasī,
  and also Karamābāī.
In this boat sat the Bhīl woman,
  and also Mīrābāī.
While all the devotees sat within,
  He gave the pole a push,
And the boat began to move ahead.
  Hari Himself ferried it
  across to the other shore.

One of the oldest testimonial songs that mixes both Kali Yug and pre–Kali Yuga saints is attributed to Kabīr. Its popularity is vouched for by the fact that it is found in most early collections including the

Kabīr bījak (pad 92), the *Kabīr granthāvalī (pad* 33), Rajjab's *Sarabaṅgī (pada* 49.1), Gopāladās' *Sarvāṅgī (pad* 63.44), and, in a rather different version, the *Gurū Granth Sāhib (gauḍī* 36). To some extent this song can be considered to be a sort of *negative* testimonial since all the saints — with the curious exceptions of Śukadev and three Nāths — are said to have been unable to truly know the (higher) Mind:[21]

Seek out that Mind, brother!
Where is the Mind absorbed when it leaves the body?
Sanak, Sanandan, Jayadev, and Nāmadev
 did bhakti but didn't know the Mind.
Śiv, Brahmā, and Nārad were all wise
 but didn't know the Mind's goal.
Dhruv, Prahlād, Vibhīṣaṇ and even Śeṣ
 couldn't see the Mind within the body.
Only a rare person[22] knows the Mind's secret.
 Śukadev got absorbed in It a little.
Gorakh, Bharatharī and Gopīchanda
 met that Mind and found bliss.
The Unconditioned is one and the bodies are many.
 Kabīr met that Mind and has kept it close.

The poet Sundaradās the younger (1596–1689), a disciple of Dādū, composed several testimonial songs including one that compares a long list of great saints and sages to warriors. Among the Kali Yuga saints in the list, Sundaradās mentions many Nāth and *nirguṇī* saints but omits any mention of *saguṇī*, Muslim, or women saints:[23]

I sing about the great heros who loved Hari,
Who subjugated the mind, the fort's commander,
 and extirpated all evil conduct.
In the *Satya Yuga* the first hero is Dhruv,
 who meditated firmly.
Crooked Māyā came with the aim to deceive,
 but failed to make him waver.
The heroes Sanak, Sanandan, Nārad and
 the nine lords of yoga are unique.
They abandoned the three *guṇas* and thought
 only about Brahman.
King Ṛṣabhadev, the best of heroes,
 went and lived in the forest.
He became absorbed in Brahman and had
 no awareness of his own body.

The devotee Prahlād's fierce warrior father
gave him no end of grief.
Prahlād held fast to the Name of Ram,
and Hari appeared for His servant.
The hero Dattātrey roams at will.
Independent, not dependent,
he wiped out all distinctions.
The esteemed hero Śukadev, the son of Vyās,
became passionless.
Rambhā could not seduce him. He remained
true to Brahman alone.
The fearless heroes Gorakhanāth, Bharatharī,
and valiant Gopīchanda,
Charapaṭ, Kāṇerī, and Chauraṅgī all
put dualism aside and became one.
Rāmānanda created heroes in Banaras,
bringing bhakti to worshippers of Śiv.
Nāmadev, Raṅkā and Baṅkā, and Trilochan became heroes.
Through bhakti they left aside fear of the world
and the drums of victory sounded.
In the *Kali Yuga* the fearless Kabīr became a hero.
He lit the fire of Brahman and in an instant
conquered the mighty fort.
The devotee Raidās became a hero and sowed
havoc among the Brahmins.
Sojhā, Pīpā, Sen, and Dhanā won many battles.
Aṅgad, Bhuvan, Paras, and Haradās
took the weapon of knowledge.
The heroes Nānak, Kānhā and Beṇ all
played [the drums of victory].
The guru Dādū was born at Sambhar.
No other hero is his equal.
Whosever's breast has been pierced
by the arrows of his words
becomes content.
In every age numberless men
become heroes.
Give Sundaradās great wisdom,
so he finds this joy.

Songs about the Holi and Basant festivals form a special class of folk songs. Many bhakti poets wrote such songs, sometimes in the form of hagiographic testimonials. Gulāl Sāhab (c. 1693–1743) of the Bhuṛakuṛā lineage included at least three such testimonial songs among those he composed for the Basant festival. His guru Bullā Sāhab (c. 1693–1768) included another among his own Basant songs. All these testimonial songs invoke the names of historical nirguṇī and saguṇī saints as well as those of mythical sages. In part, this eclecticism may reflect the spirit of social reconciliation and inclusivity that animates both the Basant and Holi festivals. Here is one of Gulāl's songs:[24]

Good mind, my king, let us play Basant.
    Hari's Name is rising, infinite Hari.
Nārad and Śukadev are playing there together,
    and the nine Lords of Yoga, who learned the secret.
Prahlād and Dhruv are playing, who never wavered.
    Ambarīṣ is playing, who kept his pride.
Nāmadev is playing, who found a state of peace.
    Kabīr is playing, who crossed to the other shore.
Nānak is playing, who learned the way to salvation.
    Pīpā is playing, who accepted faith in bhakti.
Murāridās is playing, who beat the drum.
    Malūk is playing, who reached the unknowable goal.
Chaturbhuj is playing, who cleansed his karma well.
    Tulasīdās is playing, who saw the form of God.
Yārī is playing, who found illumination.
    My satguru Bullā doesn't waver an inch.
Gulāl touches the feet of all the saints,
    and then he plays, my luck has flowered at last.

A similar song is attributed to Nābhādās (c. 1600), the famous author of the *Bhaktamāl*. It is dedicated to the Holi festival and similarly invokes all manner of sages and saints:[25]

O king of wisdom, let us happily play Holi.
    All the saints are seated on the balcony.
Mahādev is playing the *mṛdaṅga,*
    Nārad is dancing and playing his *vīnā.*
Jayadev is clapping and singing.
    Nābhā, Pīpā and Nāmadev are there.
Raidās is playing on his *rabāb*
    and singing a tune in *rāg* Basant.
Sanaka and his brothers are playing there.
    The Vedas are shouting: Hurrah, Hurrah!
The devotee Sayan is handing to each
    colored powders from a big pot.

Balibhadra's squirter is in his hand.
Prahlād is there with Bibhīṣan and Bidur.
Red powder is coloring the sky.
Anantānanda and Harikṛṣṇadās are there.
Agradās and Kīlhadev apply red color.
Amburṣi and Śukadev are also there.
Raṅkā and Baṅkā, Kālu and Kevaladās,
and His servant Divākar, the light of love.
Looking about, there near Narasī,
God's servant Mīrā sings with devotion.
Rāmānanda teaches about Brahman,
and Kabīr lets loose the arrows of the Word.
Nīmānanda and Biṣṇuśarma
converse there with Mādhavāchārya.
The fun of playing Holi increases
for all the numberless happy saints.
This time help me keep my honor.
Bestow on Nābhā the boon of bhakti.

The hagiographic songs with an *egalitarian* theme are those that refer to one or more famous saints in a context that stresses the fact that salvation through bhakti is available to everyone regardless of caste or gender, even to sinners, animals, and demons. As has been noted, this idea goes back to the *Bhagavad-gītā* and is repeated many times in the *Bhāgavata-purāṇa*. Hagiographic songs of this type are also found in South India, particularly among those of the Vīraśaiva saints.[26]

Egalitarian hagiographic songs are of two sorts. Some criticize the social ideology of *varṇāśramadharma* in a relatively indirect and muted way. The emphasis is rather on the power of God's grace, a grace that saves *even* low-caste persons, women, sinners, animals, and demons. Not surprisingly, several of these poems are by *saguṇī* saints whose social iconoclasm tends to be more timid than that of the *nirgunī* saints. In other songs, most by *nirguṇī* poets, the emphasis shifts to the praise of the religious power that such marginalized heroes win by their own efforts.

Several examples of songs that praise *God's* power to save the lowly are found among the songs of Mīrābāī and Narasī Mehatā, two saguṇī poets who partly span the *nirguṇī-saguṇī* divide. Here is one attributed to Mīrābāī:[27]

Stay in my sight, O Śyām Govinda!
You brought a cart of food for Kabīr.

You thatched the roof of Nāmadev's hut.
You cultivated Dhanā's field.
You heeded the call of the elephant king.
You took a plum from the Bhīlanī's mouth.
You accepted Sudāmā's handful of rice.
You ate Karamābāī's *khichṛī*.
All your servants were gratified.
Surrounded by the cowherd girls. O Śyām,
You shine like the moon among the stars.
You reward the efforts of all the saints,
But always keep yourself far from Mīrā.

Here is a similar song attributed to Narasī Mehatā:[28]

You, O Ram, please my soul.
No one else will do.
You take Bhīlanī's plum and Sudāmā's rice,
and lengthen Draupadī's sari.
You leave aside Duryodhan's sweets
to dine on Vidur's spinach.
You remove your devotee Sain's distress
and cultivate Dhanā's field.
You make Raidās' sacred thread appear
and deliver a cart to Kabīr.
You take Nāmadev's milk, rotate the temple,
and return the cow to life.
In the form of a dog you accept his food
and thatch Nāmadev's roof.
You rescue the elephant and crocodile
and save Ajāmil's soul.
You keep your promise to protect Prahlād
and Laṅkā bestow on Vibhīṣaṇ.
Wherever your devotees get into trouble,
you run there to save them.
Take Narasī, O Śyām, and every day
I'll awake and take your darshan.

Radical criticisms of the *varṇāśramadharma* social system and the practice of untouchability are a well-known feature of much *nirguṇī* poetry. *Nirguṇī* poets time and again stress that all human beings (or at least all males) have equal innate personal worth. Not surprisingly, many *nirguṇī* poets wrote hagiographic songs with an egalitarian theme.

One of the earliest *nirguṇī* songs of this type is one usually attributed to Pīpā.[29] It praises Nāmadev, Kabīr, and Raidās and affirms both their spiritual greatness and their low social status. It is different from most other egalitarian songs, however, in that it is more historical than hagiographic and makes no reference to any legend about the saints:

O mind, worship at Hari's feet,
the feet that remove our pain
and rid us of worldly ties.
You can chant the Vedas and endless scriptures,
but the Lord alone can save you.
Nāmadev worshipped at Hari's feet
and prevailed over all four *varṇas.*
His caste is untouchable tailor,
His glory fills the world,
Vyās and Sanak bear witness.
Kabīr is renowned in every region,
though on Id and Bakra Id
his family[30] kills cows and honors
sheikhs, martyrs and *pīrs.*
As the father did, so did the son.[31]
Raidās' victory flag flies high.
In Barnaras even today
his caste mates carry off cattle,
yet Brahmins bow before him.
At the end that One alone will remain,
who is one though creation is many.
Nobody equals the man
who prays at Vishnu's feet.
Pīpā, His slave, says: Where do I find
the One whose fame pervades
this world in the Kali Age?
I'll worship the Lord with bhakti
and get to the other shore.

Two songs in Kuṇḍaliyā meter by the *nirguṇī* poet Palaṭū Sāhab are good examples of songs that carry the shift of emphasis toward the saints themselves still further. Palaṭū's songs praise the greatness of the saints with only a passing or implicit allusion to the power of God's grace. They emphasize Palaṭū's brotherhood with some of the lowest, in terms of ritual purity, of the famous devotees of the past. Here is one of these songs:[32]

The Prostitute, the Vulture, Ajāmil,
Sadanā, and Raidās,
Sadanā and Raidās found good fortune.
Day and night they stay in His presence,
and offer devotion.
Their caste is not high yet no one
is their equal.
It is the millions of *kulīn* Brahmins,
who are really low.
No one is greater than those saints.
All others are lower.
No one can be said to be their equal
in all three worlds.
Palaṭū plays in the Imperishable's lap,
With the Prostitute, the Vulture, Ajāmil,
Sadanā, and Raidās.

The Dādū Panthī author Rajjab (traditionally, 1567–1689) also wrote many hagiographic songs with an egalitarian point of view. Here is one of them:[33]

What has caste to do with Bhakti?
Listen to me, my brother.
Like a daughter she supports her father
and goes wherever he sends her.
Nāmadev and Kabīr, Rāṅkā and Bāṅkā,
were these four anyone special?
Bhakti entered into their homes,
without any care for status.
Dyogū and Dīpū, Kītā and Kaṇerī,[34]
humble families all.
But Bhakti didn't discriminate.
She served like a slave in their homes.
Vidur was born in a family of slaves
but Bhakti stayed by his side.
She takes no note of high or low.
[. . .]
First she met Jayadev but then she entered
into Raidās's heart.
Later she went into Dādū's home.
[. . .]
Rajjab says: Once she agrees to come,
no one can hope to stop her.

For Bhakti, king and subjects are equal.
Whoever has love will win her.

The final example I want to present here is a song attributed to Kabīr that uses the examples of the Bhīl woman Śavarī and Rāmachandra, the Brahmin Tulasīdās and the Bhaṅgī Nābhādās, and the Untouchable Svapach and the Chamār Raidās to make a similar argument:[35]

O Saints, when were the saints rated?
When were the saints rated?

From what family did Śavarī come?
Her caste was lower than low.
Yet she gave attentive service to the saints,
And Ram took her *prasād*.

Tulasī was a Brahmin of the highest rank,
who people say was wise,
While Nābhā was the son of a lowly Bhaṅgī,
Yet Tulasī took his *prasād*.

If you don't believe me I'll tell you more.
Know it now, poor wretch.
Supach and Raidās were devotees.
Hari made them His own.

Kabīr says: Listen, brother sadhu.
I have given many examples.
A disciple should recognize the saints.
Without a guru you're a fool.

Many more examples of egalitarian hagiographic songs by both *saguṇī* and *nirguṇī* poets could be cited. They are in fact just one manifestation of a spirit that is implicit in the whole bhakti movement. Although the Brahmins who played a central role in developing this movement generally sought to preserve both *varṇāśramadharma* and their own role as essential mediators between man and God, bhakti is by definition a direct personal relation between the devotee and his or her object of devotion. The appeal to the mythical and legendary saints of the past in these songs is an assertion of a person's universal right, regardless of sex or caste, to win salvation through either the grace of a loving God or one's own individual effort.

4

Sain's *The Kabīr-Raidās Debate*

A rather different sort of hagiographic genre from these short songs takes the form of debates between an enlightened guru and his less enlightened rivals. The tradition of metaphysical debates, often called *śāstrārtha* in Sanskrit, is of course an ancient one. Many such debates are embodied in Sanskrit commentaries on the basic works of the six schools of Indian thought as well as other philosophic texts.

In the Kabīr Panth, the texts that contain such debates between Kabīr and various rivals are known as *goṣṭhīs* or *saṃvāds*. Only three or four of these texts have so far been published, and these are no longer available. The Kabīr Chaurā library manuscript collection, however, contains *goṣṭhīs* between Kabīr and a variety of different rivals including Rāmānanda, Gorakh, Jogājīt, Nānak, Raidās, Śaṅkarāchārya, Durvāsā, Dharmadās, and Nirañjan.[1]

Another genre of *nirguṇī* texts that takes the form of religious dialogues is that of the *bodhs*, but these texts mostly consist of a teacher's responses to a disciple's questions rather than the more equal debates found in the *saṃvāds* and *goṣṭhīs*. Many Kabīr Panthī *bodh* texts have been published in the eleven-volume *Kabīr Sāgar* edited by Yugalānanda Bihārī (1953).

The basic intention of the authors of all *saṃvāds* and *goṣṭhīs* seems to be to present a religious and social message in a form that is somewhat longer and more didactic than typical *nirguṇī* songs (*pads, śabdas, ramainīs*, etc.), but still entertaining enough to serve as a vehicle for popular religious instruction and proselytization. Since the *saṃvāds* and *goṣṭhīs* are structured as religious debates, they give valuable indications about their authors' perceptions and understanding of the doctrines of their opponents as well as their own doctrines.

Probably the oldest such text containing a debate between Kabīr and one of his rivals is the *Kabīr-Raidās kā saṃvād*, or "The Kabīr-Raidās Debate," attributed to their fellow disciple Sain or Sen.[2] Although this text asserts the superiority of Kabīr's doctrines over those of Raidās, it does not seem to be a Kabīr Panthī text. Only one copy is found in the Kabīr Chaurā manuscript collection, while a fairly large number are found in the manuscript libraries of Rājasthān. Although three versions of the Hindi text have been published, no critical edition or translation has yet appeared in print.[3]

I have located nine unpublished manuscripts of this text. Seven are in the libraries of the Rājasthān Prāchyavidyā Pratiṣṭhān (Jodhpur and Jaipur) and Rājasthānī Sodh Saṃsthān (Jodhpur). Another manuscript, originally from Rajasthan, is found in the India Office Library in London. The ninth is that in the Kabīr Chaurā Maṭh library in Banaras. Most manuscripts seem to date from the eighteenth and nineteenth centuries. All this suggests that the *Kabīr Raidās kā saṃvād* was moderately popular, particularly in Rajasthan, in this period.

Another, perhaps earlier reference to this legendary debate between Kabīr and Raidās is found in the *Raidās parachaī* by Anantadās, written about the end of the sixteenth century.[4] Two fairly modern accounts of the debate from a Raidāsī point of view are found in a version of the *Bhaviṣya-purāṇa* and in the *Ravidās Rāmāyaṇ*.[5] The debate is also briefly mentioned in two modern works by Kabīr Panthī authors: Yugalānanda Bihārī's *Kabīr charitra bodh* (1953, 11:47), probably written in the early 1930s, and Gaṅgāśaraṇ Śāstrī's *Kabīr jīvan charitra* (1976, 189–91). Today, however, this legend seems to have been mostly forgotten, even by the followers of Kabīr and Raidās.[6]

The debate between Kabīr and Raidās in Sain's *Kabīr-Raidās kā saṃvād* turns on the question of whether we should offer our worship to a *nirguṇ* or to a *saguṇ* conception of the Absolute, in other words to an impersonal and monistic Brahman or to an anthropomorphic God who sometimes becomes incarnate in the form of avatars. Kabīr argues for a strict *nirguṇ* conception, while Raidās supports a *saguṇ* conception or, more accurately, the position that *saguṇ* and *nirguṇ* are one. Despite the direct intervention of the gods Brahmā, Durgā, and Shiva on Raidās' behalf, Kabīr prevails and Raidās accepts him as his guru. With somewhat contradictory logic, the god Vishnu finally appears, mounted on Garuḍ, and Kabīr acknowledges himself to be a worshipper of this god, thus virtually accepting Raidās' original position that *nirguṇ* and *saguṇ* are one.

The Kabīr of the *Kabīr-bījak*, the *Kabīr-granthāvalī*, and the Sikh *Gurū Granth Sāhib* does refer to God by Vaishnava names such as Ram and Hari, but almost never is there any suggestion that he means by this a Vishnu mounted on Garuḍ or the avatar Ram of Ayodhya. If one accepts the debatable proposition that Kabīr does not deny the reality of *saguṇ* gods and their avatars, he simply does not deem them worthy of worship, one can perhaps make some logical sense of Sain's presentation of Kabīr's position. Nonetheless, there is little doubt that Kabīr's final acknowledgment of Vishnu "mounted on Garuḍ" as an object of devotion is not really logically consistent with Kabīr's *nirguṇī* metaphysics.

Much the same logical inconsistency is found in Anantadās' (1982; 1993) account of the Kabīr-Raidās-Sain debate in his *Raidās parachaī.* It is also found in Anantadās' *Kabīr parachaī,* which concludes with a similar *saguṇ* manifestation of Vishnu mounted on Garuḍ (Lorenzen 1991).

The social implications of the Kabīr-Raidās debate also merit comment. It is clear, from Kabīr's opening statement, that Sain sees Kabīr's insistence on the unity of Brahman as a powerful argument against caste and untouchability. Kabīr says: "The One is Brahman. The One is excrement and urine. The One is blood. The One is flesh. Perfect Brahman pervades all bodies. How can we distinguish between a Brahmin and a Shudra?" In rather contradictory fashion, however, Sain later has Kabīr and Raidās insult each other in terms of their low-caste status. Raidās calls Kabīr the son of a Muslim mother and Julāhā father, and Kabīr calls Raidās the son of Chamār parents (verses 39–40).

In Sain's text, Kabīr rejects the Vedas and Puranas as being "false" (verse 42) and also denies the reality of the avatars of Vishnu (verses 7–26). Such views are common to most of *nirguṇī* tradition and are vividly expressed in many verses and songs attributed to Kabīr. They clearly imply a rejection of the social as well as the religious ideology of more orthodox Brahminical Hinduism and of the privileged social position of the Brahmins as the guardians of that tradition.

As edited here, Sain's text contains sixty-nine verses written in *hārigītikā* meter (16/12/16/12 *mātrās* with rhyme of the last two syllables of the second and fourth *charaṇs*). The language is the mixed dialect, sometimes called "Sadhukkaḍī," that is often employed by North Indian poets and authors who write in the *nirguṇī* tradition (Mahendra 1969). There is no way to know whether or not it is really a composition of Kabīr and Raidās' fellow disciple Sain, but this is not impossible.[7] A few songs attributed to Sain are included in the *Gurū Granth Sāhib.* Some legends about his life are included in Priyādās' 1712 C.E. commentary on Nābhādās' *Bhaktamāl,* but Anantadās did not write a *parachaī* about him.

The critical edition and translation of *The Kabīr-Raidās Debate* that follow are mostly based on five manuscripts of the text. One is from the Rājasthān Prāchyavidyā Pratiṣṭhān in Jaipur (no. 9596), one from the Rājasthānī Śodh Saṃsthān in Jodhpur (no. 8633), two from the Rājasthān Prāchyavidyā Pratiṣṭhān in Jodhpur (nos. 12422 and 14741), and one from the India Office Library in London (no. A 12). Apart from minor differences in spellings and occasional alternate words, the versions of the text in these five manuscripts are almost identical.

At least four of these five manuscripts are in one way or another connected with the Nirañjanī Panth (see list below). It is possible that they represent a Nirañjanī Panth recension of the text that may be different from other recensions. Whatever the case may be, the version of the text we are presenting here clearly represents an important recension of the text, one particularly associated with the Nirañjanī Panth of Rajasthan.[8]

The other seven versions of the text that I have been able to locate and consult (three published versions and four other manuscripts) are mostly different from my text and also from each other. For the most part, their texts seem to contain rather corrupt readings and widely varying total numbers of verses. For these reasons, these other versions have been of limited use in preparing our edition and translation. They evidently represent either several quite different recensions of the text or simply anomalous and corrupt versions of it.

For my critical edition, I have chosen for each word the spellings and alternate words common to the majority of the five principal manuscripts. No attempt has been made to standardize the spellings of the same word when it occurs in different passages, much less bring any word more into line with the spellings of modern standard Hindi. When, in any specific case, no clear "majority" spelling exists, I have usually chosen that of the Rājasthān Prāchyavidyā Pratiṣṭhān (Jaipur) manuscript no. 9596 (identified in the notes as manuscript A). Though undated, this manuscript seems to be the oldest one available (see below). Where alternate readings are found in these five manuscripts, they are always given in the footnotes. Alternate spellings are not noted unless they are particularly interesting.

Uma Thukral and I have tried to make our translation both accurate and readable, but we have rendered the text in prose rather than attempt to imitate the verse form of the original Hindi text. In the translation we have used transliterations of the *tatsam* forms of modern standard Hindi for technical terms and the names of gods and goddesses. For example, we have regularly used the name Śambhu for Siṃbhū, and Hiraṇyakaśipu for Hiranākus. Interpretive additions used in the translation are put in brackets.

Photographs of all the manuscripts used, except the India Office Library manuscript (no. A 12), were taken by me on visits to Rajasthan in 1990 and 1992 and Banaras in 1994 while in India on fellowships from the American Institute of Indian Studies. Thanks are owed to Dr. Nārāyaṇ Siṃha Bhāṭi of the Rājasthānī Śodh Saṃsthān in Jodhpur, Dr. Padmadhar

Pāṭhak of the Rājasthān Prāchyavidyā Pratiṣṭhān in Jodhpur, Dr. Dwārka Nāth Śarmā of the Rājasthān Prāchyavidyā Pratiṣṭhān in Jaipur, and Achārya Gaṅgāśaraṇ Śāstrī of the Kabīr Chaurā monastery in Banaras for arranging for permission to photograph the manuscripts.

The nine manuscripts and three published versions of the text are the following:

1. Manuscript A: Rājasthān Prāchyavidyā Pratiṣṭhān (RPP) (Jaipur) manuscript no. 9596. This manuscript has only three folios (written on both sides) and contains no other composition nor any colophon. The RPP catalog estimates it to belong to the nineteenth century (V.S.), but my opinion is that it is older, probably the oldest manuscript of the text that I have seen.

2. Manuscript B: RPP (Jodhpur) manuscript no. 12422. The *Kabīr-Raidās kā saṃvād* is found on folios 443–48 of a larger manuscript dated 1831 V.S. (1774 C.E.). The copyist's name is Ugamadās, and he copied the manuscript at Didvana. Since Didvana is the traditional seat of the Nirañjanī Panth, it can be assumed that the copyist was a Nirañjanī Panth sadhu.

3. Manuscript C: Rājasthānī Sodh Saṃsthān (RŚS) (Jodhpur) manuscript no. 8633. The *Kabīr-Raidās kā saṃvād* is found on pages 430–32 of a larger manuscript that the RSS catalog estimates to belong to the eighteenth century. The other compositions in this interesting manuscript are mostly by well-known authors of the Nirañjanī Panth.

4. Manuscript D: RPP (Jodhpur) manuscript no. 14741. The *Kabīr-Raidās kā saṃvād* is found on pages 222–30 of a larger manuscript that the RPP catalog estimates to belong to the nineteenth century, once listing the copy date as 1814 V.S. (1757 C.E.). I did not see any passage containing this date in the manuscript. The catalog also once lists the name of the copyist of the larger manuscript as Digambaradās, born at Bansabareli. The manuscript contains compositions by a number of authors associated with the Nirañjanī Panth, the Dādū Panth, and the Nāth Panth, as well as several of Anantadās's *parachaīs*. Its text of Anantadās' *Kabīr parachaī* belongs to the Nirañjanī Panth recension of that text (Lorenzen 1991, 73–91).

5. Manuscript E: India Office Library (London) manuscript no. A 12. This *Kabīr-Raidās kā saṃvād* forms part of a much larger manuscript that includes many of Anantadās's *parachaīs* as well as various *nirguṇī* works. It was copied at Pokara (Pushkar) by Baiṣṇav Nirañjanī Sobharām Svāmī, a sadhu of the Nirañjanī Panth, in 1843 V.S. (1786 C.E.). I examined this manuscript directly in 1982, but worked from a paper copy of a microfilm of the text.

6. Kabīr Chaurā Maṭh (Banaras) manuscript no. 062 (pp. B177a–79b). This manuscript contains dates ranging from 1915 V.S. to 1923 V.S. (1858 to 1866 C.E.). Its version of the *Kabīr-Raidās kā saṃvād* is somewhat anomalous but is similar to the text in RPP no. 13494 (see next item). The reputed author Sain is nowhere mentioned. The Kabīr Chaurā manuscript is a large and lengthy one that contains a number of compositions associated with the Kabīr Panth including several other Kabīr *goṣṭhīs*.

7. RPP (Jodhpur) manuscript no. 13494 (pp. 45–51). The catalog estimates that it belongs to the nineteenth century (V.S.). Its version of Sain's text contains several passages of several verses each not found in other versions. The text nonetheless contains the same total of sixty-nine verses as the manuscripts used for my critical edition. One curious feature of the numbering of these verses is that the copyist usually writes the number "4" as a "5."

8. RPP (Jodhpur) manuscript no. 15755 (pp. 88–93). This is estimated to belong to the nineteenth century (V.S.) by the RPP catalog. Its version of Sain's text also seems to be generally corrupt. My photographs of this text are not always legible.

9. RŚS (Jodhpur) manuscript no. 7608. This version of Sain's text seems to show the influence either of Khaḍī-bolī or modern standard Hindi and gives *tatsam* spellings of many words. The manuscript is probably little or no older than the early part of this century (C.E.). The text is short (34 verses) but contains several verses not found in other versions.

10. The version of Sain's text published by B. P. Śarmā (Sain 1978, 143–46). This is apparently based on an otherwise unidentified single manuscript said to be dated 1743 V.S. (1686 C.E.). The text contains only thirty-nine verses and seems to be somewhat corrupt despite the reputed antiquity of the manuscript.[9]

11. Shukdeo Singh's (Sain 1994, 39–54) recently published version. This is a good text but has not been used here since it seems in fact to be based mostly on the India Office manuscript (here manuscript E) and perhaps on an earlier version of the present critical edition that was circulated in unpublished form in 1991.

12. Shukdeo Singh's (Sain 1986, 37–40) earlier published version. This presents a rather corrupt text of sixty-one verses. Singh told me that he used a single manuscript found in the University of Poona library.

The Kabīr-Raidās Debate

Translated by David N. Lorenzen and Uma Thukral

No, Mādhav, there is no welfare for me. How am I to get a vision of you, Oh Ram?

Kabīr: The One is Brahman. The One is excrement and urine. The One is blood. The One is flesh. Perfect Brahman pervades all bodies. How can we distinguish between a Brahmin and a Shudra?

Raidās: A cloud-burst appears on the horizon of bad thoughts. Light appears on the horizon of good thoughts. Keep knowledge and meditation in your heart and you'll see. Raidās speaks the truth.

Kabīr: Unless one has knowledge of Brahman; unless one meditates on Brahman, consciousness will never arise in one's heart. Perfect Brahman pervades all bodies. There is no one else.

Raidās: Sir, why do you say that the One is all there is? What do you do with Prakṛti? I am formed from Prakṛti. This is what the sadhus say.

Kabīr: Flowers are always accompanied by perfume; the wind always brings the rain. If the universe is [periodically] destroyed, where does Prakṛti disappear to?

Raidās: Prakṛti is absorbed in the Great Spirit. That Spirit appeared as Krishna in Vrindavan. Accompanied by the milk maids, he snapped his fingers and sang.

Kabīr: [The Highest Spirit] neither dances nor sings, nor does He play the flute. The Lord Nārāyaṇ is neither man nor woman.[10] He doesn't appear in the form of an avatar.

Raidās: If He doesn't appear in the form of an avatar, then how will living beings achieve salvation? They won't even realize their own ignorance. All living beings will fall into hell.

Kabīr: Where is hell? Where is heaven? Who has ever come back from there? Who has seen it? The soul is a traveller who has set off on a journey. After he leaves, he sees no one.

Raidās: He sees [Krishna] standing in the shade of the Kadamba tree, holding a lotus stalk in his hand, wearing a yellow robe and his Baijantī garland, with a peacock crown placed on his head.

Kabīr: If one's mind is certain that [the soul resides] within the lotus of eight petals in one's heart, [and if] one keeps [one's mind] firm in the junction of the *trikuṭī,* then the cycle of rebirths will end.

Raidās: Sir, you should let rebirth be. Let's sing to Gopāl. He is Mohan, Nanda's son, whose beauty bewitched the women of Braj.[11]

Kabīr: Who is this Nanda's son?[12] Tell me, where did he come from? The imperceptible Spirit is indestructible and perfect. I say that it's a rare person who knows [this secret].[13]

Raidās: Nanda's son is everywhere.[14] The Vedas proclaim that He is everywhere. Wherever sin appears, sir, there he comes running.

Kabīr: There [in the world of Brahman] there is neither sin nor merit, neither Vedas nor sacred songs. I, Kabīr, say, listen Raidās. Light is absorbed in light.

Raidās: . . . .[15]

Kabīr: He whom you call an avatar was subject to death. You haven't found the secret of the Indestructible. You are drowning in the river of the three *guṇas.*

Raidās: Nirguṇ and *saguṇ* are one, sir. No distinction can be imposed on Him. We've seen Him as the cowherd in the forest [of Vrindavan]. He is Nanda's cowherd in Nanda's house.

Kabīr: Who is Nanda? Who is Yaśodā? Tell me, from whom was He born? The Vedas proclaim that He is formless, spotless, unconditioned, and without attributes.

Raidās: He is the Creator. He is the Sustainer. He is the Unique. He is Krishna. The Formless and He who has form are one. Keep His [name] on your tongue.

Kabīr: Such a silly story doesn't interest me. I always keep the truth before me. I bow down before the Formless. I taste Its inexhaustible nectar.

Raidās: Listen Kabīr. . . .[16] He fostered the work of [King] Bali.[17] [He grabbed] Kaṃsa by the hair. He killed Hiraṇyakaśipu and saved the devotee Prahlād.[18]

Kabīr: I have no faith in anyone who incarnates himself in a body. The Imperceptible doesn't come to earth as an avatar. In the void, a light shimmers. It is that light that pleases me.

Raidās: For the sake of devotion, He has become incarnate in bodies. For the sake of praising Brahman, He killed Rāvaṇ and all his family and gave his kingdom to Vibhīṣaṇ.[19]

Kabīr: He neither kills nor is killed, neither destroys nor is destroyed. He is the Indestructible. The Lord Nārāyaṇ is neither man nor woman.[20] He is neither the Sun nor Fire.

Raidās: [If] He neither kills nor is killed, neither destroys nor is destroyed, then how can one praise Him? [If] Lord Nārāyaṇ is neither man nor woman,[21] tell me, how then can one find him?

Kabīr: His epithets are so many, they cannot all be told.[22] Whoever seeks Him will find Him. In every body there exists the bodiless, indestructible, imperceptible, King Nirañjan.

Raidās: O Knower of Brahman, you have gone astray. You do not understand His essence. You have abandoned Añjan and sing only of Nirañjan.[23] You are wasting your birth in vain.

Kabīr: If a guru makes a mistake, then his disciple corrects him. If the pupil makes a mistake, the guru scolds him. I, Kabīr, say, listen Raidās. Understand and worship the Formless.

Raidās: Everyone says that they have understood the Vedas through mental concentration,[24] [but] they do not respect what is said in the Vedas and the Koran. They keep to their own opinions.

Kabīr: I've studied the Vedas and the Koran and have seen all [their contents]. They're all imperfect hopes.[25] By placing its faith in the Vedas, all this world is sinking into hell.

Raidās: He enters into many bodies, not just a few.[26] He is fickle; He is steadfast. He is a youth, an old man, a child. He is a scoundrel; He is a *pīr*.

Kabīr: He enters into bodies neither a lot nor a little. He neither moves nor desires. He is unborn. Hari never becomes [incarnate]. This is how my Lord is.

Raidās: You have spoken the truth.[27] He is the real truth. He punishes the powerful. He destroys the powerful and saves the weak. Listen Kabīr, my fellow disciple.

Kabīr: He is separate from passion and hate, from pleasure and pain. He is unmoving. He neither commits errors nor enjoys anything. That Spirit, full of bliss, doesn't act. He is a yogi bearing the form of light.

Raidās: O sadhu, the Vedas and the *Bhāgavata-purāṇa* tell how He destroyed many gods and men. The Beloved of His devotees is under the power of those devotees. Don't deny [the reality of] His avatars.

Kabīr: Brahmā, Vishnu, Śeṣ, Śaṅkar, the gods, and men offer service to Him. He is the cowherd of infinite worlds,[28] O ascetic. This is how my God is.

Raidās: Your mother was a Muslim, your father a Julāhā.[29] Their son became a knower of Brahman. He doesn't respect what is said in the Vedas or in the Koran. He sticks to his own opinions.

Kabīr: Your mother and father were both Chamārs.[30] How can you practise devotion? You cannot know the essence of Ram's Name. You are impertinent![31]

The god Brahmā arrived mounted on a swan. He called on the Vedas as his witness: "Raidās has practised true devotion. Kabīr doesn't understand the secret."

Kabīr: This witness is false. Brahmā is false. The Vedas and Puranas are false. Go away, Brahmā! Go home! Even you don't know the secret.

[Durgā,] the Goddess who rides on a lion, then [came] to debate [with Kabīr]. Speaking sweetly, she said: "Raidās has practised true devotion. Kabīr doesn't understand devotion."

Kabīr: You have people cut throats on the seventh and eighth days [of the Navarātrī festival]. You go about eating from door to door. Go away, Mother of the world! Why do you give false witness?

Durgā: I lowered the royal umbrella of the mighty king [Kaṃsa].[32] I was a slave in Krishna's house.[33] [Krishna eventually] became dispassionate and went and sat in the forest. [There] the hunter killed him.[34]

Kabīr: Mother, those who you send down to hell belong to Māyā. I have abandoned wealth and women. Do whatever you want [to me].

Durgā: I keep control of all the three worlds. I am the mother of all: gods, men, demons, and beggars. Whom have I not eaten?

Kabīr: O foolish one, you have spoken without [having acquired] a guru, without [knowing] the secret. I have been saved by being attached to Hari. If service to you is the way to salvation, then why did Pīpā abandon [your worship]?[35]

Mounted on a bull, Shiva then [came] to debate [with Kabīr]. Speaking immortal words, he said: "Raidās has practised true devotion. Kabīr doesn't understand devotion."

Kabīr: You are the master of ghosts and spirits. Since when have you earned devotion? Go away, Śaṅkar! Go home! Who is it who has falsely misled you?

Shiva then went off to where Garuḍ and Gopāl were. [*Shiva:*] "I created ghosts and spirits, but the Julāhā's secret is infinite."

[*Vishnu:*][36] You, O Śambhu, are debating. . . .[37] The bird is singing of the branches and leaves. Why are you destroying the root?[38]

Durgā stood up displaying her anger everywhere. Shiva got up furious. Shiva said: "In an instant, I bring about the destruction of the universe.[39] The four ages of the world honor me."

Kabīr: Who do you really kill? Who do you really save? Who will really die after you kill him? O Śambhu, you are debating foolishly.[40] I don't fear you.

Shiva: The ten avatars came after me. I neither take nor abandon any body. You, Kabīr, are a man of bad conduct. Don't compete with me.

Kabīr: The ten avatars accomplished their tasks. They took bodily form and restored dharma. [Meanwhile] you fled from Bhasmāsur. Then Hari came and saved you.[41]

Shiva: The three worlds are absorbed in me. How can they compare to me?[42] When Rāvaṇ came and fell at my feet, I gave him Laṅkā.

Kabīr: Rāvaṇ was destroyed through his faith in you. By serving you, he got his whole family killed. The fool made a bad decision.

Śaṅkar: Fool, I am the giver of treasure and magic powers. I am the god who gives everything. You are low and badly behaved. Don't compete with me.

Kabīr: No one has been saved by being enlightened by you. Listen, Lord Śaṅkar. [Your devotees] stay separated from devotion and salvation. It is difficult [for them] to meet Hari.[43]

Raidās: What is knowledge according to you? What is meditation? What are the Vedas and sacred songs according to you? With [the help of] what and against what do you struggle? From whom did you learn your doctrine?

Kabīr: The mind is knowledge. The mind is meditation. The mind is the Vedas and the sacred songs. One struggles against the mind by means of the mind. It is by the mind that one knows the goal.

Raidās: The doctrine that you proclaim, I will proclaim it as well. I accept your knowledge. I, Raidās, declare that Kabīr is my guru. I will wash away both illusion and karma.

Kabīr: Give up illusion! Give up karma! Give up the doubts of living beings. Rely on your own Self. We are both fellow disciples.

Raidās: You churned the butter and showed me the essence. All illusion and karma have vanished. I, Raidās, say. You are my guru and my *pīr*. I've gotten my doctrine from you.

Kabīr: Nirguṇ Brahman is the giver of everything. Keep It in your mind and concentrate your intellect on It. Who is inferior? Who is superior? You and I are both brother disciples.

Vishnu came along to where Kabīr and Raidās were. [*Vishnu:*] "Get up Kabīr! Look me in the face! What do you desire from me?"

Kabīr: Listen, Vishnu! You are intelligent and wise. I, whether bad or good, am your devotee. Who [except you] has seen the truth?

Mounted on Garuḍ, Gopāl says: "You two are my true devotees. Kabīr possesses the truth. Raidās is blessed." It is Sain who has sung this [story].

The Kabīr-Raidās Debate

कबीर-रैदास का संवाद

नही नही हो माधौ हित मोरा ।
मैं कैसैं दरसण पाऊं रांम [1] तोरा ॥ **1** ॥

कबीर कहै जी ॥ ऐक ही ब्रह्म ऐक मल मुत्र ।
ऐक लोही ऐक गूदा ॥
पूरण ब्रह्म सकल [2] घटि [3] ब्यापक ।
कुंण बांभण कुंण सूदा ॥ **2** ॥

रैदास कहै जी ॥ कुमति तणां दल बादल फूटा ।
सुमति तणां प्रकासा ॥
हिरदै ग्यांन ध्यांन धरि देषौ ।
सति भाषै रैदासा ॥ **3** ॥

कबीर कहै जी ॥ ब्रह्म ग्यांन बिन ब्रह्म ध्यांन बिन ।
हृदा सुध न होई ॥
पूरण ब्रह्म सकल घट ब्यापक ।
और न दुतीया कोई ॥ **4** ॥

रैदास कहै जी ॥ तुम ऐक ही ऐक कहा कहौ स्वांमी ।
दूजी प्रकृति कहां जाई [4] ॥

---

1. C omits रांम .
2. A सब .
3. D मैं .
4. AE जहां जाई ; D कहां समाई .

दूजी प्रकृत मैं रूप धर्या है ।
साधां ऐह बताई ॥ **5** ॥

कबीर कहै जी ॥ जेता फूल र तेती बासनां ।
जेता पवन र पांणी ।
जे या उतपति प्रलै होती ।
तौ प्रकृत कहां समांणी ॥ **6** ॥

रैदास कहै जी ॥ प्रकृति समांनी परम पुरष मैं ।
सो बनराबन मैं आया ॥
गोपनि कै संगि ग्वालनि कै संगि ।
चिटकी दे दे गाया ॥ **7** ॥

कबीर कहै जी ॥ नां वै नाचै नां वै गावै [5] ।
नां वै बेणि बजावै ॥
पुरष न [6] नारि नाथ नारांइण ।
वै औतार न आवै ॥ **8** ॥

रैदास कहै जी ॥ जे लीला औतार न होती ।
तौ जीव कहां निसतरते ॥
अंध धंध की षबरि न होती ।
सब जीव नरक परंते ॥ **9** ॥

कबीर कहै जी ॥ कहां नरक है कहां सुरग है ।
कौ आया को देष्या ॥

---

5. B inverts नाचै and गावै .
6. C omits न .

हंस बटाऊ कीया पयांनां ।
चलत न काहू पेष्या ।। **10** ।।

रैदास कहै जी ।। ठाढा देष्या कदम की छहीयां ।
कंवल नाल कर लईयां ।।
पीतांबर बैजंती माला ।
मोर मुकट सिर दईयां ।। **11** ।।

कबीर कहै जी ।। अष्ट कंवल दल हृदा [7] भीतरि ।
जे यौ मन पतियावै ।।
त्रिकुटी संगम दृढ करि राषै ।
तौ आवागवण चुकावै [8] ।। **12** ।।

रैदास कहै जी ।। तुम आवागवण ह्वैण द्यौ स्वांमी ।
गांवण द्यौ गोपाला ।।
वा कै रूप छली [9] बृज बनिता ।
मोहण नंद के लाला ।। **13** ।।

कबीर कहै जी ।। कहां नंद अरु कहां के लाला ।
कहौ कहां तैं आया ।।

---

7. A हिरदा . Manuscripts BCD are difficult to read but seem to have हृदा or हुदा .

8. B मिटावै .

9. AD पछली . B is not completely legible. For sense छली seems the better reading.

अलष पुरस अबिनासी पूरण ।
कहूं क [10] बिरलां पाया ॥ **14** ॥

रैदास कहै जी ॥ चहुं दिस नंद रु चहुं दिस लाला ।
चहुं दिस बेदां गाया ॥
जहां जहां पाप प्रगट्या स्वांमी ।
तहां तहां उठि ध्याया ॥ **15** ॥

कबीर कहै जी ॥ नही तहां पाप पुनि भी नांही ।
नही तहां बेद र बांणी ॥
कहै कबीर सुनौ रैदासा ।
जोति मैं जोति समांणी ॥ **16** ॥

रैदास कहै जी ॥ कौंण पचि मरै गुडी कै वोटै ।
कौंण गहै पियाला ॥
बडी लूटि मैं रतन षजीनां ।
रांम कृष्ण औतारा ॥ **17** ॥

कबीर कहै जी ॥ जा कूं तुम औतार [11] कहत हौ ।
सो होता जम झोर्या ॥
अबिनासी का मरम न पाया ।
त्रिगुण नदी मैं बोर्या ॥ **18** ॥

रैदास कहै जी ॥ नृगुण सुरगुण ऐक गुसांई ।
जा मैं रेष न रोपा ॥

---

10. B कहू क ; CE कहौ क ; D सौ कहूं क .
11. CE repeat औतार .

सो हम देष्या बनराबन मैं ।
नंद घरां नंद गोपा ॥ **19** ॥

कबीर कहै जी ॥ कहां नंद रु कहां जसौदा ।
कहौ कहां का जाया ॥
निराकार निरलेप नरंजन ।
नृगुण बेदां गाया ॥ **20** ॥

रैदास कहै जी ॥ वै है करता वै है भरता ।
वे केवल वै कृष्णां ॥
निराकार आकार ऐक ही ।
सो रटि ल्यौ हो रसनां [12] ॥ **21** ॥

कबीर कहै जी ॥ काची कथा न रीझूं राचूं ।
साची सिर परि राषूं ॥
निराकार कूं नवणि हमारी ।
अघट अमी रस चाषूं ॥ **22** ॥

रैदास कहै जी ॥ सुणौ कबीर पीर मति वै ही ।
वै बलि काज संवारण ॥
कंस केस हिरणाकुस हतीया ।
भक्त [13] प्रहलाद उधारण ॥ **23** ॥

कबीर कहै जी ॥ देह धरै ता कूं नही धीजूं ।
अलष न औतरि आवै ॥

---

12. C रष्णां .
13. A भगत ; D भगति ; E भक्ति .

सुनि मंडल मैं जोति झिलमिलै ।
सो म्हारै मनि भावै ॥ **24** ॥

रैदास कहै जी ॥ भगति [14] हेत उन देह धरी है ।
ब्रह्म बिडद कै काजा [15] ॥
रांवण कुल कुटंब सब काट्यौ ।
दीयौ बभीषण राजा ॥ **25** ॥

कबीर कहै जी ॥ वै मरै न मारै षिरै न षारै ।
वै अबिनासी ऐसा ॥
पुरष न नारि नाथ नारांइण ।
नां ऊ भानां बैसा ॥ **26** ॥

रैदास कहै जी ॥ वै मरै न मारै षिरै न षारै ।
वानैं कौंण बिडद दे गाजै ॥
पुरष न नारि नाथ नारांइण ।
कहौ किसी बिधि पाजै ॥ **27** ॥

कबीर कहै जी ॥ बिडद बहुत है अकथ कथत है ।
जिन षोज्या तिन पाया ॥
घट घट मैं अघट अबिनासी ।
अलष निरंजन राया ॥ **28** ॥

रैदास कहै जी ॥ तुम भूला छौ ब्रह्म ग्यांनी ।
वा का मरम न पाया ॥

---

14. BD भगत ; C भक्ति .
15. A छाजा . E ज .

अंजन छाडि निरंजन गाया ।
मिथ्या जन्म गमाया ॥ **29** ॥

कबीर कहै जी ॥ गुर भूलै तौ सिष समझावै ।
सिष भूलै गुर तारै [16] ॥
कहै कबीर सुनौ रैदासा ।
समझि भजौ निराकारै ॥ **30** ॥

रैदास कहै जी ॥ मै तौ निगम नृति होइ बूझ्या ।
सो तौ सब यूं भाषै ॥
बेद कतेब कौ कह्यौ न मांनै ।
टेक आपणी राषै ॥ **31** ॥

कबीर कहै जी ॥ बेद कतेब षोजि सब देष्या ।
ऐ सब ऊली आसा ॥
यौ संसार नरक सब बूडौ ।
करि [17] बेद बिसवासा ॥ **32** ॥

रैदास कहै जी ॥ घट तन बधत घणां नही थोडा ।
वै चंचल [18] वै थीरा ॥
तरुन बृध बालापन वै ही ।
वै पाजी वै पीरा ॥ **33** ॥

कबीर कहै जी ॥ घट तन बधत घणां नहि थोडा ।
वै निहचल निहकांमी ॥

---

16. C लारै ; D नारै .
17. CD करि करि .
18. A निहचल .

अण होता हूवा हरि नांही ।
इसा हमारा स्वांमी ॥ **34** ॥

रैदास कहै जी ॥ तुम साची कही सही सति वा ही ।
सबलां सज्या लगाई ॥
सबल सिंघार्या निबला तार्या ।
सुनौ कबीर गुर भाई ॥ **35** ॥

कबीर कहै जी ॥ राग दोष [19] दुष सुष तैं न्यारा ।
वै नृवरति भरम न भोगी ॥
प्रवर्ति नही पुरष परमांनंद ।
वै [20] जोतिस रूपी [21] जोगी ॥ **36** ॥

रैदास कहै जी ॥ साध बेद भागौत बतावै ।
सुर नर बहुत संघारा ॥
भगत बछल भगतां बसि हूवा ।
मति मेटौ औतारा ॥ **37** ॥

कबीर कहै जी ॥ ब्रह्मा बिष्ण सेस अरू संकर ।
सुर नर जा [22] की सेवा ॥
अनंत लोक के ग्वाल गुसांई ।
ऐसा [23] हमारा देवा ॥ **38** ॥

---

19. C दौ .
20. C omits वै .
21. D रुसी .
22. B ता .
23. C इसा ; E एसा .

रैदास कहै जी ॥ तेरी माइ तुरकणी बाप जुलाहा ।
पुत्र भया ब्रह्म ग्यांनी ॥
बेद कतेब कौ कह्यौ न मांनैं ।
बात आपनी ठांनी ॥ **39** ॥

कबीर कहै जी ॥ तेरी माइ चमारी बाप चमारा ।
कहा भगति तुम कीनी ॥
रांम नांम का मरम [24] न जांन्यां ।
माथै बेठि तुम लीनी ॥ **40** ॥

हंस चढया ब्रह्मा जी आया ।
साषी बेद बुलाया ॥
सति भगति रैदास करी है ।
कबीरै भेद न पाया ॥ **41** ॥

कबीर कहै जी ॥ झूठा साषी झूठा ब्रह्मा ।
झूठा बेद पुरांनां ॥
जा जा ब्रह्मा घरां आपनैं ।
तुम भी भेद न जांनां ॥ **42** ॥

सिंघ बांहणी बाद करत है ।
बोलत मुधरी बांनी ॥
सति भगति रैदास करी है ।
कबीरै भगति न जांनी ॥ **43** ॥

---

24. B भेद .

कबीर कहै जी ॥ तूं आठैं सातैं गला कटावै ।
घर घर षाती डोलै ॥
जा जा जगत की जननी ।
कूडी साषि क्यूं बोलै ॥ **44** ॥

दुरगा कहै जी ॥ भोपति अनड मैं छत्र नवाया ।
हूं र कृष्ण घरि दासी ॥
बिरकत होइ बनां जाइ बैठा ।
दे गलि मार्या पासी ॥ **45** ॥

कबीर कहै जी ॥ जो तुम पास्या [25] नरक गरास्या ।
जा कै माया माता ॥
कनक कांमणी दोऊं त्यागी ।
करि चे जौ ले [26] लाता [27] ॥ **46** ॥

दुरगा कहै जी ॥ तीन लोक मैं बसि करि राष्या ।
हू र सकल की माई ।
सुर नर दांणां देव भिष्यारी ।
हूं र किनूं नही षाई [28] ॥ **47** ॥

---

25. This is probably related to फांसना ("to trap or snare"), as is the पासी of the previous stanza. It may also be related to उपासना ("to worship"), or be a miswritten पारया ("caused to fall").

26. C ल्यौ .

27. D जाता .

28. C पाई .

कबीर कहै जी ।। तैं निगुरा बाष्या भेद बिन भूंदू ।
हम उबर्या हरि लागी ।।

तौ सेयां जे गति मुक्ति है ।
तौ पीपै क्यूं त्यागी ।। **48** ।।

बृष [29] चढया सिव बाद करत है ।
बोलत इम्रत बांणी ।।
सति भगति रैदास करी है ।
कबीरै भगति न जांणी ।। **49** ।।

कबीर कहै जी ।। तूं तौ भूत प्रेत कौ दाता ।
कदि तैं भगति कमाई ।।
जा जा संकर घरां आपणैं ।
मिथ्या कांइ भरमाई ।। **50** ।।

चाल्या सिव जहां गया जी ।
जहां गरड गोपाला ।।
हम तौ भूत प्रेत करि थाप्पा [30] ।
जुलाहा भेद अपारा ।। **51** ।।

तुम तौ सिंभू बाद [31] करत हौ ।
कहां चकवै वै [32] भोला ।।

---

29. A बिर्षम ; C बृषम ; E बूषम . RPP 13494 वेहल ; RSS 7608 बैल .
30. B थरप्पा .
31. B अजूंनी बाद ; C अजौंनी बाद .
32. C omits वै .

डाल पांन कै पंछी बोलै ।
क्यूं मेटत हौ मूला ॥ **52** ॥

चहुं दिस ऊभी दुरगा कोपै ।
महादेव षरा रिसांनां [33] ॥
पलक मैं परलै करि रालां ।
चहुं जुगां हम [34] मांनां ॥ **53** ॥

कबीर कहै जी ॥ कहा तुम मारौ कहा तुम तारौ ।
को तेरा मार्या [35] मरिहै ॥
तुम तौ सिंभू अजूंनी बाद करत हौ ।
हम तुम सैं नही डरि हैं ॥ **54** ॥

संकर कहै जी ॥ दस औतार हूवा [36] मो आगैं ।
देह धरूं नही छोडा ॥
तुम लुघ मनिष कुचल [37] कबीरा ।
न करि हमारी होडा ॥ **55** ॥

कबीर कहै जी ॥ दस औतारां कारिज कीया ।
देह धरि धरम दिढाया ॥
भसमागर आगैं तूं भागौ ।
तब हरि आंणि छुडाया ॥ **56** ॥

---

33. E सिना .
34. E ह .
35. E र्या .
36. C repeats हूवा .
37. C कुल .

संकर कहै जी ॥ तीन लोक समांनी मेरै ।
कहा सरभर [38] उहां कीनी ॥
रांवन आइ पाइ जब लागौ ।
तब वा कूं लंका दीनी ॥ **57** ॥

कबीर कहै जी ॥ तुम र भरौसै रांवन बूडौ ।
करि करि सेव तुम्हारी ॥
कुल के सब कुटंब कटाऐ ।
भूंदू बुरी बिचारी ॥ **58** ॥

संकर कहै जी ॥ हूं र अजूंनी रिधि सिधि कौ दाता ।
हूं [39] भगवंत भंडारी ॥
तूं कुचल [40] कमीण कबीरा ।
न करि होड हमारी ॥ **59** ॥

कबीर कहै जी ॥ तुम परमोध्या तिर्या [41] न कोई ।
सुणि हो संकर स्वांमी ।
भक्ति मुक्ति सूं न्यारा रहि गया [42] ।
हरि सूं हुई हरांमी ॥ **60** ॥

रैदास कहै जी ॥ कौंण तेरै ग्यांन है कौंण तेरै ध्यांन है ।
कौंण तेरै बेद र बांणी ॥

---

38. C भरभर .
39. D adds र .
40. C कुल .
41. C सुण्यां .
42. C रया .

कौंण ले कौंण आगैं झूझै ।
या मति कौंण सूं जांणी ॥ **61** ॥

कबीर कहै जी ॥ मन ही ग्यांन है मन ही ध्यांन है ।
यौ मन बेद र बांणी ॥
यौ मन ले मन आगैं झूझै ।
या गति मन सूं जांणी ॥ **62** ॥

रैदास कहै जी ॥ सो तुम गावौ सो हूं गांऊं ।
तेरा ग्यांन बिचारूं ॥
कहै रैदास कबीर गुर मेरा ।
भरम करम धोइ डारूं ॥ **63** ॥

कबीर कहै जी ॥ भरम ही डारि दे करम ही डारि दे ॥
डारि दे जीव की दुबध्याई ॥
आत्म रांम करौ बिसरांमां ।
हम तुम दोन्यूं गुर भाई ॥ **64** ॥

रैदास कहै जी ॥ मांषण मथि रु तत दिषलाया ।
भरम करम सब जाई ॥
कहै रैदास पीर गुर मेरा ।
या मति तुम सूं पाई ॥ **65** ॥

कबीर कहै जी ॥ नृगुण ब्रह्म सकल कौ दाता ।
सो सुमरौ चित लाई ॥
को है लुघ दीरघ को नांही ।
हम तुम दोन्यूं गुर भाई ॥ **66** ॥

चल्या चल्या बिष्ण जी आया ।
जहां कबीर रैदासा ॥
उठौ कबीर सनमुष ह्वै देषौ ।
करौ कौंण की आसा ॥ **67** ॥

कहै कबीर जी सुणौ बिष्ण जी ।
तुम हौ चतुर बबेकी ॥
हम तौ बुरा भला जन तेरा ।
या तत बस्त किन देषी ॥ **68** ॥

गरड चढे गोपाल कहत है ।
सति भगत [43] म्हारै दोई ॥
सति कबीर धनि रैदासा ।
गावै सैंनां [44] सोई ॥ **69** ॥

ईति श्री सैंन बिरचित कबीर अरू रैदास संबाद संपूर्ण ।।[45]

43. A सत भगत ; BE सति भक्त ; C सत भग भगति ; D सति भगत .
44. B सेना .
45. This is exact wording of C. A and D are almost the same. does not mention Sain.

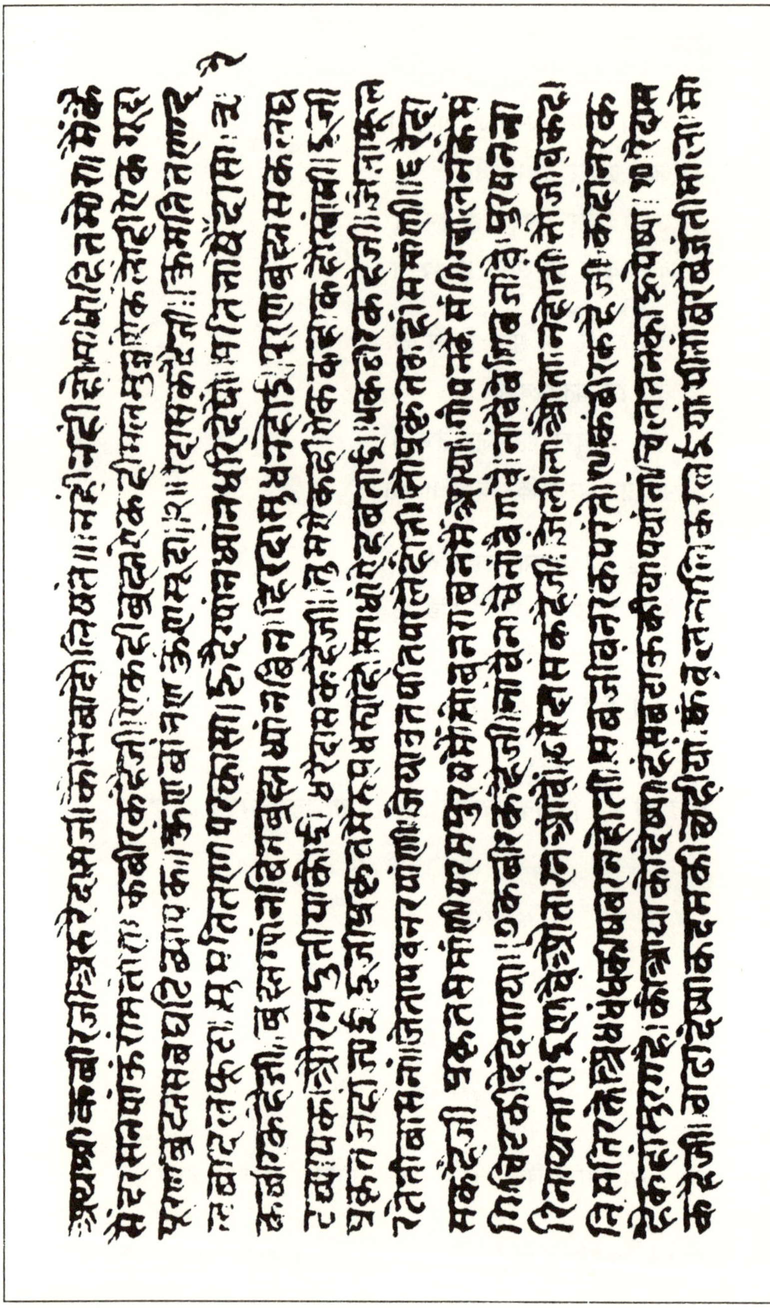

Fig. 1a. Kabīr-Raidās kā saṃvād, manuscript A (photos by D. Lorenzen).

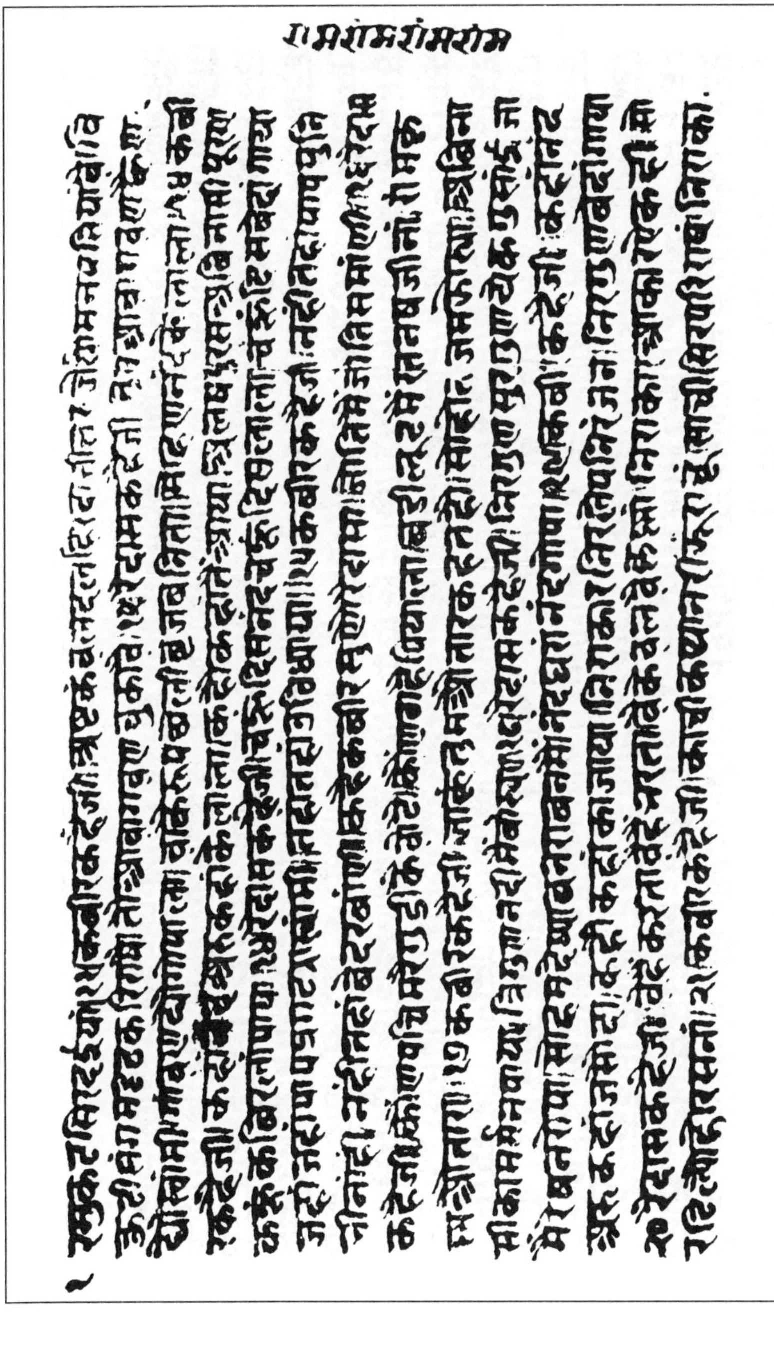

Fig. 1b. Kabīr-Raidās kā saṃvād, manuscript A

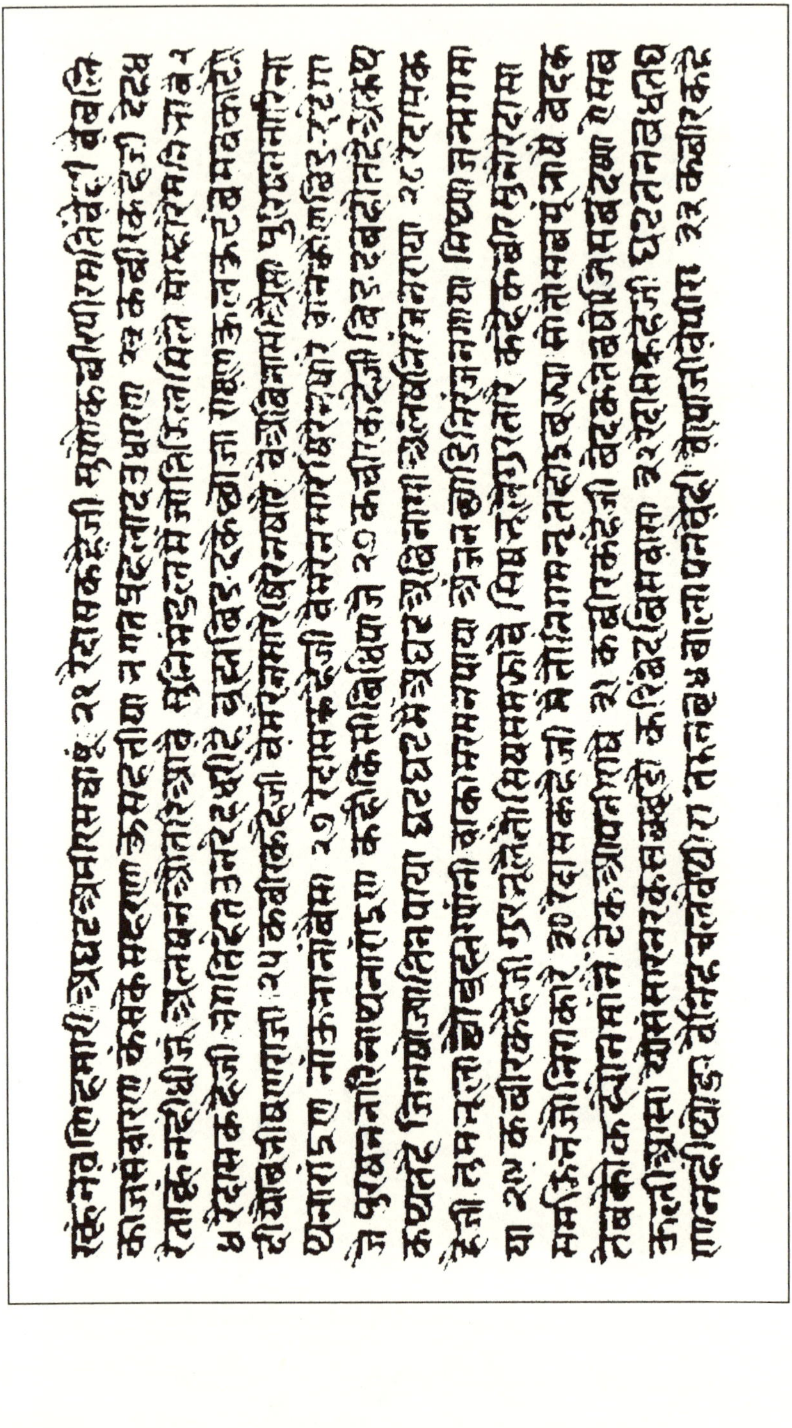

Fig. 2a. Kabīr-Raidās kā saṃvād, manuscript A

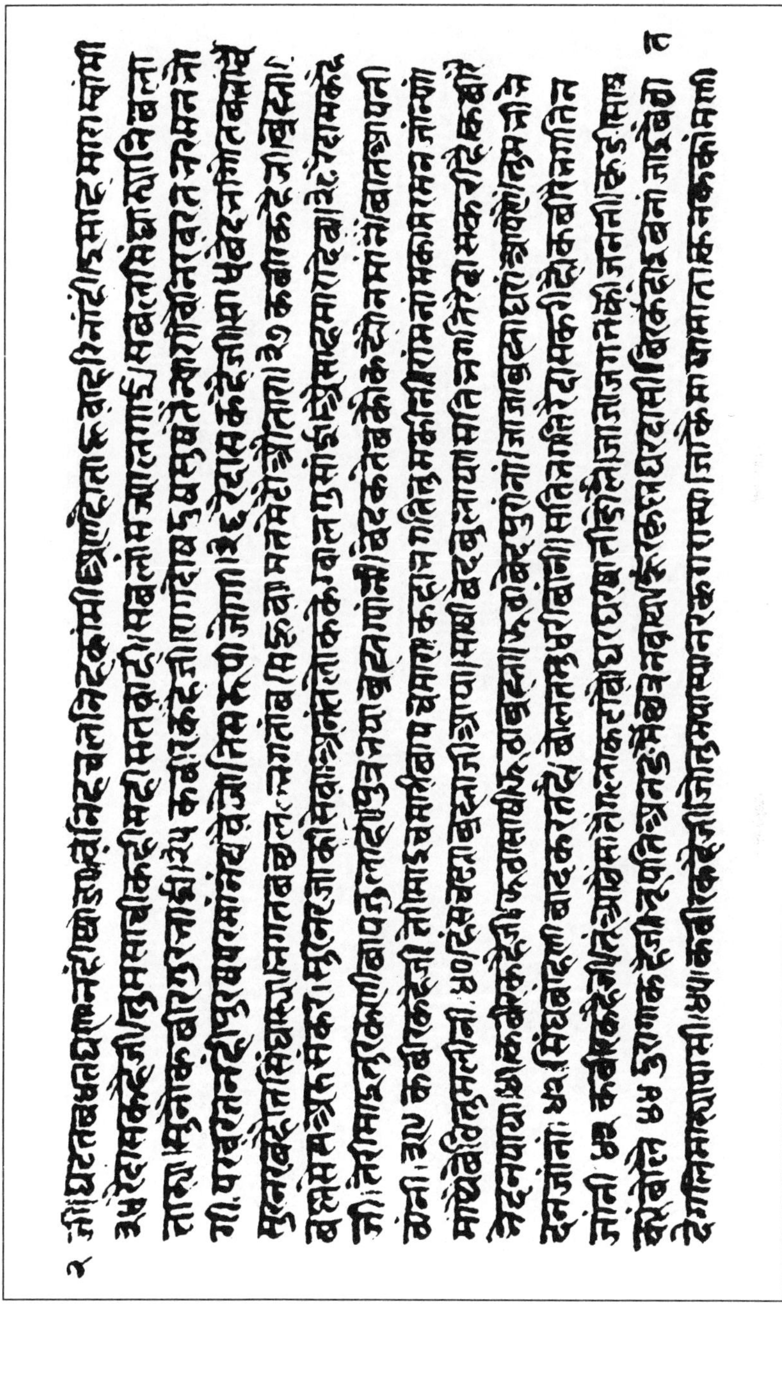

Fig. 2b. Kabīr-Raidās kā saṃvād, manuscript A

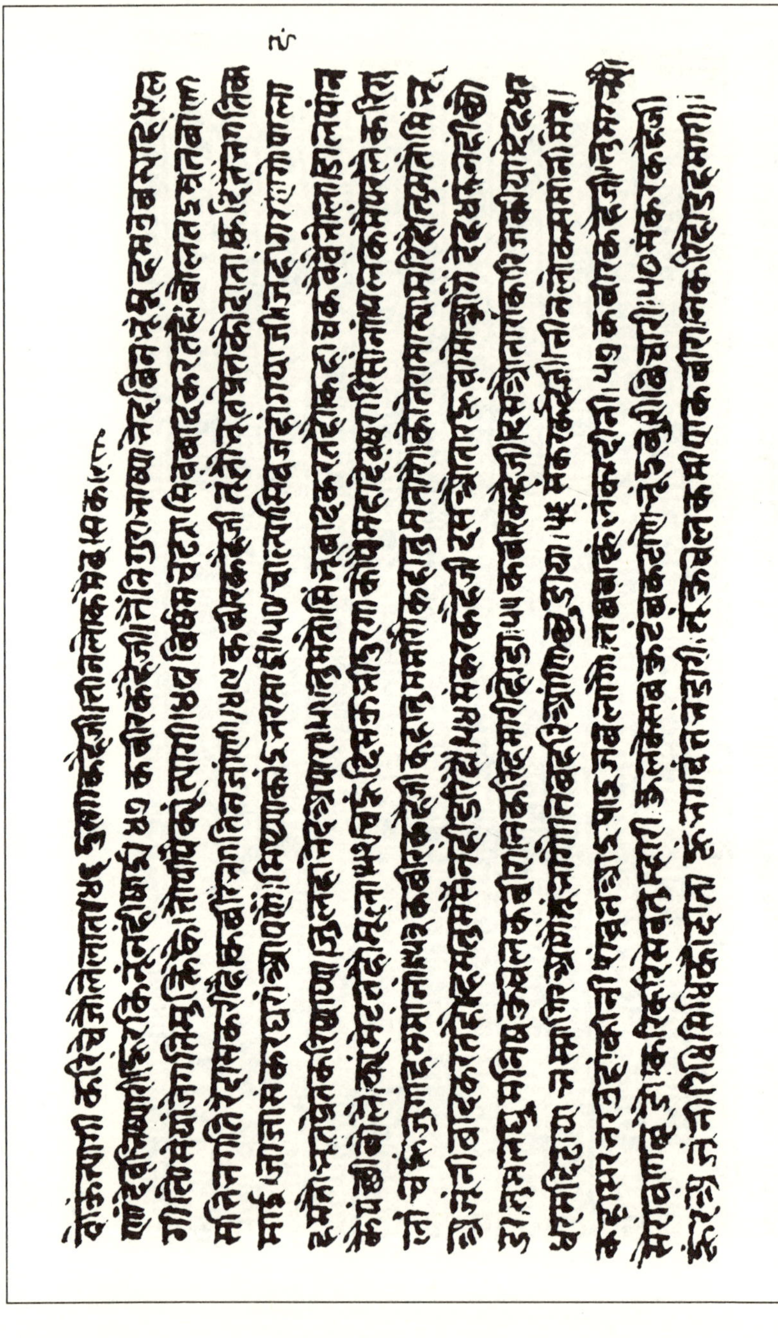

Fig. 3a. Kabīr-Raidās kā saṃvād, manuscript A

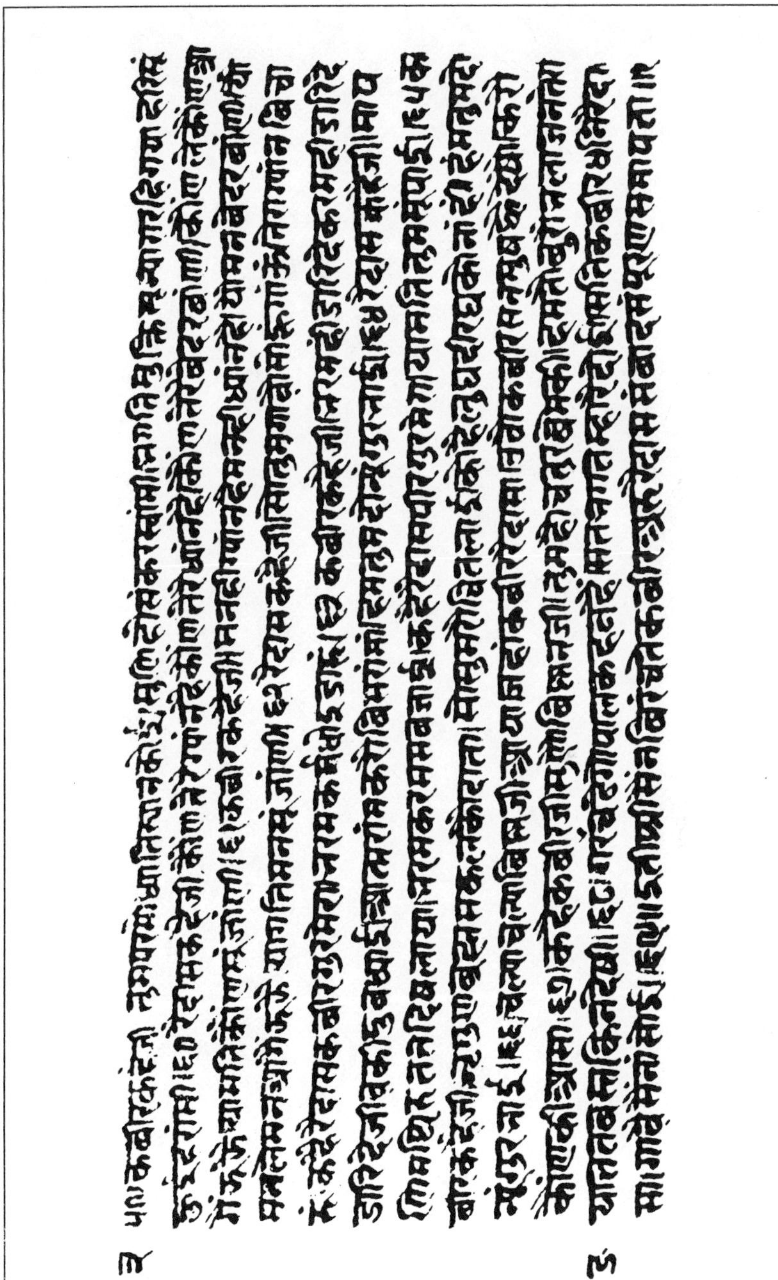

Fig. 3b. Kabīr-Raidās kā saṃvād, manuscript A

5

Kabīr's Most Popular Songs

Probably over two thousand religious songs (*pads,* bhajans, *śabdas,* and *ramainīs*) attributed to Kabīr have so far been published.[1] Many more are found in oral tradition and in unpublished manuscripts. Academic scholars have concentrated their study almost exclusively in the three oldest known collections of Kabīr's songs and verses: the *Kabīr bījak* associated with the Kabīr Panth, the *Kabīr granthāvalī* associated with the Dādū Panth, and the songs and verses found in the *Gurū Granth Sāhib* of the Sikhs. With only a few exceptions, however, the songs attributed to Kabīr that are most popular today are not those found in these three collections.

To put together an album of "Kabīr's Greatest Hits," we must turn instead to the more modern collections of his songs. It is in fact doubtful the Kabīr himself composed these songs, usually called bhajans, except perhaps for the few that are also found in the older collections. Even Kabīr's authorship of the songs in these older collections is impossible to verify. Nonetheless, all the songs, old and new, have been given signature phrases *(bhaṇitā)* — most commonly "Kabīr says" — that identify Kabīr as the author, and all the songs express aspects of the larger body of ideas that defines Kabirian tradition.

Among the published modern collections, three are particularly important. First is a collection of 256 Kabīr bhajans included as an appendix to H. Dvivedī's *Kabīr* (1971). This appendix is apparently based on an earlier collection of Hindi texts with Bengali translations that the scholar K. M. Sen published in 1910–11. Sen's collection is no longer available virtually anywhere, but a new edition is being planned by Visvabharati University.

In 1915 Rabindranath Tagore published an English translation of one hundred of these songs (numbers 1–100 of H. Dvivedī's appendix) in a book that has achieved considerable popularity (Kabīr 1961). Tagore based his translation on Sen's Hindi texts and Bengali translations and on unpublished English translations by A. K. Chakravarty (Kabīr 1961, xliii–iv). Although Tagore's translations read quite nicely, in a Victorian English sort of way, V. C. Mishra (1987) has criticized them for their semantic looseness and theistic bias.

The second important modern collection of Kabīr bhajans was first published by the Belvedere Press of Allahabad in about the 1930s and has been reprinted several times since (Kabīr 1987–89). The third important collection is a more recent one published by the Kabīr Chaurā monastery in Banaras (Kabīr 1988). Several additional modern collections have also been published.[2] Another interesting source are the many commercial recordings of Kabīr's songs by a variety of singers including Kumar Gandharva, Bhupendra, Bhimsen Joshi, Laxmichand, Hari Om Sharan, and Anup Jalota.

Apart from the one hundred songs translated by Tagore, relatively few songs from the modern collections of Kabīr bhajans have been translated into English. The musicologist Edward Henry has transcribed and translated about twenty songs from recordings of itinerant singers of the Jogī caste in the Bhojpuri-speaking region of Uttar Pradesh (Henry 1988; 1991; 1995). Henry has also discussed the musical performances of the singers, a subject that other scholars have entirely neglected. Other translations to English of various popular Kabīr bhajans are found in books by V. K. Sethi (1984), P. Machwe (1977), and in the monthly magazine, *Kabir Voice,* published by the Kabir Association of Canada.

Many of the songs in these collections of Kabīr bhajans are known to a sizeable percentage, perhaps even a majority, of the adult population of Hindi-speaking North India. Some songs have considerable merit as literature, and some of the itinerant sadhu and Jogī singers that sing them are skilled musicians. For all these reasons, the songs clearly deserve closer study by academic scholars.

During fieldwork in Banaras in 1990 and 1992, I asked a number of Kabīr Panthī sadhus and *bhagats* (lay devotees), as well as several people not directly connected with the Panth, to identify the Kabīr bhajans they knew best. Some of the more knowledgeable sadhus also went through the entire contents of the larger published bhajan collections with me in order to give their estimate of the popularity of each bhajan. They sometimes commented that a certain bhajan was particularly popular with sadhus, with *bhagats,* or with women. I cannot claim that the survey has the statistical validity of a Gallup poll, even for the Banaras region, but in fact the responses about which bhajans are the most popular ones were quite consistent.

According to my survey, easily the most popular Kabīr bhajan is the one that begins "Jhīnī jhīnī." It was known by heart by almost everyone I talked to. The next most popular bhajans, ones that many persons also knew by heart, formed a group of seven including "Chādar ho gayī," "Moko kahāṃ," "Man tūṃ phūlā phūlā," "Pīle pyālā ho matavālā," "Dhobiyā jal bīch," "Man lāgo mero yār," and "Saiyāṃ nikasi gayo" (this last one usually attributed to Kabīr's daughter Kamālī).

After this came a group of twenty or thirty bhajans that most persons recognized, but that less than half knew by heart. Finally, there was a group of twenty or thirty more bhajans that one or two persons claimed were fairly popular but whose popularity was not confirmed by others. Not surprisingly, Kabīr Panthī sadhus often know many rarely sung bhajans and can recite from memory most or all of the *Kabīr bījak,* the text that the sadhus staying in the larger Kabīr Panthī monasteries (but not the monasteries of the Dharmadāsī and Burhanpur branches) chant every evening during the *Sandhyā pāṭh* (see chapter 6).

The religious and social themes and the stylistic devices found in these most popular of Kabīr's popular bhajans largely overlap with those of the songs found in the three oldest collections of Kabīr's compositions. Nonetheless, differences do exist. The most obvious one is that the bhajans of the modern collections generally soften the sharp, often sarcastic social and religious criticism found in many songs of the older collections. Such criticism is not absent from the modern collections, but in them it tends to be muted and expressed with less aggressivity and wit.

A theme that becomes more prominent in many popular modern bhajans is a preoccupation with death and the transience of human life. Among those translated here, "Man tūṃ phūlā," "He lakaṛī" and "Sādho yah muradoṃ" are good examples. For the average Hindi speaker today, Kabīr is above all the poet of death. Life is short and human relations do not endure, he says. Use this life to good advantage, for death is certain and a human birth is hard to get.

Another common theme of the modern bhajans is an insistence on the importance of inner faith over external rituals and observances. Among the songs translated here, "Moko kahāṃ" and "Man nā raṅgāye" are typical examples. Although this theme is also prominent in the early songs, the defiantly iconoclastic tone common in them is generally replaced by a plea for a faith that goes beyond, rather than directly against, traditional religious practices.

The rest of this chapter presents translations of twenty popular bhajans attributed to Kabīr together with a short commentary on each. These bhajans include all the eight rated as most popular as well as twelve more that have mostly been chosen from the group of moderately popular bhajans. These twelve were selected on the bases of personal preference and historical interest. As in other chapters, the first one or two lines of most songs have been put into italics to indicate the refrain. In sung performances, this refrain is normally repeated after every verse.

1. "Jhīnī jhīnī bīnī chadariyā"

This most popular of all Kabīr bhajans compares our human bodies, even the bodies of the gods, to a finely made but perishable blanket, a theme found in several other bhajans attributed to this weaver-saint. Kabīr insists that the body must be kept in good condition, not only the physical body but also the mystic yogic body containing *chakras* in the form of lotuses and the "veins" called Iṅgalā, Piṅgalā, and Suṣumnā. One must not waste one's priceless human birth in accumulating negative karma. This bhajan has been recorded by Kumar Gandharva, Anup Jalota, and others. The only other English translation I have found is in *The Kabir Voice* of October 1991. The Hindi text appears in most modern Kabīr bhajan collections.[3]

Thin, thin, the blanket is woven.

Of what is the warp, of what the woof?
With what thread is the blanket woven?
Iṅgalā is the warp and Piṅgalā the woof.
With the thread Suṣumnā the blanket is woven.

The eight-petaled lotus is the spinning wheel.
With *tattvas* and *guṇas* He makes the blanket.[4]
For ten months the Lord keeps weaving.
Checking it well He weaves the blanket.

That blanket covers both gods and men.
They wrap it round and the blanket gets dirty.
Kabīr has covered himself with care.
He keeps his blanket as good as new.

2. "Man lāgo mero yār phakīrī meṃ"

In my survey, "Man lāgo mero yār" came out as the second most popular Kabīr bhajan, better known than any except "Jhīnī jhīnī." The singer laments that he is overwhelmed by the worries and cares of a householder's life and longs for the simplicity and liberty of the life of a religious ascetic. The use of many Persian-Arabic words is a notable feature of this bhajan, strongly suggesting Muslim influence. As far as I know, it has not been previously translated into English, but several commercial recordings of it exist. The Hindi text is found in various modern Kabīr collections:[5]

All I want, my friend, is a fakir's life.

Heed what everyone says is good or bad
    but live in poverty.
At the end of life this body will turn to dust.
    How can you strut with pride?

I've gone and made my home in the city of love.
    By luck I found satisfaction.
In my hand a bowl and under my arm a staff.
    My fief is all the world.

I found my joy, my friend, in worshipping Ram.
    Such joy is not in wealth.
Kabīr says: Listen, brother sadhu.
    The Lord is in satisfaction.

3. "Chādar ho gayī bahut purānī"

The theme and imagery of this bhajan are quite similar to those of "Jhīnī jhīnī." Although "Chādar ho gayī" is less popular than "Jhīnī jhīnī," it still can be counted among the most popular Kabīr bhajans. It has been commercially recorded at least twice. The only English translation I have found appears in *The Kabir Voice* of December 1991. The Hindi text is included in most modern bhajan collections.[6]

Your blanket has gotten old, so old.
Think and understand, proud friend.

A strange weaver wove this blanket.
The thread of karma makes the warp.
Surati and Nirati make the woof.
Then everyone says it looks just fine.

But sins, like dirty spots, will stain it.
Whatever we touch will leave a smudge.
With the soap of wisdom wash the blanket
in the water of fellowship with the saints.

Your blanket's beauty has gone for good.
You let it get mixed up with greed and folly.
With this sort of covering your life is a waste.
You don't seem to know what's good and what's bad.

Endure your doubts and know your self.
This is a thing that's hard to find.
Says Kabīr: Protect it with all your might.
It won't come into your grasp again.

4. "Man tūṃ phūlā phūlā phire"

This is one of the most moving of Kabīr's songs and is a favorite of many modern bhajan singers. The theme is the inevitability of death and the transitory nature of human relations. The image of the funeral pyre is central to this song, as it is to many other Kabīr bhajans such as "He lakaṛī" (no. 16 below). Although three oldest collections of Kabīr's songs do not include "Man tūṃ phūlā," they do contain versions of a song that is quite similar in terms of imagery, sentiment, and even language.[7] Rather surprisingly, I have not found any commercial recording of the modern bhajan and only one previously published translation (Behari 1971, 229). The Hindi text appears in various modern collections:[8]

O mind, you merrily strut your stuff,
But who in this world can you find to trust?

The mother says: This is my son.
The sister says: He is my hero.
The brother says: He is my rock.[9]
The woman says: He is my man.

His mother cries for the rest of her life.
His sister cries for less than a year.
His woman cries for a couple of weeks
Then goes to live with someone else.

The shroud they begged was four yards long.
The pyre was lit, just like at Holi.
The bones burned up like firewood.
The hair burned up like dried grass.
The body that once was gold is burnt
And no one wants to come near to it now.

The women of the house begin to cry,
Wandering all over, searching in vain.
Says Kabīr: Listen, brother sadhu.
Give up the hopes you hold for the world.

5. "Pīle pyālā ho matavālā"

This is one of several Kabīr bhajans that describe the successive stages of human life, only to conclude that all our hopes for this world are in vain. Another bhajan with a similar theme that is translated here is "He lakaṛī" (no. 16).

"Pīle pyālā" contains two important tropes that are found in many *nirguṇī* bhajans. One is the comparison of religious ecstasy with being drunk on liquor or marijuana. Another popular Kabīr bhajan that uses this trope is "Man masta huā to kyo bole."[10] An interesting hagiographic song of the *Kabīr bījak* is built around this trope and has a first line quite similar to the refrain of "Pīle pyālā."[11] The second trope is the image of the musk deer who searches the forest for the perfume that comes from his own navel. This symbolizes our search for the divine spirit within us whose discovery brings mystic illumination.

At least one commercial recording has been made of "Pīle pyālā." A quite short version of it was translated by Tagore (Kabīr 1961, 63–64) and a long one by B. Behari (1971, 240–41). The Hindi text is found in various modern collections:[12]

Drink from the cup and get yourself drunk.
The cup of the Name is filled with nectar.

You came to enjoy both sin and merit.
You are whose? And who is yours?
As long as you breathe, take God's Name.
Money and youth are but one night's dream.

Your childhood was lost in endless games.
As a youth you were caught in women's clutches.
You get old and the body begins to shake.
At the end you go nowhere, not even crawling.

The deer goes looking from forest to forest,
Seeking the musk that's within his navel.
Without the guru, you got so much pain,
But couldn't find the doctor to cure it.

If you want to be saved from birth and death,
Then give up lusts and other fancies.
Says Kabīr: Listen, brother sadhu.
From head to foot you're full of poison.

6. "Dhobiyā jal bīch marat piyāsā"

A washerman stands in the middle of a tank or river washing clothes while he dies of thirst. This is the striking central image of this very popular bhajan. In symbolic terms, the water is Brahman and/or mystic illumination and the washerman is the human soul that has not achieved illumination because of its ties to negative karma. Another popular Kabīr bhajan, "Pānī meṃ mīn piyāsā" ("In the Water the Fish is Thirsty"), features a similar central metaphor.[13] "Dhobiyā jal bīch" is found in most modern Kabīr bhajan collections, but I have not found any English translation:[14]

A washerman stands in the water, dying of thirst.

Standing there in the water the fool doesn't drink.
    The water's plenty good.
He doesn't know that that's the body's essence.
    He only wants to wash.

One minute the washerman weeps aloud,
    the next he's still and sad.
He himself is braiding the noose of karma,
    and tying it round his neck.

The fool forgets to pick up the soap of Truth
    that good men always use.
The cloth's got an ancient stain that won't go away,
    washing for twelve full months.

He uses up all his strength for a milligram
    and gives up a thousand times more.
Kabīr says: Listen, brother sadhu.
    In the presence of food you fast.

7. "Moko kahāṃ ḍhūṇḍhe re bande"

The words of this popular bhajan belong to the voice of God Himself. Its theme is the uselessness of the external religious practices —

worship in temples and mosques, idolatry, pilgrimages, asceticism, and yoga — of both Puranic Hinduism and traditional Islam. It has been translated to English both by R. Tagore (Kabīr 1961, 1) and by P. Machwe (1977, 55). Bhupendra and Laximichand have made commercial recordings of it. The Hindi text is found in various modern collections:[15]

Where will you find me, my friend?
I'm always near.

Not in idols or sacred spas,
not in secret places,
I'm not in temples or mosques,
not in Kāśī or Kailāś.

I'm not in prayer or penance,
not in vows or fasts.
I don't stay in yoga, in rites,
or renunciation.

Look and you'll find me as quick
as the wink of an eye.
Says Kabīr: Listen, sadhu.
I'm found in faith.

8. "Saiyāṃ nikasi gayo, maiṃ nā laṛī thī"

This is the last of the bhajans that the persons I questioned tended to put in the "most popular" group. Its theme is highly emotional: the confusion and loss felt by a wife who has been inexplicably abandoned by her husband. In symbolic terms, the husband is the soul, and the abandoned wife is the body. The five younger sisters-in-law are probably the five material elements and the twenty-five older sisters-in-law are the twenty-five *tattvas* of Sāṃkhya metaphysics. The city of ten doors is the body with its ten (often counted as nine) openings, including the mystic *brahmarandhra* at the top of the skull.

As one would expect, this bhajan is said to be particularly popular among women. I have recorded a version of it by a singer of Banaras named Kāśī Bhagat. He attributes the song to Kabīr himself. Usually, however, the signature phrase identifies Kabīr's daughter Kamālī as the author. As far as I know, this bhajan has not been translated into English. I have found only two printed versions of this bhajan, both of which attribute it to Kamālī:[16]

My husband left, though I didn't quarrel.

I hardly said a word to him at all.
I got in the blanket and slept alone.
His sisters, all five and twenty-five,
I don't know what they said against me.

This city has ten different gates.
I don't know which of the windows was open.
Kamālī, Kabīr's disciple, says:
My life was better before I married.

9. "Ghūṅghaṭ kā paṭ khol re"

This bhajan is quite popular, perhaps belonging with the most popular group. Its basic trope is a comparison between the experiences of mystic illumination and sexual union. The "unstruck drum" of the final line is a variant of a common *nirguṇī* image of the "unstruck sound." This sound is a symbol of the experience of illumination. "Ghūṅghaṭ kā paṭ" has been recorded by Hari Om Sharan. Several English translations have been published, and the Hindi text is included in most modern collections.[17]

Open up the veil that covers your face,
so you can meet your lover

In each and every body the Lord is present.
Don't utter a spiteful word.
Abandon pride in illusions of wealth and youth.
Even five-color robes are false.[18]
When a lamp is lit inside the empty palace.
Don't flounder about in hope.

By the power of yoga, in a room of the pleasure palace,
you've met a priceless lover.
Kabīr says: Bliss is here at last.
The unstruck drum is sounding.

10. "Man nā raṅgāye, raṅgāye jogī kapaṛā"

This bhajan is also popular. It attacks the hypocrisy of the yogis who perform the exercises and penances prescribed by the rules of their orders, but who fail to "color their minds" with the spirit of true devotion. I have not found any commerical recording of this bhajan. It has been translated by Tagore (Kabīr 1961, 69–70) and by B. Behari (1971, 237). The Hindi text is found in various modern collections:[19]

O yogi, you've colored your clothes but not your mind.

You take a yogic pose and sit in the temple.
You abandon Ram and worship a lifeless stone.
You split your ears and do up your hair in knots.
You've grown a beard, yogi, just like a goat.

You go off to the jungle for penances before a fire.
You've burnt up your lust, yogi, just like a eunuch.
You shave your head, yogi, and color your clothes.
You recite the *Gītā*, gaily babbling away.

Kabīr says: Listen, brother sadhu.
At Death's door you'll be caught, bound, and gagged.

11. "Rahanā nahīṃ deś virānā hai"

This bhajan uses three striking metaphors to highlight the transience and futility of mundane existence. The saving alternative is to find the Name of the True Guru, which is none other than Ram's Name. This bhajan has been translated by Machwe (1977, 48) and by B. Behari (1971, 238). Anup Jalota has made a commercial recording of it. The Hindi text is found in various modern collections.[20]

Let's not stay, it's a foreign land.

The world is a fragile paper cachet,
 a single drop and it falls apart.
The world is a garden filled with thorns,
 whoever gets snared will never get loose.
The world is a heap of dried-out brambles.
 Set it on fire and it jumps into flame.
Says Kabīr: Listen, brother sadhu.
 The True Guru's Name is the destination.

12. "Nāhīṃ dharmī nāhīṃ adharmī"

The voice of this bhajan is the Soul, both universal and individual, a being whose existence surpasses all attributes, both negative and positive. This song has been translated by Tagore (Kabīr 1961, 85) and by

Machwe (1977, 53). At least one commerical recording of it has been made. The Hindi text is found in several modern collections.[21]

I'm not religious and I'm not not religious
I'm not a monk and not a libertine.

I never speak, nor do I sit and listen.
I'm not a servant, nor am I anyone's boss.
I'm neither tied to the world nor liberated.
I'm not indifferent, I'm not enthusiastic.

I'm never apart from any single thing.
I'm never joined to any single thing.
I'll never go to the hells beneath the earth,
Nor set off for the heavens of the gods.

I have performed every sort of action,
But stay apart from any action at all.

The person who understands this is hard to find.
He must be firm, he must be seated well.
Says Kabīr: I don't create a single thing,
Nor do I destroy a single thing.

13. "Avadhū kudarat kī gati nyārī"

This is definitely an old song since it is included in the *Kabīr bījak* as well as in various modern collections.[22] This makes it about 400 or more years old. My translation here is based on the *Bījak* text. One can also consult the excellent translation by Linda Hess and Shukdeo Singh (Kabīr 1983, 49). Kumar Gandharva has made a commercial recording of it.

Some *Bījak* commentators interpret the "divine power" *(kudarat)* of the refrain as equivalent to the Vedantic concept of "illusion" *(māyā)*. The word *kudarat,* however, is borrowed from Persian and is usually associated with a Muslim context that is theistic and realist. The usual Advaita context of the word *māyā,* on the other hand, is monistic and idealistic.

The song presents several "absurd" images such as the fish that goes hunting in the jungle. These images are meant to amuse the listener and to illustrate the limitless power of God. This sort of absurd image is often called *sandhā bhāṣā,* a term that has been translated as "upside-down," "twilight," or "topsy-turvy" language (Hess 1983). The commentators attribute various symbolic meanings to such absurd images, but these equivalences are ambiguous and not all commentators agree about what means what. In any case, one can appreciate the song's humor and message without having to identify the symbolic meanings of these images. As in "Ghūṅghaṭ kā paṭ," the "unstruck sound" refers to the experience of mystic illumination.

This divine power, O sadhu, is something else.

It raises the humble making them into kings,
    then makes the king a beggar.
It stops the clove tree from giving any fruits,
    and the sandal from giving flowers.

It makes the fish go hunting in the forest,
    and the lion go swimming in the ocean.
It turns the castor tree to sandalwood
    and spreads its perfume all over.

It puts the whole world into a single clod,
    and a blind man sees the show.
It allows a cripple to jump over Meru mountain,
    and souls to roam the world.

By it a mute acquires an eloquent voice,
    and the unstruck sound is sounded.
It ties up the sky and sends it to lower worlds,
    and the king of snakes to heaven.

Kabīr says: Ram is the king of kings.
    Whatever he does it works.

14. "Rām nirañjan nyārā re"

This is another old song that has somehow managed to survive. It is found in the old Rājasthānī *Kabīr granthāvalī* collection as well as in several modern bhajan collections.[23] Kumar Gandharva has recorded a beautifully sung version of it.

The word *nirañjan* is difficult to translate. Literally it means "without stain." In *nirguṇī* texts from western India such as the *Kabīr granthāvalī,* it is generally used as an attribute or proper name of the "unconditioned" Absolute or one supreme God. In the eastern *Kabīr bījak* and many later Kabīr Panthī works, however, *nirañjan* more often refers to the secondary creator god who is also known as Kāl or Kāl-Nirañjan.[24] The word *añjan* as used in the present song is simply the opposite of *nirañjan.*

It refers to all that is "conditioned," to the physical universe including human minds.

Nirañjan Ram remains apart.
Añjan is every other thing.

Añjan is the creation, the syllable OM.
Añjan is all the things we see.
Añjan is Indra, Brahmā, and Śaṅkar.
Añjan is Govinda and all the gopīs.

Añjan is the songs, Añjan is the Vedas.
Añjan has made so many secrets.
Añjan is knowledge, texts and traditions.
Añjan gives lessons in worthless wisdom.

Añjan is the offerings, Añjan is the gods.
Añjan offers its service to Añjan.
Añjan dances, Añjan sings.
Añjan puts on endless disguises.

Tell me: How far and how many is Añjan?
As many as gifts, penances, spas and virtues.
Says Kabīr: It's an uncommon person who awakes,
Abandons Añjan and sticks to Nirañjan.

15. "E ab koi hīrā ratan gaṃvā ke"

E. O. Henry has transcribed, translated, and compared three different versions of this bhajan from performances by three different Jogī mendicants of eastern Uttar Pradesh.[25] Although "E aba koi hīrā ratan" is evidently quite popular among the Jogīs, it was not mentioned by the persons I surveyed. I have also been unable to find it in any published collection. Apparently it belongs exclusively to oral tradition and is not a part of the bhajan repertoire associated with the Kabīr Panth. Since this song and the following one are transcriptions of actual performances, the repetitions of the refrains are included in the translations and are not italicized.

The poetic images in this poem are all common tropes in nirguṇī literature. The diamond is a symbol both of the difficult to achieve human birth, and of mystic illumination. The parrot who is drawn to the delicious-looking, but inedible, silk-cotton fruit, represents the persons who are caught in the ties of worldly existence.

Someone has wasted the diamond,brother,
    and now leaves the world.

Take care to keep that diamond secure,
    safe under lock and key.
Today some saint will come to buy it.
    The diamond will cost him plenty.

You'll have to leave this world, brother,

When a fly alights on sticky molasses,
    its feet get hopelessly stuck.
In the end he won't have the strength to fly
    and he'll die without knowing why.

You'll have to leave this world, brother.

Look at the parrot, brother, so happy
    in a forest of silk-cotton trees.
In the end he won't have the strength to fly
    and he'll die without knowing why.

You'll have to leave this world, brother.

Says Kabīr: Listen, brother sadhu.
    Fix your mind on worship.
Without it salvation will never be won.
    Your birth will have been in vain.

You'll have to leave this world, brother.

16. "He lakaṛī tu ban lakaṛī"

This is another bhajan that was transcribed and translated by E.O. Henry (1988, 166–67, 277–78) from a performance by a Jogī mendicant. In this case, however, the song was identified as a well-known one by several of the persons I surveyed. Somewhat unexpectedly, the only other printed version I have found is in a small collection by the Kabīr Panthī sadhu Bhadaīdās, a resident of Damakheda in Raipur District, Madhya Pradesh.[26] Whereas the previous bhajan "E ab koi hīrā" uses standard *nirguṇi* tropes, the central metaphor of "He lakaṛi" is quite original. Poetically, it is one of the best of the bhajans attributed to Kabīr.

It's wood, my friend, nothing but wood.
Take a look, it's all a show of wood.

When you left the womb and entered the world,
The cradle that rocked you was made of wood.
By the time that you reached the age of five,
The toy in your hand was made of wood.

It's wood, my friend, nothing but wood.
Take a look, it's all a show of wood.

By the time you reached the age of twenty,
Your only worry was getting married.
The wedding palanquin was tulasī wood.

By the time you reached the age of forty,
Your only worry was getting old.
By the time you reached the age of sixty,
The cane in your hand was made of wood.

By the time you reached the age of eighty,
Your only worry was leaving this life.
When the men arrived to lift up the stretcher,
The funeral carriage was made of wood.

When they gave you a bath in Ganges' water
And brought your body to the Yamuna's bank,
They put wood below and wood above.
The pyre they built was made of wood.

It burned like the fires that light up Holi,
As they broke your skull with a pole of wood.
Says Kabīr: Listen, brother sadhu.
All this play is a show of wood.

It's wood, my friend, nothing but wood.
Take a look, it's all a show of wood.

17. "Chalanā hai dūr kyoṃ sovai re"

The message of this bhajan is quite direct. The path that leads to salvation is long and hard to travel. Our time here on earth is much too short. After our death no one can travel with us. Get your act together and depart. "Chalanā hai dūr" has been commercially recorded by Hari Om Sharan. The Hindi text is found in various modern collections.[27]

There's a long way to go, so why are you sleeping?

Wake up, you dreamer! Think, you fool!
Stop sleeping away, caught in the traps
Of lust and anger, frenzy and greed.
Open your eyes, you're wasting your life.

Illusions and delusions are piled on your head,
And murderers travel along at your side.[28]
When the pile you carry gets snatched away,
Why do you grab your head and cry?

The road to that city is full of dangers.
From the moment you leave you'll travel alone,
And no one will walk along at your side.
Who do you think you're waiting for?

The river is deep and the boat is old.
How will you cross to the other shore?
Says Kabīr: Listen, brother sadhu.
Don't gamble on profit and lose what you've saved.

18. "Mukharā kyā dekhe darapan meṃ"

In this bhajan, the face reflected in a mirror represents human vanity and the transient nature of beauty and physical pleasure. The alternative, here suggested only indirectly, is the life of an ascetic. The sense of the last two stanzas is somewhat enigmatic. The first contrasts domestic life with life in the forest, but to what end is unclear. The second brings in a pretty woman, a representative of the life of vain pleasures and concludes the person addressed won't be ready for death. I have not found any commercial recordings or English translations of this song. The Hindi text appears in various modern collections.[29]

What is the face you see in the mirror?
Your mind is devoid of compassion and dharma.

The river is deep and the boat is old,
    but you want to cross in a second.
The love boat has crossed to the other shore,
    and the sinners have drowned in the current.

You look in the mirror, curling your mostache,
oiling up your curls.
Before you know it that day will come
when crows will pick your bones.

The koyal sings on a mango branch.
The parrot sings in the forest.
The head of the house is happy at home.
The wanderer prefers the forest.

The pretty woman brings a betel treat,
you want to enjoy her body.
Says Kabīr: Listen, brother sadhu.
How will they battle [with death]?

19. "Avadhū gagan ghaṭā ghaharānī"

This song features an extended series of agricultural metaphors structured somewhat like the weaving metaphors of "Jhīni jhīni" (no. 1) and "Chādar ho gayī" (no. 3). The terms *surati* and *nirati* refer to aspects of the experience of mystical illumination. Kumar Gandharva has made a commercial recording of this song. It is included among the songs translated by R. Tagore, and the Hindi text is found in several collections.[30]

Sadhu, the sky is full of thunder.

In the East the clouds have begun to appear.
It sprinkles then starts to rain.
Take care of the bunds between your fields
so the water cannot escape.

Make Surati and Nirati your oxen,
nirvana the land you plough.
Pull up the weeds of doubt by the roots
and sow the rice of the Name.

Let consciousness guard the fields against
the deer who nibble the crop.
When the grain is ripe and he takes it home,
the farmer's joy is complete.

Then the five women come cook the meal
and the saints and the sages eat.

Says Kabīr: Listen, brother sadhu.
    The burning desire has been quenched.

20. "Sādho yah muradoṃ kā gāṃva"

This bhajan is quite popular and was featured in a recent television series on Kabīr's life. Its theme is death and the transience of human life as in "Man tūṃ phūlā" (no. 4) and "He lakaṛī" (no. 16). Nonetheless, it has not been translated and I have managed to find only one published version of the Hindi text (Kabīr 1988, 244–45).

Sadhu, this village belongs to the dead.

The *pīrs* are dead, the prophet is dead,
    the *jindā* yogis are dead.
The king is dead, his subjects are dead.
    Both doctor and patients are dead.

The moon has died, the sun has died.
    Both earth and sky have died.
The head of the fourteen worlds has died.
    What can others hope for?

The nine are dead, the ten are dead,
    the eighty-eight thousand are dead.[31]
The thirty-three crores of gods are dead,
    snared in the noose of time.

The Unnamed Name remains forever.
    Nothing else is real.
Says Kabīr: Listen, brother sadhu.
    No one should die in vain.

6

The Rituals of the Kabīr Panth

Another category of *nirguṇī* texts that has been mostly neglected by modern scholars is that of the songs and chants that accompany the performance of rituals.[1] One reason for this neglect may be the fact that rituals have a somewhat ambiguous role in *nirguṇī* religion. In their songs, Kabīr, Raidās, Gurū Nānak, and other early *nirguṇī* poets often reject rituals as manifestations of a false, exterior religiosity. Animal sacrifices, circumcision, pilgrimages, untouchability, death pollution, and the like are all disparaged or condemned. Nonetheless, many simple rituals have inevitably become a part of the religious life of the modern *nirguṇī* devotees.

In the case of the Sikhs, new life-cycle rites performed by Sikh officiants have replaced those performed by non-Sikh priests. In most *nirguṇī* sects, however, life-cycle rites like marriages and cremations are still performed by Hindu priests. Sectarian rituals are mostly limited to a few simple ceremonies. The rituals I want to examine here are those associated with the sadhus and lay initiates of the Kabīr Panth, the sect of the followers of Kabīr.

The rituals of the Kabīr Panth can be conveniently divided into those that are performed daily and those that are performed on special occasions: annually, monthly, or at irregular intervals. In the Kabīr Chaurā monastery in Banaras and other large monasteries of the Panth, the principal daily rituals are the morning and evening *āratī-pūjās* (adoration with a lamp or incense), the pre-meal chant, and the *sandhyā-pāṭh* (evening recitation) and its accompanying *kathā* (sermon). In most branches of the Kabīr Panth, the principal occasional ritual is the *chaukā* (literally "square"). It is performed at night during the annual *melās* (festivals) celebrating the birth and death anniversaries of Kabīr, on the full moon day of Jyeṣṭh (May–June) and the eleventh day of the bright fortnight of Māgh (January–February) respectively, and on every month's full moon night. Often these monthly *chaukās* are financed by lay devotees, usually in honor of some relative who has recently died. Another important, though simple, ritual is the initiation of *bhagats* (lay devotees) into the Panth. This often takes place during the *chaukā,* but may in fact be performed at any time.

A few other occasional rituals exist, but will not be discussed in this chapter. One is the simple ritual for the initiation of a sadhu, little more than his receiving a new name and a mantra from the *mahant* (abbot). This may take place at any time but, unlike lay initiations, is not performed during the *chaukā.* Another important occasional ritual is the funeral of the sadhus and *mahants* of the Panth. The *mahants* are usually buried, while the sadhus may be either buried or "floated" in a sacred river. As in most other Hindu sects, sadhus' corpses are not cremated. The funerals, marriages and other life-crisis rites of the lay *bhagats* of the Kabīr Panth are the same as those of the members of their respective castes who do not belong to the Panth. Kabīr Panthī sadhus do not normally take part in such rites.

Other religious activities of the *bhagats* and sadhus alike share certain features of rituals, but they are not usually identified as rituals by either the Kabīr Panthīs themselves or outside observers. These activities include the singing of bhajans (religious songs, often of Kabīr), religious study and meditation, the offering of *bhaṇḍārās* (feasts) to the sadhus, and visits to the monasteries to pay respect to their guru (usually the mahant and especially on the date of Guru-pūrṇimā in the month of Śrāvaṇ (July–August, and religious discussion and informal preaching *(satsaṅga).* For the sadhus it can even be said that almost all their regular daily activities take on a ritual character: from defecating and bathing in the morning to washing their dinner plates and going to bed at night. Nonetheless, the sadhus and *bhagats* do make a distinction between activities that are "secular" *(vyavahārik)* and those that are "religious" *(dhārmik),* and between religious activities that are "ritual" *(vidhyātmak)* and those that are not. All these partly ritualized religious activities will be mostly ignored in this chapter.

My principal aims here are to describe the rituals of the Kabīr Panth in some detail, to offer translations of some of the texts that are recited or sung as part of their performance, and to discuss how these texts modify, and even intentionally subvert, the semantics of similar or analogous rituals associated with more orthodox Hindu traditions.[2]

For this, two general points about ritual behavior need to be remembered. First is the obvious fact that ritual has a verbal as well as a physical component. As W. A. Lessa and E. Z. Vogt (1972, 323) observe: "Speech (prayers, spells, chants) comprises an integral part of ritual behavior, as much so as gesture and the manipulation of objects. Ritual is not the dumb, silent cousin of myth."

Second is the fact that any given ritual, or the various individual components of that ritual, can be associated with a variety of different cognitive and ideological messages by the persons who perform them (not to mention outside observers). Ruth Benedict (1934) long ago noted that "the rite is . . . more stable and fundamental than the rationalizations that universally accompany it. . . . In the rituals that have been studied most thoroughly the instability of the associated symbolism is as striking as the stability of seemingly arbitrary ritual acts." What is particularly interesting in the case of the Kabīr Panthī rituals is the way in which they are constructed using typical components found in more orthodox Hindu rituals but at the same time are imbued with an iconoclastic and generally egalitarian ideological message that stands in opposition to the basic religious and social ideology of a dominant *saguṇī* Hinduism that fosters reverence for the Vedas and Brahmins, image worship in temples, and *varṇāśramadharma.*

The descriptions here of the daily and occasional rituals of the Kabīr Panth are based primarily on personal observation in the large Kabīr Chaurā monastery in Banaras during eight periods of fieldwork there between 1976 and 1994. In other large monasteries of the Kabīr Panth, similar rituals are performed although the spoken and sung texts that accompany them are somewhat different in those monasteries belonging to other branches of the Panth. At smaller monasteries, both types of rituals may be partly or completely dispensed with.

The first daily monastic ritual is the morning *āratī-pūjā,* sometimes called the *"samūhik-pūjā"* (assembled worship) since this is when the sadhus first assemble together. At about 5:00 a.m., one sadhu, who has been chosen as *pujārī* (ritual officiant), places flowers on several sacred sites in the monastery courtyard. These include the *samādhi* (burial shrine) of Kabīr, the shrine to Kabīr's *Bījak,* the *gaddī* (throne) of the *mahant,* and four *samādhis* of past *mahants.* The other sadhus gradually line up in two lines in front of the *Bījak* shrine. Two or three sadhus bang small gongs while the *pujārī* visits each of the mentioned places ringing a small bell and waving a small censer of smoking incense over each of them. Finally he walks up and down between the two facing lines of sadhus allowing each of them to pass their hands through the incense smoke. The sadhus then chant in unison the "Prārthanā-pañchak se" attributed to Rāmeśvarānanda Sāhab:[3]

O Gurudev, give me peace. Give
 worthy feelings, worthy intelligence.

Give mutual cooperation.
    Give purity to my heart.
Let there be pure feelings in my mind.
    Let there be pure conduct by my body.
May my speech be free of falsity and slander.
    May the sentiment of devotion increase.

May my thoughts not be agitated
    by the ripening of innate karma.
May my body and mind be healthy,
    may my worship be free of obstacles.
May I remain in the presence of saints
    and be filled with the sentiment of devotion.
May I swim across the ocean of *saṃsāra,* the ocean
    filled with passion, hate, change and fear.

Let there be neglect for wicked persons
    and compassion for the destitute,
Happiness among those of good conduct
    and friendship with good people.
May buffoonery cease and may we delight
    in the words that lead across *saṃsāra*.
May we be merry in the study of wisdom;
    may we keep our minds under control.

May we have hope of refuge with the Satguru,
    may we have no fear of lust and other vices.
May we ever yearn for self-awakening
    and have faith the the words of revelation.
May the darkness of ignorance be destroyed;
    may the lamp of knowledge be lit.
May the law of death be forgotten,
    and immortality be expanded.

May there be no harm done to living beings
    through my words or my actions.
May I never feel the least attachment
    to the objects of my senses.
May there always be happiness
    and the absence of desire.
May there be an end to the power of *saṃsāra,*
    and a beginning to the knowledge of God.

This chant is followed by a call for "Victory to the Satguru Kabīr! Victory to the holy Satguru! Victory to the saints and devotee! Victory to Ram, the all-powerful Self!"

The sadhus, and any lay *bhagats* who may have lined up with them, then go to offer a greeting to the *mahant*, who all the while has been sitting on his *gaddī*. They squat before the *mahant*, with arms extended between their knees and hands cupped together, and repeat three times the phrase "Sāheb bandagī." On other occasions, this same greeting, often shortened to simply saying "Sāheb" and cupping one's hands, serves as the regular salutation between all sadhus and devotees of the Panth. After the "Sāhab bandagī," they touch the foot of the *mahant* and then their own foreheads with their right hands. Finally they do a clockwise circumambulation around the *Bījak* shrine and somewhat randomly greet each other with the same *"Sāheb bandagī."*

The sadhus then retire to carry out whatever individual activities and duties they may have — from study and meditation to gardening and kitchen chores — until the drum *(nagāṛā)* for the morning meal is sounded at about 11:00 a.m. The sadhus then rinse out their eating utensils *(thālī* and *kaṭorā)* and sit or squat down in the eating area *(laṅgar)*. Before this meal, they recite two short chants. The first is called the "Bhojan samay kā bhog śabda":[4]

When an offering is made to the Satpuruṣ,
the bell of the unstruck sound rings out.

The cooking is done with the *surati* of love.
The food is the key to immortality.
The Lord shares his food with the saints.
The devotee sings the joy of supreme bliss.

The pitcher is of gold and the plate well-made.
The Lord Creator sits to take his meal.
He took the *prasād* and rinsed his mouth,
and gave the great *prasād* to his devotees.

From the time the soul became alert,
Death became submissive.
Kabīr says: Your good fortune was complete
when the Satguru put his hand
on your head.

The second chant recited before the morning meal is called the "Añchaman kā śabda." It is a somewhat curious poem, full of semantic puzzles:[5]

You should rinse your mouth, O guru,
abode of mercy.

The servant took the water pitcher of love
and the straw[6] of knowledge of Brahman.

With great devotion, he takes the betel leaf,
a breath of life for the saints.
He gives the great *prasād* to the devotees,
their supreme reward.

Spread your bed within the lotus of the heart,
where the ancient Puruṣ lies at ease.
Offer service to his lotus-like feet,
this is the role for the devotee's body.

Standing here, I swing the braid of *surati.*
Unblinking, I concentrate my mind.
O Lord Kabīr, my guru, show me compassion.
The perfect abode is nirvana.

The principal daily ritual activity of the sadhus of the Kabīr Panth is the *sandhyā pāṭh* (evening recitation). The *pāṭh* begins at about 7:00 p.m. and lasts for about 45 minutes. The *mahant* and most of the Kabīr Panthī sadhus who happen to be staying in the monastery — together with a few lay persons and visiting sadhus from other sects — sit in facing rows on the raised porch on which Kabīr's *samādhi* is located. Each night the recitation begins with a short poem called "Vandan" in praise of Kabīr as the Satguru:[7]

I praise the true Kabīr,
the blessed, the maker of blessings.
I beg you to take away the pain of *saṃsār.*
Be a giver of sons, a teacher of boons.

Listen to my request.
I bow to you with joined hands.

O guru, I come to you for refuge.
    Remove the errors from my heart.

The threefold pains of birth and death,
    the terrible pain of the path of error,
Remove this great torment
    and bestow your *pārakh,* full of mystery.

O symbol of the soul,
    abode of compassion and mercy,
Give deliverance to all.
    Pass judgment on each.

Don't let a speck of darkness remain,
    O firm guru, the light of *pārakh.*
Enter within our hearts,
    O ocean of wisdom and mercy.

Appear before us. Bestow on us
    the hidden treasures of the *Bījak.*
Day and night I touch your feet,
    O guru Kabīr, my bondage breaker.

After this introductory hymn, the assembly begins a recitation of one-twelfth of Kabīr's *Bījak,* the collection of Kabīr's compositions that most branches of the Kabīr Panth regard as authoritative.[8] When this is finished, the assembly recites one-twelfth of a small collection of songs and verses by various authors called, like the recitation itself, the *Sandhyā pāṭh.*

Each branch *(śākhā)* of the Kabīr Panth has its own *Sandhyā pāṭh* booklet.[9] The Dharmadāsī branches use this text alone, recited in full each evening, and do not regularly recite the *Bījak.* The *Sandhyā pāṭh* of each branch contains a different selection of texts. Most of these texts are in Hindi, but the Kabīr Chaurā *Sandhyā pāṭh* also includes a "Sadguru-Kabīra-śatakam" in Sanskrit. A few of the poems are included in *Sandhyā pāṭh* booklets of several different branches of the Panth. Only the somewhat anomalous *Sandhyā pāṭh* of the Burhanpur branch contains no material found in the booklets of other branches. Most booklets contain several poems attributed to Kabīr, but not found in the *Bījak,* and other poems by other authors expressing devotion to Kabīr and imparting moral and religious instruction. Other authors included in the Kabīr Chaurā booklet are Rāmarahasya, Śrutigopāl, Sant Sāhab, Nābhā,

Ratnabāī, and Rāghavadās. All the verses for the last six days of the twelve-day recitation are by Gaṅgāśaraṇ Śāstrī, the current *mahant* of the Kabīr Chaurā.

One poem is found in all the *Sandhyā pāṭh* booklets I have seen except that of Burhanpur. This is the "Jñān gudarī" or "Quilt of Knowledge," an anonymous composition of uncertain date.[10] Each verse suggests symbolic meanings for the sadhus' quilt and other material possessions:[11]

When the invisible Puruṣ began to think,
he spread eighty-four *lakh* threads.
He wove the quilt with the five elements.
He sized it with the three *guṇas.*

In it are living souls, Brahman, and Māyā.
The Mighty One created it in play.
The souls held on to the five and twenty-five,
soaked in lust, anger, egotism, and pride.

Look at this quilt's expanse, the material world,
and its astounding beauty.
The moon and sun are stuck on it like patches,
sleeping and waking by the Guru's power.

Creation is sewn with the needle of *śabda,* the thread
of *surati,* the stitch of knowledge.
Take good care of the quilt, make sure
you don't get it stained.

Wash creation with the soap of good thoughts
and wipe away the dirt of bad thoughts.
Whoever takes good care of the quilt,
that person will meet the Creator.

Make patience your holy fire, meditation your pose,
truth your loincloth, *sahaj* your seat
Grasp the water pot of logic, the arm-rest of love,
This is the mark of a wise person.

Make virtue your scarf, analysis your garland,
mercy your cap, the body your pilgrims' inn,
Kindness your elephant, thought your crutch,
and mind your deerskin mat.

With resolve as his garment and air his sacred thread,
 he recites the name and knows its secret.
He who ever relies on the Satguru's mercy
 keeps company with saints and gets it all.

He makes affection his staff, a good heart his bag,
 and puts on the sandals of forgiveness.
Making salvation his belt and good deeds his rosary,
 the silent sage drinks the cup of love.

Let quarrels be stemmed by the staff of equanimity
 and the dogs of egoism be defied.
When the chains of logic are well tied,
 one finds the window to unknown worlds.

A store of asceticism, self-denial, and wisdom,
 the mark of truth on one's brow, one finds nirvana.
With a flint, the guru's words, and the cotton of intellect,
 the fire of Brahman appears.

There he burns all doubt, sorrow and error.
 The five and twenty-five arise and die.
Doubt vanishes in the mirror of the heart,
 and he becomes a perfect monk.

He roams about in the palace of the void.
 He takes the alms of immortal nectar.
The world's essence is mixed with pain and joy.
 On the steps of the *triveṇī* take your bath.

When body and mind are purified and knowledge arisen,
 it is then that one gets nirvana.
When he perceives the lotuses of the eight *chakras,*
 the yogi finds his knowledge in himself.

He goes from the house of Iṅgalā and Piṅgalā
 and in the Suṣumnā vein he makes his home.
There he contemplates the truth of the *oham soham*
 and controls himself within the Baṅkanāl.

He takes control of his mind, mounts to the sky,
 and bathes in Mānasarovar.
This monk worships the Name with the unstruck sound.
 Besides Brahman he has no other god.

He eliminates impurities born of karma.
    With his own eyes he sees the Lord.
He disperses all his egotism and pride,
    as he lights his body's *chaukā*.

Making mind the sandalwood, intellect the flowers,
    welfare his bow of respect, he finds the root.
Making faith the flywhisk, love the incense,
    he finds the pristine name, the form of the Lord.

The indescribable Lord put on the quilt
    and displayed this apparel to all.
When Lord Kabīr offered to donate the quilt,
    gods, men and sages accepted the gift.

Reciting this "Quilt of Knowledge" each morning,
    one's sins will vanish from birth after birth.
Reciting this "Quilt of Knowledge" each noon
    one reaches the abode of nirvana.

The person who recites it each evening
    crosses the ocean of old age and death.
Kabīr says: Listen, Dharmadās.
    Set this "Quilt of Knowledge" in the light.

Every evening the sandhyā *pāṭh* of the Kabīr Chaurā monastery concludes with five Sanskrit verses called the "Śloka pañchakam." This is probably a composition by the current *mahant,* Āchārya Gaṅgāśaraṇ Śāstrī, who has fostered many Sanskritizing innovations within the Panth. He was the *adhikārī* of the monastery when the 1977 *Sandhyā pāṭh* booklet in which this "Śloka pañchakam" first appears was compiled. The first verse should suffice to give an idea of its style and contents:[12]

I praise the supreme Kabīr, the best of ascetics,
    who took a body through divine play,

    whose permanent nature is awareness,
    the guru all the three worlds should worship,
    who analyzed well the knowledge of reality,
    who gives the essence of auspiciousness,
    who is served by his disciples,
    as he sits on his pleasing lotus seat
    of similar charming form.

After the recitation of this "Śloka pañchakam," one of the sadhus present generally gives a religious *kathā* (sermon) based on a religious text considered to be compatible with the teaching of Kabīr. The text chosen may be a commentary on Kabīr's *Bījak,* a hagiographic text such as Nābhādās' *Bhaktamāl* and Gaṅgāśaraṇ Śastrī's own *Kabīr jīvan charita,* and occasionally a well-known Sanskrit text such as the *Bhagavadgītā* or an Upaniṣad. More saguṇī-oriented texts such as the *Mahābhārata,* Vālmīki's *Rāmāyaṇa,* the Puranas, and Tulasīdās' *Rāmacharitamānas* are considered to be incompatible with Kabīr's message and are rarely used. During one of my stays in the Kabīr Chaurā, one sadhu once tried to base his *kathā* on Tulasīdās' *Rāmacharitamānas,* but several senior sadhus objected and stopped it.

At about 8:00 p.m., shortly after the kathā has finished, a few sadhus begin to beat the gongs, and the sadhus line up for the evening *āratī-pūjā* or *samūhik-pūjā.* The ritual is virtually identical to that performed in the morning, except that a small oil lamp is used in place of the incense. In addition, in place of the morning "Prārthanā pañchak se," the sadhus chant the "Āratī-uparānta stuti," a poem attributed to a Rāghavadās and notable for its use of repeating phrases and its increasingly emotional tone:[13]

Victory to the king, the divine Guru!

Victory to the divine Guru, the store of mercy,
    a benefactor to the saints,
    our Lord, a benefactor to the saints.
The devotees' distress, the devotees' distress,
    he destroys these chains to the world.
Victory to the king, the divine Guru!

The giver of blessings, the world's savior,
    you take the form of our Guru,
    O Lord, you take the form of our Guru.
Seeing you destroys sin, seeing you destroys sin,
    our Guru, heavy with greatness.
Victory to the king, the divine Guru!

You crush our pain, you smash our error,
    you give joy to the saints,
    O Lord, you give joy to the saints.
You broke the chains of error, you broke the chains of error,
    our great examiner.
Victory to the king, the divine Guru!

All our souls are carried
away in a river of delusions and frenzy,
O Lord, all our souls are carried away.
Your refugees take the boat, your refugees take the boat.
Across the ocean of existence,
the Guru ferries us all.
Victory to the king, the divine Guru!

You are an ocean of compassion,
you destroy the wretcheds' pain.
O Lord, you destroy the wretcheds' pain.
Your grant all desires, you grant all desires.
Show us mercy, O master.
Victory to the king, the divine Guru!

You, O Guru, are my mother and father,
an ocean of compassion, my master,
O Lord, an ocean of compassion, my master.
Save us from birth and death, save us from birth and death,
O Lord, the inner controller.
Victory to the king, the divine Guru!

You alone can enlighten me.
Who else will give me refuge?
O Lord, who else will give me refuge?
I see no one else, I see no one else,
give me hope.
Victory to the king, the divine Guru!

You roam about in a perfect form,[14]
a child ascetic,
O Lord, a child ascetic.
You will save our souls, you will save our souls,
O best of men in bodily form.
Victory to the king, the divine Guru!

Friend of the wretched, ocean of bliss,
Kabīr, my Guru,
O Lord, Kabīr, my Guru.
Protect your devotees, protect your devotees.
I come to you for refuge.
Victory to the king, the divine Guru!

Full of faith, we sing the *āratī*
    of true Kabīr.
    The devotees sing, full of faith.
One gets the stuff of salvation,
    one gets the stuff of salvation,
    and never returns to this world.
Victory to the king, the divine Guru!

This poem is followed by the recitation of single stanza written in Sanskrit:[15]

I worship the venerable, unborn Kabīr,
    the very form of intellect.
May we ever meditate on the Guru's lotus feet.
May we sing his glorious words,
    that take away the sins of this evil age.
May we be led to him who great sages adore.

As in the morning *āratī-pūjā,* the evening ritual ends with the *bandagī* to the *mahant* and the circumabulation of the *Bījak* shrine. This ends the daily round of ritual activities in the Kabīr Chaurā monastery. Before making a few comments on the character of these observances, I would like to describe the most important occasional ritual of the Kabīr Panth, the *chaukā.*

The *Chaukā*

The principal actor in the *chaukā* ritual is the *mahant.* He is assisted by a sadhu who takes the temporary title of *dīvān* (minister). At the same time, all other persons who are present — sadhus, male and female devotees and friends, even visiting foreign scholars — are also expected to participate. At least for the duration of the rite, all become essentially equal members of a single community. It is this practical *communitas,* combined with the theatrical show of the ceremony, that makes the *chaukā* a memorable and unifying experience for its participants.

The historical origins of the *chaukā* are unknown. Kabīr Panthī legends attribute its foundation to Kabīr itself.[16] This is rather unlikely, in my opinion, given the express rejection of all forms of external ritual in Kabīr's songs and verses. In addition, the *chaukā* is nowhere mentioned in the older collections of these songs and verses or in early hagiographic texts about Kabīr's life such as those of Anantadās, Priyādās, and Rāghavadās.[17]

The earliest reference to the *chaukā* seems to be that of the above translated "Jñān gudarī" ("Quilt of Knowledge"), which states:

He disperses all his egotism and pride,
as he lights his body's *chaukā*.
Making mind the sandalwood, intellect the flowers,
welfare his bow of respect, he finds the root.
Making faith the flywhisk, love the incense,
he finds the pristine name, the form of the Lord.

Although these items of worship are not necessarily exclusive to the *chaukā,* all are connected with it. The flywhisk — in the *chaukā* weilded by a "servant" of the "king-guru" — is particularly characteristic since it is not used in other Kabīr Panthī rituals.

Unfortunately, the composition date of the "Jñān gudarī" is unknown. Copies of this text are found in ten manuscripts belonging to the Kabīr Chaurā library in Banaras. The oldest manuscript (no. 015) is dated 1895 V.S. (1838 C.E.) (Lorenzen 1994). The presence of the "Jñān gudarī" in the *Sandhyā pāṭh* booklets of almost all branches of the Kabīr Panth, however, suggests that it is an old composition, perhaps older than the split of the Kabīr Panth into its Kabīr Chaurā and Dharmadāsī branches. This split cannot be dated with any assurance either, but it probably took place over 300 years ago.

Another interesting question is that of the sources for the *chaukā* in Hindu tradition beyond the Kabīr Panth. Most of the basic elements of the *chaukā* — offering sweets and fruits to God, breaking coconuts, doing *āratī* over the guru-*mahant,* distributing *prasād* — are common to many Hindu rituals. The overall structure of the *chaukā* bears a definite resemblance to several simple "domestic" Hindu rituals such as the popular *Satyanārāyaṇ vrat.* Some scholars have claimed that a close resemblance exists between the *chaukā* and certain Tantric rituals. Since they have offered few if any specific details, however, I remain unconvinced.[18]

More specifically, there is a rite of this type actually called the *"chauk"* that is discussed by U. Arya (1968, 14–16) in his account of the religious practices of the South Asian Indians settled in Surinam. Since these Indians are mostly descended from low-caste laborers from Bihar, the same social and geographical base as much of the Kabīr Panth, it is likely that both this *chauk* and the Kabīr Panthī *chaukā* share a common origin. As far as I know, however, this non-Kabīr Panthī *chauk* has not been described in anthropological literature from India itself. The Kabīr Panthī sadhus from this region that I asked about it had no knowledge of it. Nonetheless, the anthropologists R. S. Freed and S. A. Freed (1980, 385–86) have noted the use of the term *chauk* for the ritual "squares" used in domestic rituals in a monograph on the life-crisis rituals of a village near Delhi.

These Kabīr Panthī sadhus did mention the fact that two minor religious sects centered in the Bhojpurī region of eastern Uttar Pradesh and northwestern Bihar, the Śivanārāyaṇī Panth and the Dariyā Panth, both practise their own *"chaukā"* rituals. Another sect to have its own *chaukā* is that of the Satnāmīs of the Chhattisgarh region of Madhya Pradesh. Since these are all three low-caste *nirguṇī* sects related to the Kabīr Panth, however, it is likely that their *chaukās* derive from that of the older Kabīr Panth.

The Kabīr Panthī *chaukā* is mentioned in several of the Kabīr Panthī texts collected by the sadhu Yugalānanda Bihārī and published under the general title, *Kabīr Sāgar* (1953). These include the *Jñānasāgar, Bhopālabodh, Jagajīvanabodh, Chaukāsvaroday, Amaramūl,* and *Sumiranabodh.* The age of these texts is uncertain, but most probably date from the eighteenth and nineteenth centuries C.E. Different branches of the Kabīr Panth have also published more modern ritual manuals that describe the *chaukā* in detail. Two important manuals that I have had access to are the *Chaukā paddhati* of Sudhādās "Sukavi" Dehalavī (1970) and the *Chaukā-chandrikā* of Sukṛtadāsajī Barārī (1980). Both these manuals are from the Dharmadāsī branch of the Panth. Gaṅgāśaraṇ Śāstrī of the Kabīr Chaurā has published a somewhat less detailed description of this branch's version of the *chaukā* in his *Āchār-saṃhitā* (1983, 34–43).

Several modern academic scholars have also discussed aspects of the Kabīr Panthī chaukā. These include G. H. Wescott (1953 (1907, 83–88), F. E. Keay (1931, 156–59), K. Dvivedī (1965, 196–205), Umā Ṭhukarāl (1979, 35–38, 173–75), V. P. Gilaḍā "Śaival" (1985, 126–27, 156–62), D. Gold (1987, 96–97), and myself (1988, 445–68). My description of the ritual here is based on all these sectarian manuals and academic accounts as well as on personal observation of about ten chaukās held in the Kabīr Chaurā monasteries of Banaras and Magahar. I have still not been able to observe a *chaukā* of the Dharmadāsī branch of the Panth.

The *chaukā* manuals of the Dharmadāsī branch of the Panth indicate that its *chaukā* does not differ dramatically from that of the Kabīr Chaurā except in two respects. First, the Dharmadāsī manuals distinguish four types of *chaukā* while the Kabīr Chaurā manuals distinguish only two. The four Dharmadāsī *chaukās* are: (1) the *ānandī chaukā,* performed during the principal festivals of the Panth and at the time of the initiation of new *bhagats;* (2) the *janmauti* or *solah sut kā chaukā,* performed for those who wish to have a child or to celebrate the birth of a child; (3) the *chalāvā chaukā,* performed to insure the peace of the soul of a person who has recently died; and (4) the *ekottarī chaukā,* performed for the peace of 101 ancestors. In the Kabīr Chaurā, only the *ānandī chaukā* and the *chalāvā chaukā* are practiced. The second important difference between the Dharmadāsī and the Kabīr Chaurā versions of the *chaukā* is in the songs sung during its performance. Many of these songs are quite different although a few are common to the *chaukās* of both branches of the Panth.

In terms of their nonverbal components, all the four (or two) types of *chaukā* are quite similar. Each type does, however, have its own set of songs appropriate to its specific ritual purpose. The remaining differences between the different types of *chaukā* maining concern minor details such as the quantities of the various offerings of fruit, sweets, cloth, and so on that the sponsor of the rite is expected to provide for its performance. Here I will limit my discussion to the *chalāvā* and *ānandī chaukās* as celebrated in the Kabīr Chaurā monasteries in Banaras and Magahar.

The *chalāvā chaukā* does not form an integral part of the cycle of funeral rites *per se.* It is an optional, supplemental ritual that is performed sometime after the person's death, preferably on the following full-moon night. Its sponsor is usually a close relative of the deceased. The *chalāvā chaukā* does invite comparison with certain parts of the standard Brahminical cycle of funeral rites, especially the *sapiṇḍīkaraṇa,* but this comparison is relevant mainly to the *purposes* of the rites, not to their respective structures and procedures.[19]

The performance of all the different types of Kabīr Panthī *chaukās* can be divided into nine stages or episodes. First is the preparation of the *chaukā* itself, the "square" from which the ceremony takes its name. This task is directed by the *dīvān* (minister) who aids the *mahant* throughout the performance. A white canopy is hung over the square. From this canopy several strings of mostly white flowers are strung, each reaching to about 25 or 30 cm. above the floor. Next the *dīvān* and two or three sadhus spread out a white cloth, about one and one-half by two meters, on the floor under the canopy. The canopy and the cloth are oriented so that each side corresponds to a cardinal direction. On the cloth they place about two kilograms of wheat flour. The flour is spread out and a design traced in the four in a sort of low-relief "sand" painting. The design is specified in detail in the ritual manuals and is virtually identical in all the Kabīr Chaukā and Dharmadāsī *chaukās.* Five small squares are marked out within the larger one of the cloth itself, all oriented in the same directions. One is put in the center and the other four on each side of it. From each corner of the central square diagonal lines are marked out that extent almost to the corners of the cloth. "Lotuses" are drawn at the end of each diagonal line and in the center of the small squares. On each of these lotuses the *dīvān* places a betel leaf and a metal rupee. The sides of the five smaller squares and the diagonal lines are all formed with *kaṅgure* (scallops) whose number is exactly specified in at least the Dharmadāsī version of the ritual. The complete design can be seen in figure 1.

Once the square and canopy are properly set up, the various materials and implements used during the ritual and placed on or near each of the small squares. In the center are placed dried and fresh fruits, sweets, and betel leaves. A *kalaś* (a particular kind of pot) filled with water is placed on the eastern square. An oil lamp with five wicks and docorated with mango leaves is placed on top of the pot and a small

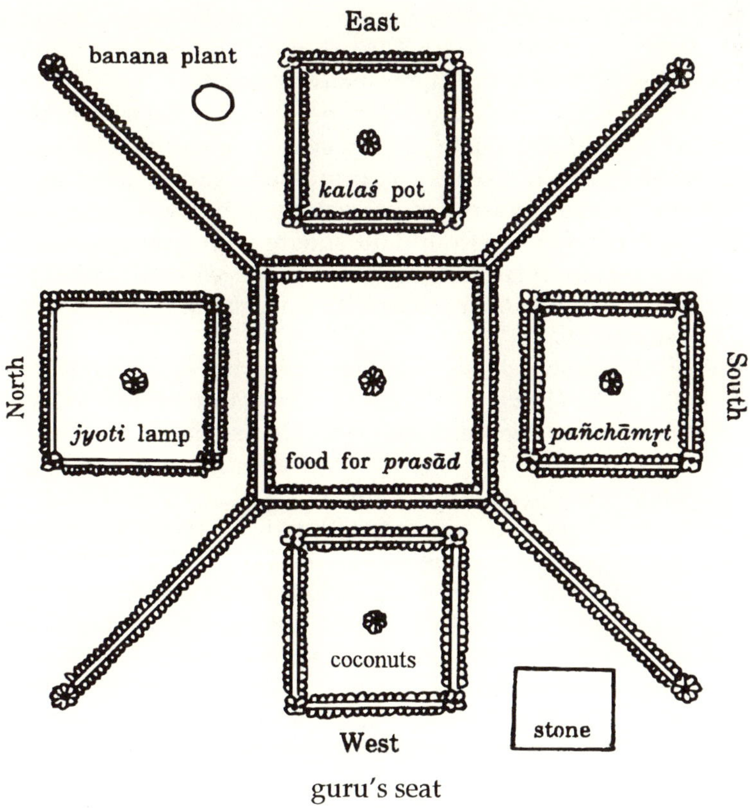

Fig. 1. The Chaukā Ceremony.

potted banana plant is placed nearby. A *jyoti* (oil lamp) fueled with ghee, its bowl lined with flour paste, is placed in the northern square. On the southern square they place a glass of *pañchāmṛt* ("five nectars," called *amīdal* in Dharmadāsī manuals). This is a mixture of milk, sugar and five ground spices: clove, cardamon, black pepper, *chiroñjī,* and raisins. On the western square they put from five to ten or more coconuts. The *mahant* later sits in front of the western side of the cloth. To his right is placed a heavy flat stone on which he breaks the coconuts.

In the Dharmadāsī manuals, each of the five small squares is dedicated to a different guru: the central square to the Satyapuruṣ (i.e., God and/or Kabīr), the eastern square to the guru Baṅkejī, the southern square to the guru Chaturabhujajī, the western square to the guru Sahatejī, and the northern square to the guru Dharmadāsajī. Baṅkejī, Chaturabhujajī, and Sahatejī are otherwise unknown. Dharmadāsajī is, of course, Kabīr's famous disciple, the reputed founder of the Dharmadāsī branch of the Panth. The Kabīr Chaurā ritual manuals do not accept these dedications but do not suggest any alternatives.

While this *chaukā* square is being prepared, the *mahant* dresses himself in a special embroidered garment, the *selī,* puts on his pointed hat, sits on his *gaddī,* and recites a *jap* (muttered chant) of various prayers and mantras. As the time for the ceremony to begin approaches, *bhagats* and sadhus assemble around the square and a group of musicians and singers, mostly recruited from among the sadhus, begins to sing bhajans, accompanying themselves with a harmonium and various percussion instruments.

When all is ready, the second stage of the rite begins, the *padharaunī* (procession) of the *mahant.* Bells and cymbals are sounded and a *turahī* (trumpet) is blown to announce the event. On the square, the *dīvān* lights the oil lamp with five wicks. The *mahant* rises from his *gaddī* and marches to the site of the square accompanied by a group of sadhus and by a *bhagat* who fans him with a *chaṃvar* (flywhisk). When he arrives, his feet are washed by the *dīvān,* he sits on a cushion on the western side of the square, and garlands of flowers are placed around his neck.

The third stage of the chaukā is the *jyoti jalānā* (lighting the lamp). The seated *mahant* lights the *jyoti,* an oil lamp whose bowl is lined with a dried dough made of flour and water. This is filled with ghee and a large lump of camphor. This *jyoti* must be lit with burning ghee that drips from a wad of cotton wrapped on the end of a thin stick about 50 to 60 cm. long made of mango, *beṛ,* sandalwood, *tulasī,* or *madar* wood. The sadhus and *bhagats* then recite a verse in honor of the lighting of the *jyoti:*

Play the music of the unstruck sound.
The *jyoti* has been lit.
Guru Kabīr has stood up within,
the Lord, the benevolent slave.

In the Dharmadāsī version of this part of the ritual, several other verses are recited in addition to this one, followed by the recitation of three longer *ramainīs* attributed to Kabīr. The *jyoti* is kept lit for the rest of the ritual, adding more ghee when necessary.

The fourth stage of the *chaukā* is the *nāriyal bheṇṭa* (offering of coconuts). The assembled *bhagats* and sadhus one by one approach the *mahant* from the north side (i.e., his left) and receive from him one of the coconuts. Holding it, they circumambulate the square and then return the coconut to the mahant as an offering. They are expected to add a few rupees to the offering before handing to the *mahant*. Offerings of fruit, sweets, and cloth may also be made at this time. The *mahant* keeps the coconuts circulating until everyone who wishes to has made his offering.

During this time, the *bhagats* and sadhus sing a set of five songs called the "Haṃsāvalī" ("Row of souls"). In the *ānandī chaukā,* a set of five songs called the "Maṅgal" is used instead. This difference in songs is in fact the principal difference in performance between the *chalāvā* and *ānandī chaukās.* A translation of all ten of these songs used in the Kabīr Chaurā *chaukās* has been provided at the end of this chapter.

The songs of the "Haṃsāvalī" are sung to help guide the soul of the dead person as it passes either from one life to the next, or from this life to an eternal salvation beyond the cycle of rebirths. In the Dharmadāsī version of the rite, these five songs are replaced by seven *ramainīs* followed by eight *śabdas* (i.e., *pads*) called *ḍorīs,* and then eight more *śabdas* intended to guide the soul. Only one of these songs is common to both the Dharmadāsī and Kabīr Chaurā versions of the rite.[20]

The most interesting of the Kabīr Chaurā "Haṃsāvalī" songs is the first one. It offers a dramatic revision of an important part of the Brahminical cycle of funeral rites. In the *sapiṇḍīkaraṇa* part of this cycle, the soul is instructed about the nature of its journey from this world to the palace of Yama, the god of death, and from there to the world of the *pitṛs* (fathers). As described in the *Garuḍa-purāṇa* and other Sanskrit texts, this journey involves numerous obstacles. Among them, the soul has to cross the Vaitaraṇī, the river of death. To help the soul cross the river, his relatives are traditionally expected to offer a cow to a Brahmin as a sort of toll.

The Kabīr Chaurā song directly challenges these Brahminical beliefs. It advises the soul to strike and kill Yama and then go straight on to the "ocean of bliss." The song claims that the path to this ocean has "no jungles, mountains, nor ravines." The soul will meet no "messengers, ghosts, robbers," and "no toll collector" will stop it. The soul will go on unimpeded to the feet of the divine Satguru and will attain "the unique abode" for all time.

The fifth stage of the *chaukā* ritual is the *nāriyal moranā* (breaking the coconuts). The *mahant* picks up each coconut and waves over it a betel leaf which he has first dipped in the glass of *pañchāmṛt*. Then he waves the coconut over the *jyoti* flame and finally smashes it on the stone slab placed to his right. At this time, the *bhagats* and sadhus sing the "Nāriyal morane kā śabda" ("Song of breaking the coconut"), a text that features a number of philosophical riddles typical of *nirguṇī sandhā-bhāṣā* (topsy-turvy speech):[21]

The shop girl makes a request.
    Listen, sir.
She takes the coconut in her hand.
    Listen, good sir.

There is a tree without a seed.
    Listen, sir.
Its sprout is not in the ground.
    Listen, good sir.

Its roots are in the infernal regions.
    Listen, sir.
The coconut fruit is auspicious.
    Listen, good sir.

I bring the coconut as an offering.
    Listen, sir.
Its task is to save the *haṃsa*.
    Listen, good sir.

Break it with the Guru's word.
    Listen, sir.
Take the *haṃsa* to the other shore.
    Listen, good sir.

The five and twenty-five.
    Listen, sir.
Three persons are headmen.
    Listen, good sir.

Five girls are companions.
    Listen, sir.
Nine women the creation.
    Listen, good sir.

Kabīr says to king Baghel.
    Listen, sir.
The Satguru is the headman.
    Listen, kind sir.

The sixth stage of the ceremony is the *bhog aur jap* (enjoyment and muttered chant). The *mahant* puts a cloth over the offerings of fresh and dried fruits, the coconut meat from the broken coconuts, and the sweets piled up in the middle small square of the *chaukā.* He dips a betel leaf in the *pañchāmṛt* and sprinkles it over the covered pile. Then he repeats this action with plain water. Next invokes the *bhog,* the mystic "enjoyment" of the offerings by the Satyapuruṣ, with a muttered chant of prayers and mantras during ten or fifteen minutes. Meanwhile the assembled people sing the "Bhog lagāne kā śabda" ("Song of taking enjoyment"):[22]

The Satyapuruṣ takes enjoyment.
The unstruck sound rings out,
    and the blare of a horn.

Arrange the plantain and betel leaves
Accompanied by cooling words,
    the *jyoti* is lit.

Beautiful sweets, delicious sweets.
Offer them to Him
    with great affection.
Cloves, cardamons, sultanas, bananas.
Beautiful, sweet tasting,
    abundant raisins.

With crystaline water from the ocean of bliss
By which our mortal body
    becomes content.

This we have offered to the Satyapuruṣ.
Someone is playing a *vīnā*
    and blowing a conch.

His devotee has taken the betel leaf
By which the god of Death
becomes controlled.

He who gets the betel passport
Becomes immortal and travels
to Satyalok.

Kabīr says: Listen, brother sadhu.
Always offer your worship
to the heroic Name.

The Dharmadāsīs sing roughly the same song although a few verses are different. Afterwards, the *bhagats* and sadhus sing various bhajans of their own choosing, usually popular bhajans attributed to Kabīr.

After the *mahant's jap* has finished, any persons who have arranged to be initiated into the Kabīr Panth come forward, squatting to the *mahant's* right. They bring with them whatever they wish to offer as a *dakṣiṇā* (gratuity) to the *mahant* for their initiation. The *mahant* then gives them some long thin straws and the following mantra:[23]

āsan bāsan man kalapanā, khedo sarvā bhūt
kahai Kabīr sataguru mile, mithyā ke mukh thūk

[. . .][24]
Kabīr says: Meeting the Satguru, one spits in falsehood's face.

The new initiates are told to break the straws and throw them over their shoulder. After this, the *mahant* puts around their necks the *kaṇṭhī,* a multi-strand string with a single bead of *tulasī* wood. Finally he gives them a betel leaf, called the *pān parvānā* (betel passport), an important symbol of Kabīr Panthī identity.

According to the Dharmadāsī *Chaukā-chandrikā,* initiations of lay *bhagats* are not given as part of any *chaukā* except the *ānandī chaukā.* In the Kabīr Chaurā, however, I have seen such initiations given during both the *ānandī* and *chalāvā chaukās* as well as in a simple ceremony without any *chaukā* at all. In all branches of the Panth, both men and women receive the complete initiation.

The seventh stage of the chaukā is the *añchaman* or *añchavan* (Sanskrit *āchamana*). Literally this refers to the sipping of water to purify one's mouth before meals or religious ceremonies. In fact, no such *añchaman* actually takes place. The *mahant* takes the cloth off the sweets, coconuts, and fresh and dried fruits. This is now called *"prasād,"* the grace-giving leavings of the Satyapuruṣ. The assembled *bhagats* and sadhus then sing the "Song of the *añchaman.*" This is same song as that sung at the daily morning meal and has been translated above in that context. The song used by the Dharmadāsīs is virtually identical, but the *Chaukā-chandrikā* identifies this stage of the rite with the sprinkling of water by the *mahant* on the covered *prasād* before he imparts the initiations. In any case, once the *prasād* is uncovered, the *dīvān* and some of the sadhus begin to cut up the fruit and coconut meat so that it can be distributed to those present.

The eighth stage of the *chaukā* is the *āratī.* For most of those present, this marks the emotional climax of the ritual, and the occasion on which they participate most directly. First the *dīvān,* and then, one by one, all the assembled sadhus and *bhagats* and guests, male and female alike, take the *jyoti* lamp and perform *āratī,* the waving of the lamp, in front of the *mahant*. Those who can afford to do so generally offer a few rupees in the plate that hold the lamp. The song sung on this occasion is the "Maṅgal chaukā āratī":[25]

When you see the beautiful face
take the fruit with your eyes.
Perform the āratī well,
for Kabīr, the bondage breaker.

Prepare a sandalwood square,
and draw a *tilak* on your brow.
Wear a crest of peacock plumes,
display a flourish of frills.

In the beloved city of Kāśī
he set the Panth in motion.
The guru went off to Magahar
and enlightened both religions.

He has brought a passport of *pān*
for the sake of saving lives.
He breaks our souls' bondage
and sends us to Satyalok.

For us who are tied to the world
he shows what never will perish.

Kabīr is our bondage breaker.
He shows what cannot be seen.

The ninth and final stage of the *chaukā* is the distribution of the *prasād*. The singing stops and all the sadhus, *bhagats,* and guests come up one by one and receive from the mahant a handful of the cut-up fruits, coconut meat, and sweets. The initiated members of the Kabīr Panth, both *bhagats* and sadhus, also receive a *pān parvāna,* the "betel leaf passport" that brings them a promise of immortality. Each person takes their *prasād* with them and eats it at leisure in his rooms or in the monastery courtyard. Among the Dharmadāsīs, the patrons of the *chaukā* are later given what is known as the *jot prasād,* the remains of the bowl of dough used to line the *jyoti* lamp.

Conclusions

There is no doubt that the songs and verses attributed to Kabīr express his fierce opposition to virtually all external manifestations of religion, especially to the rituals that provide external marks of a generally nonexistent inner purity and religious faith. Kabīr valiantly rails against Muslim circumcision, Hindu untouchability practices, animal sacrifice, sacred threads, daily prayer, pilgrimages, idol worship, *haṭha* yoga, even (in at least some contexts) against discrimination against women. It is easy to regard the introduction of rituals within the Kabīr Panth as a betrayal of Kabīr's radical iconoclasm and his insistence on inner faith and moral integrity.

Nonetheless, it should be evident from the discussion here that Kabīr Panthī rituals are not simply the product of an abject capitulation to the social and cultural pressures that foster Sanskritization, Hinduization, and socioreligious homogenization. In the first place, the rituals of the Kabīr Panth are quite simple and inexpensive compared to those of more orthodox Hindu monasteries and temples. More important, however, is the fact that the Kabīr Panthī rituals express, in both actions and words, an implicit opposition to many of the accepted religious and social norms of more orthodox Hinduism at the same time that they incorporate the basic structure and many formal elements of more orthodox rituals.

One of the ways in which this opposition is expressed is in the active participation of both lay *bhagats* and sadhus in the same rituals, regardless of caste, and the absence of Brahmin officiants. Even more striking is the near equal participation of female *bhagats*. All *bhagats*, male and female alike, high-caste and low-caste, even non–Kabīr Panthīs, are allowed to participate in the *sandhyā pāṭh,* to eat in the same "line" at meal time, to receive initiation, to wave the *āratī* lamp in the *chaukā,* and to join in the singing of bhajans during the *chaukā*. Although there are only a few nuns in the Panth, the male sadhus may come from any caste including Untouchable castes. In theory, all sadhus are social and ritual equals, and all are allowed to serve as *pujārīs* and work in the monastery kitchens. In practice, however, conservative *mahants* sometimes discourage Untouchable sadhus from doing these ritually sensitive tasks.

It is in their songs and verses that the oppositional (or "contestatory") side of Kabīr Panthī rituals is most explicit. The radical iconoclasm of the social and religious ideology articulated in Kabīr's own compositions is well known, and examples need not be cited here.[26] In the principal daily ritual of the Panth, the *sandhyā pāṭh,* the sadhus and *bhagats* recite, over twelve days, Kabīr's entire *Bījak,* generally the most radical of the three oldest collections of his songs and verses,[27] as well as other typical *nirguṇī* compositions such as the "Jñān gudarī." During the performance of the *chaukā* ritual, the assembled sadhus and *bhagats* sing a varying selection of typical *nirguṇī* bhajans by Kabīr and other poets as well as the special *chaukā* songs. In the case of the songs of the *chalāvā chaukā,* we have seen that they offer a more or less direct challenge to many aspects of the more orthodox beliefs concerning the fate of the soul after death.

Some of the details of Kabīr Panthī rituals are esoteric in the sense that they are understood only by more knowledgeable sadhus and *bhagats*. The symbolic meanings given to the *chaukā* squares, implements, and materials provide one good example. These are specified, with considerable differences of opinion, in the ritual manuals, texts that very few participants in the rituals have read. What really matters, however, is the public performance of the rituals. Their significance does not lie in their secret symbols but in the implicit and explicit meanings conveyed by the actions of the participants and articulated in the words of the songs they sing.

Appendix: The *Chaukā* Songs

A. *Maṅgal:*[28]

1

Today is the full-moon day. Come sing the *maṅgal*.
Touch the feet of the guru and reach the Supreme.

First clean the temple and smear on the sandalwood paste.
Then bring new cloth and spread out the canopy.

Put the *kalasā* there, adorned with mango leaves,
And upon it light the lamp with five bright flames.

Arrange there the *chaukā* of "elephant pearls,"
And offer upon it coconuts, cloth, and sweets.

Then prepare a throne-like seat where the guru will sit.
You must wash the guru's feet and invite him to sit.

Bring banana, camphor and many other things.
Offer betel-nuts, betel-leaves, and eight perfumes.

Wash the stone with water and light the light.
Beat the *mṛdaṅga* drum and sing the *maṅgal*.

The sadhus and saints are all here, let the *āratī* start.
When the *āratī* is done, then break the coconuts.

When the Spirit has taken his fill, you friends will be fed.
When the age-old hunger is gone, you'll get what you want.

When bliss is complete, you should gratify the guru.
Says Kabīr: With good thoughts, set off for heaven.

2

The true guru came to the world to save it.
He appeared in Kāśī and took the name Kabīr.

He made Rāmānanda his guru, then started the Panth.
By the of his wit he took *dīkṣā*, and then he taught.

The sannyasis and the Brahmins then made a request.
The holy guru appeared and gave them a darshan.

He broke the chains of the world and imparted wisdom.
Leaving Kāśī he went to Magahar where no one knew him.

The Lord came to Magahar village, not far from Gorakhpur.
He enlightened Hindus and Turks, and started the Panth.

Bijjalī Khān Paṭhān sealed shut the tomb.
King Vīr Siṅgh Baghel arrayed his troops.

The queen Kamalāpati wrote and sent a letter.
Kabīr's corpse had vanished, but quarrels flared.

They opened the tomb and looked, but he had gone.
The men and women wept and felt remorse.

In Orissa Kabīr halted the ocean's advance.
Lord Jagannāth and Lakṣmī came to meet him.

With the *paṇḍā* as pretext, he worked a manifold wonder.
At the same moment he appeared in many places.

He calmed contrary emotions and nourished justice.
All who met him found grace. He destroyed all error.

Listen people, Kabīr speaks sacred truth.
He takes our countless souls across the ocean.

3

Take refuge in the true guru and cast off folly.
And whether praised or scorned, keep your temper in check.

When tempers get loose we quarrel, and quarrels are vile.
When a body is filled with anger, that body is vile.

When anyone rails against you, try not to reply.
When nectar is in your reach, you should swallow it down.

When immortal fruit is at hand, it's foolish to quarrel.
It's nature that a dog will grab and grab at a bone.

One's nature is so engrained, that life won't leave it.
A neem tree watered with treacle won't become sweet.

Your hand may hold a garland, but a knife's at your side.[29]
Don't think that the fire is out, it lurks in the ashes.

[. . .]

Kabīr says: Consider this well, O mind.
The soul has gone to heaven, and won't return.

4

If you're off to the guru's market, bring along your wits.
If you call on the Lord's Name, you'll get to His place.

The Lord gave us all we know. What's more to give?
What unlucky women we are, who give up joy for pain.

You went to your lover's palace, but didn't stay.
You still keep deceit in your heart and shameful thoughts.

If the guru gets angry at you, then rush to please him.
If you always serve the humble, your faults won't count.

If the guru shows mercy, then seek that out in your heart.
Your karma will vanish, the moment you turn your mind.

By a lucky chance He's put on the robe of love.
If you offer your head, the Lord will smile and speak.

Kabīr says: Consider this message well.
To rule through the ages, uproot all evil intent.

5

The Lord's Name is unbroken, all else is in pieces.
Sumeru and Meru are broken, the world is in pieces.

Our homes and wealth will crumble, our lives at odds.
Millions of lives are caught in Yam's deadly snare.

If we steady our fickle minds, then things will be better.
If we look within we'll drink a Ganges of nectar.

If we live for the Lord, our bondage will end.
In the fellowship of sadhus there's joy forever

The mercy we keep in our hearts is the body of bhakti.
Kabīr says: Keep in mind the world's like a moth.

B. *Haṃsāvalī*:[30]

1

O brother soul, once you have understood,
it's then you should start your journey.
Once Kāl's chains have all begun to break,
it's then you should move ahead.

Once you grasp the power of the rod of firm resolve
the head of Yam will fall.
Once you smash your foes and reach the ocean of bliss,
then Yam's tricks will fail.

The road to the ocean of bliss is quite delightful,
no jungles, mountains, nor ravines.
And when you go to cross this ocean's waters,
the waves will not rise up.

You'll meet no messengers, ghosts, or robbers.
No toll collector will stop you.[31]
Destroy your fear and journey on to your home
where your bumps and bruises will vanish.

Every soul will touch the guru's feet
and reach that single place.
Kabīr says: Whoever understands and goes on
will find peace in age after age.[32]

2

O soul, meeting other souls will make you happy.
Whoever breaks with his family and meets with the saints
will enter into me.

The people hide behind the six faiths[33]
and ninety-six heretic cults.

The four *varṇas,* the Vedas and the Muslim book
have nothing to do with the soul.

The soul will feel not a bit of thirst for water
if the water is drawn from a well.
This water is the water of total self-indulgence.
The soul should discard it like chaff.

Though King Yam holds all three worlds in bondage
and noble justice as well.
Our soul will defeat him and then set off on its way
while Yam stays behind and cries.[34]

Our soul puts all its trust in the holy word.
The holy word is its food.
I will make it sit in the world of eternal life
where its comings and goings will end.

Kabīr says: You must have faith in the truth
that the soul will not be destroyed.
I will make it sit with me in the gleaming light[35]
and soul will merge with soul.

3

O soul, when you come to our country the food you get
is the nectar of eternal life.

The path to our country is very hard to travel.
To whom can I explain it?
To whoever depends on me like a humble child
I'll give him the courage he needs.

The soul has come from the ocean of worldly existence
and is going to the flower island.
If you keep your thoughts on the island amid the water
then that island will come into view.

If one makes a great effort one's life will come home
to the door of the ocean of bliss.
Open the door panel and enter the body.
See the secluded door.

Kabīr says: Listen brother sadhus!
    Congratulate that soul.
On a white throne he has now taken his seat.
    He's found a subtle body.

4

O soul, steady your mind and remember the Name.[36]
Unless you reach the city at the root,[37] *O soul.*
    Your life will perish forever.

Much is told about knowledge and meditation.
    Fools will die explaining it.
The moment one tastes just a drop of the nectar of life,
    one gets set apart forever.

Our essence is like a tiny mustard seed,
    as subtle as half a seed.
Like the water in every wave, that spirit our root
    resides within the body.

The *chaukā* is made on a lotus of pure white petals
    and there our spirit sits.
The thousand-petaled lotus is set apart
    with its cords and secluded door.[38]

On the tree an immortal fruit has ripened.
    Make that fruit your food.
Kabīr says: Listen brother sadhu!
    Conquer and stay apart.

5

O body, why cry when the lifebreath departs?
O soul, you've begun to make the journey home.
    When you go, you'll destroy me.

Joined with you, my daily joys were many.
    Getting up I washed and scrubbed.
That body has gotten thin and is turning to dust.
    No one is calling its name.

The soul says: Listen, moronic body!
    I've never been one with you.
I've left millions of lovers like you behind.
    Not one could come with me.

Shiva, Sanak, and others, even Brahmā
    and Śeṣ with his thousand heads,
Whoever has taken a body in all three worlds,
    Not one will keep it forever.

Both sin and merit, O people, are partners with birth.
    Think and see for yourself.
Kabīr says: The ways of the perfect Lord
    are known to only a few.

EPILOGUE

If nothing else, the discussion and translations presented here should give some idea of the enormous amount of basic scholarly work that remains to be done on *nirguṇī* texts. Many important texts have not yet been edited and published, much less translated. Other texts that have been published are available only in crude "chapbook" type editions that have no critical apparatus and are full of mistakes. Careful transcriptions of oral performances of songs and verses are almost nonexistent.

If such primary work is lacking, what can we expect from studies *about* these texts? Among the many topics yet to receive adequate treatment are the poetic meters and literary genres used by *nirguṇī* poets, their metaphors and metonymy, the oral and musical performance of the texts, the intertextual dialogue between *nirguṇī* and *saguṇī* poets, and the history and social bases of the movements to which the poets belong.

Nonetheless, much of the foundation for such work has been laid. Workable editions of several basic texts already exist. A few have even been translated. The edited texts include the Nāmadev's *pads,* the *Kabīr bījak,* the *Kabīr granthāvalī,* Raidās' *pads,* the *Gurū Granth Sāhib,* the *Dasam Granth Sāhib,* the *Dādū granthāvalī,* the *Sundaradās granthāvalī,* the Dādū Panthī *Pañchavāṇī,* the *Rajjab vāṇī,* Rajjab's *Sarabaṅgī,* Gopāladās' *Sarvāṅgī,* a modern anthology of *pads* of earlier poets of the Nirañjanī Panth, the *Dariyā granthāvalī,* Nābhādās' *Bhaktamāl,* Rāghavadās' *Bhaktamāl,* several of Anantadās' *parachaīs,* Jan Gopāl's *Dādū janma līlā,* and an anthology of the *pads* of the poets who lived at Bhuṛakuḍā.[1]

None of these editions utilizes a critical apparatus as sophisticated as the one that Kenneth Bryant has planned for his forthcoming edition of the *pads* of the *saguṇī* poet Sūradās. The editions are, however, adequate for most purposes. Also helpful for future studies are W. M. Callewaert and B. Op de Beeck's (1991) word index to several basic *nirguṇī* texts and Callewaert's forthcoming word index to the *Gurū Granth Sāhib.*

Important texts associated with the *nirguṇī* movement that remain unpublished include several *parachaīs* by Anantadās and others, the *Dhruv charitra* and *Jaḍ Bharat charitra* by Jan Gopāl, many songs and verses by the Nirañjanī Panthī poets Sevādās and Turasīdās, several Kabīr Panthī *goṣṭhīs,* and the songs and verses of a host of minor poets belonging to a variety of different sectarian movements. In addition, many published works deserve more scholarly editions. One such text is the so-called *Sākhī granth* attributed to Kabīr. The sadhus of the Kabīr Panth consider this work to be almost as authoritative as the *Kabīr bījak.* Other texts that need scholarly editions include the songs and verses of the poets published in the Belvedere Press series such as Malūkadās, Garībadās, Palaṭū Sāhab, Dharanīdās, Dharmadās, and Jagajīvan Sāhab as well as the Kabīr Panthī works published by Yugalānanda.

Given the linguistic difficulties of most early *nirguṇī* texts, another important scholarly task is that of preparing translations and commentaries on the texts, either in modern standard Hindi or English. Although most of the older songs and verses attributed to Kabīr, Raidās, Gurū Nānak, and Dādū have been translated, three major *nirguṇī* poets — Sundaradās, Palaṭū Sāhab, and Dharmadās — remain almost completely untranslated. This is also true of virtually all the works mentioned in the previous paragraph.

Secondary works about *nirguṇī* poets and sects are numerous but of uneven quality. Three great Indian scholars can be said to be the founders of modern *nirguṇī* studies: P. D. Barthwal, Hajārī Prasād Dvivedī, and Paraśurām Chaturvedī. Two scholars who played key roles in the development of modern Sikh studies were M. A. Macauliffe and Kahan Singh Nabha. More recent scholars working on *nirguṇī* literature who deserve mention include R. K. Varmā, Pārasanāth Tivārī, Mātāprasād Gupta, Charlotte Vaudeville, Shukdeo Singh, Winand Callewaert, and Monika Thiel-Horstmann (now Boehm-Tettelbach). Important recent scholars working in the field of Sikh literature include W. H. McLeod, Harjot Oberoi, and Gurbachan Singh Talib.

In the introduction to this book, I noted the existence of a "logical contradiction inherent in a religious movement that insists on offering heart-felt devotion to a God without attributes, without even any definable personality." I would like to conclude with some further discussion on this point.

The theological doctrines accepted in given religious movement must, of course, operate within the general limits of the conceptual universe of the civilization of which it forms a part. In at least one sense, however, the theological choices are arbitrary: almost any theological doctrine can be used to justify almost any set of social and political values, any ideology. In the case of medieval Hinduism, one of the principal theological choices available in the Indian air was between *saguṇ* and *nirguṇ* bhakti: devotion to a God with or without attributes.

Both *saguṇ* and *nirguṇ* doctrines could, and were, used to justify a social ideology more liberal than that offered by Vedic and *śāstrik* Hinduism. In the case of *saguṇ* bhakti, the concept of God's grace *(prasād)* was used to short-circuit the long cycle of rebirths based on karma. For some *saguṇī* thinkers, God is said to bestow His saving on those who practice moral conduct combined with a personal surrender to God. For other thinkers, God required only faith and surrender, without the need for moral conduct. For yet others, God's choice of the persons on whom He would bestow His grace was totally inscrutable, as in Augustinian and Calvinist Christianity.

In the case of the *nirguṇ* bhakti of poets like Kabīr, Raidās, Gurū Nānak, and Dādū, a doctrine influenced by the theology of the Brahmin school of Advaita Vedānta was used to draw similar egalitarian conclusions. If all the visible universe is somehow grounded in Brahman, and if this Brahman resides in every human heart, then all men are, in essence, equally pure and equally worthy of salvation. They are in fact already saved, provided they can look within and find the Truth.

If one wishes to speculate on a grand scale, it can be argued that the *advaita-nirguṇī* idea first appeared as part of a Upanishadic rebellion against the excesses of Vedic sacrifice; then itself became the doctrine of a small, rigid, social establishment; then was rebelled against in turn by persons advocating an essentially dualist theology of *saguṇ* bhakti; and finally this *saguṇ* bhakti was rebelled against in its turn by the proponents of *nirguṇ* bhakti. All this seems to me to be a quite plausible way of looking at the long-term historical dialectic between these *saguṇ* and *nirguṇ* theologies, provided that we remember that at each stage the choice of which theology to follow was made by different social groups under the influence of their differing social, economic, and political needs. In other words, the ideas and their dialectic are not self-propelling. Each idea is wielded by different groups at different times for different purposes.

It was basically low-caste groups and persons who first adopted *nirguṇ* bhakti in fifteenth- and sixteenth-century North India. In this book, I have argued that although their choice of a *nirguṇ* theology was in one sense arbitrary, it was also a logical choice given the conceptual universe of medieval India and given the basic desire of the advocates of *nirguṇ* bhakti to protest against what they felt to be an unjust social, economic, and political establishment backed by a Brahmin priesthood that preached a doctrine of *saguṇ* bhakti.

If it is true, as I am claiming, that a social protest against *varṇāśramadharma* lies behind the *nirguṇī* rejection of *saguṇ* bhakti and of the puranic mythology of the avatars of Vishnu, this can help a great deal to explain not only the choice of *nirguṇ* bhakti, but also the interpretative working out of this theology by poets like Kabīr, Raidās, Nānak, Dādū, and their followers. For instance, whereas the Advaitin philosopher Śaṅkarāchārya interprets his version of *nirguṇ* metaphysics in such a way that the everyday *(vyavahārik)* world in which *varṇāśramadharma* ideology operates has a *relative* validity, *nirguṇī* thinkers deny this. Similarly, whereas Viśiṣṭādvaita philosophers like Rāmānuja insist on the importance of God's grace *(prasād)* to escape the cycle of karma and *saṃsāra*, *nirguṇī* thinkers generally either deny the necessity of God's grace or give it very little emphasis. Any human birth is rare and equally valuable, say the *nirguṇī* poets, the important thing is to take advantage of this unique chance to win salvation.[2]

One of the most ambiguous and interesting aspects of *nirguṇī* theology is the reaction of *nirguṇī* thinkers to the *saguṇī* world of puranic mythology. Nirguṇi poets and thinkers employed a variety of strategies that attempted to neutralize, or at least modify or co-opt, the great popularity that this mythology evidently enjoyed among the common people. Sometimes several of these strategies were adopted simultaneously, despite the logical contradictions among them.

One strategy is simply to deny that the mythology — even the Vedas themselves — of mainstream Hinduism is true. This, for example, is the strategy of many of Kabīr's songs such as "Rām nirañjan nyārā re" (above, p. 217). This has also been the principal strategy of Sikh theology since its reformation by the Singh Sabha movement in the latter part of the nineteenth century.

A related strategy is to substitute an alternate, sectarian mythology that mimics the style and content of the Puranas. The stories of the former births of the Satpuruṣ in Dharmadāsī texts like Paramānanda-dās' *Kabīr manśūr* is the clearest example of this strategy. The hagiographic lives of figures like Kabīr, Raidās, and Gurū Nānak represent a historicized variant of the same strategy. In the *chalāva chaukā* of the Kabīr Panth (above, chapter 6), the mythical journey of the soul after death is redesigned in a way that subtlely subverts that mainstream puranic version of the same journey.

Other strategies are somewhat more ambiguous. One involves an attempt to incorporate the great gods of Hinduism in a subordinate position. In the developed theology of the Kabīr Panth, Brahmā, Vishnu, and Shiva are said to have been created by Kāl-Nirañjan, who was in turn created by the supreme Satpuruṣ (above, p. 217).

A similar strategy is to pick and choose among the existing stories and heroes of puranic mythology. Those stories and heroes that, for one reason or another, are acceptable are retained, and the rest are largely forgotten. This is the strategy used by the many *nirguṇī* texts that allude to or retell the myth of the demon devotee Prahlād. As argued in chapter 1, Prahlād's role as pious demon and victim appears to have been interpreted by *nirguṇī* poets as a metaphor of their own marginal status as low-caste dissenters. The many references to other mythical heroes in the hagiographic songs discussed in chapter 3 provide another good example of this pick and choose strategy. By the same token, *nirguṇī* texts only rarely mention the *saguṇī* avatars, Ram and Krishna, the two principal divine heroes of puranic mythology.

Let the Dādū Panthī poet Rajjab have the last word with "Nirguṇ Rām na āvai jāī," a song that nicely captures a *nirguṇī* view of the contrast between the supreme *nirguṇ* Ram and the incarnate *saguṇ* Ram (1967, 1073–73):

Nirguṇ Ram doesn't come or go.
Saguṇ earns karma again and again.

Nirguṇ Ram isn't born nor dies.
There's danger, then Saguṇ takes a body.

Nirguṇ Ram won't descend to earth.
Saguṇ is born and roams the world.

Nirguṇ is the master, Saguṇ the slave.
The sadhus and saints extol his virtues.

Saguṇ's form will be destroyed.
Rajjab runs in Nirguṇ's direction.

A GLOSSARY OF DEVOTEES

For further information on these devotees and saints, the reader can consult a number of works including those of J. Dowson (1961), P. Chaturvedī (1964), Mahipati (1982), Nārāyaṇadās (1980; 1982), S. Dasgupta (1962), G. Garga (1963), K. M. Sen (1974), Nābhādās (1969), and Rāghavadās (1969).

Agradās. (c. 1575). A Rāmānandī sādhu and saguṇī author who lived at the Galatā monastery near Jaipur. He is listed as the disciple of Kṛṣṇadās Payahārī and was the brother-disciple of Kīlhadev and the guru of Nābhādās.

Ajāmil. A pre–Kali Yuga Brahmin of Kānyakubja who was seduced by a prostitute and became an evil doer. At the time of his death he was frightened by Death's messengers and began to call his son named Nārāyaṇ. This pleased the god Vishnu-Nārāyaṇ who saved Ajāmil from hell.

Ambarīṣ. A pre–Kali Yuga Vaishnava king and hero. The sage Durvāsā became angry with him and created a demon named Kṛtyā to kill him. Vishnu killed the demon with his discus and in the end Durvāsā must ask Ambarīṣ to forgive him.

Anantānanda. (c. 1500). The chief disciple and successor of Rāmānanda.

Aṅgad. A friend and devotee of Rāmachandra. He fought with Ram against the demons of Laṅkā. Another Aṅgad (1504–52) was the second of the Sikh gurūs. A third Aṅgad, Aṅgadasiṃha, was a famous warrior and a nephew of King Dīnasalāhasiṃha of Sainagaṛh. He became a devotee through his wife's influence (Nārāyaṇadās 1982: 89–90, 619–20, 534–37).

Balibhadra or *Balabhadra*. A name used for Rāmachandra's brother Balarāma and also for the serpent Śeṣa. Also various authors.

Beṇ, Beṇī or *Beṇīdās*. Some references may be to a poet-saint perhaps earlier than Nāmadev. This Beṇī's compositions show the influence of Haṭha yoga (Garga 1963: 192–93). Other references may be to a poet who was disciple of Mākhū and great-disciple of Dādū. Although connected to the Dādū Panth, he is said to have been a *saguṇī* devotee (Nārāyaṇadās 1980: 44–45).

Bharatharī. A king who renounced his queen and became a ascetic disciple of Gorakhanāth.

Bijjalī Khān. A Muslim nawab who is said to have become a lay follower of Kabīr.

Bhīkhā Sāhab (died 1791). A poet of the Bhuṛakuṛā lineage, a disciple of Gulāl Sāhab. He was born in a Brahmin family of Azamgarh district.

Bhīlanī, Bhīl woman, or *Śavarī.* A woman of the socially low Bhīl tribe who offered to King Rāmachandra *ber* (plum) fruits that she had previously tasted in order to find him the sweetest ones. Through Rāmachandra's favor, she won heaven.

Bhuvan. Bhuvanasiṃha Chauhān was a warrior vassal of the king of Udaipur. He is said to have taken a vow of *ahiṃsā* after killing a pregnant deer (Nārāyaṇadās 1982: 532–33).

Bīrū Sāhab (died c. 1659). A poet and the guru of Yārī Sāhab of the Bhuṛakuṛā lineage.

Bullā (or *Bulā*) *Sāhab* (died in 1709?). A poet in the lineage of the Bhuṛakuṛā monastery of Gazipur district. He was born in a Kurmī family and worked on the farm of Gulāl Sāhab, who became his disciple. With Gulāl's help, he founded the monastery at Bhuṛakuṛā. In addition, a Sufi poet-saint named Bullā Śāh lived in the Punjab in 1680–1752 (Behari 1971: 121–42).

Charpaṭ. A Brahmin who became an ascetic disciple of Gorakhanāth (or of Bālānāth).

Chaturbhuj Sāhab (died 1818). A disciple of Bhīkhā Sāhab of the Bhuṛakuṛā lineage. He was born in a Brahmin family of Banaras district. Another Chaturbhuj (c. 1550) was one of the Aṣṭachhāp poets, a disciple of Viṭṭhalanāth.

Chauraṅgī or *Pūran Bhagat.* A disciple of Gorakhanāth who was forced to spend twelve years buried in a well before being rescued by his guru.

Chokhāmeḷā (died 1338). A famous Maharashtran poet-saint. He was from the Untouchable Mahār caste and has been associated with the Vārakarī Sampradāy, a Vaishnava movement that tends to straddle the *nirguṇī-saguṇī* divide.

Crocodile (*makar* or *grāh*). The Gandharva Hūhū was cursed to be born as a crocodile who fought with an elephant. When Lord Vishnu came to the elephant's aid, both animals won salvation.

Dādūdayāl or *Dādū* (1544–1603). A well-known *nirguṇī* poet of Rājasthān. His disciples founded the Dādū Panth.

Dattātrey or *Datta.* Generally considered to be an avatar of Vishnu. He was born in the house of Atri and Anasūyā. He is said to have rescued the Vedas and to have been a teacher of Prahlād.

Dhannā or *Dhanā* (c. 1500). A *nirguṇī* poet, said to have been a disciple of Rāmānanda. He was a farmer of the Jāṭ caste from the Ajmer region. He fed his seed wheat to some sadhus, but God saw to it that his crop grew anyway.

Dhruv or *Dhū.* A pre–Kali Yuga Vishnu devotee, the son of King Uttānapād. He is noted for the firmness of his devotion and is identified with the polar star.

Dīpū. A devotee and poet of the Kāyastha caste of scribes (Nārāyaṇadās 1980: 187).

Divākar. A disciple of Agradās of Rāmānanda's line.

Draupadī. The wife of the five Pāṇḍavas. Krishna magically lengthened her sari when the Duḥśāsana, on the orders of Duryodhana, tried to undress her.

Dyogū. A devotee of the *mīṇā* caste of Rajasthan, a caste associated with banditry. He always gave food to the saints (Nārāyaṇadās 1982: 573).

Eighty-four Siddhas. A standardized list of early saints of the Nāth and Tāntrik Buddhist movements.

Elephant (*gaj* or *gajendra*). The elephant king, a reincarnation of King Indradyumna, fought with a crocodile and was rescued by Lord Vishnu.

Farīd, sheikh (1175–1265). A famous Sufi scholar and poet who settled at Ajodhan in the Punjab. His songs are found in various *nirguṇī* collections including the Sikh *Gurū Granth Sāhib.*

Gaṇikā. See "Prostitute."

Gopīchanda. A Bengali king who was a son of Bharatharī and Maināvatī. He renounced the throne and became an ascetic disciple of Jālandharanāth.

Gorakhanāth. A famous Nāth yogi, a disciple of Matsyendranāth.

Gulāl Sāhab (died 1759). A poet in the lineage of the Bhuṛakuṛā monastery of Gazipur district. He was a rich zamindar of the Chhatrī caste but became a disciple of Bullā Sāhab, a servant on his farm. Gulāl remained a householder.

Haridās or *Haradās.* There are several important poet-saints with this name. References are often ambiguous. The three most important Haridāses are Haridās Nirañjanī (died c. 1550?), the Haridās/-

Haradās (c. sixteenth century) whose poems are collected in the Dādū Panthī *Pañcha vāṇī,* and the Haridās (c. 1560) associated with the Nimbārka Sampradāy. It is possible that the first two are the same person.

Harikṛṣṇadās. Not listed by Nārāyaṇadās.

Ibrāhīm bin Adham, sultan of Balkh (c. 730–78). A famous Sufi saint. In Kabīr Panthī legends he becomes a disciple of Kabīr.

Jaḍabharat or *Bharat.* The son of King Ṛṣabhadev. Jaḍabharat gave his name to India (Bhāratavarṣa). He was reborn as as Brahmin ascetic who wandered about "dead to the world" *(jaḍavat).* This Bharat should not be confused with Bharat, the brother of Rāmachandra, or Bharat, the son of Śakuntalā.

Jayadev (fl. c. 1150). A devotee of Krishna famous for his Sanskrit devotional poem about Krishna, the *Gītagovinda.* Jayadev was from a Brahmin caste.

Kabīr (c. 1450–1518). A famous *nirguṇī* poet of Banaras. He was raised in a Muslim family of low-caste Julāhā weavers. His life is the subject of a complex cycle of legends.

Kālu or *Kālū.* This name probably usually refers to a devotee named Kālū of the fowler *(kīr)* caste (Rāghavadās 1969: 278). Another possibility is the Aughaḍ saint Kālūrām (Chaturvedī 1964: 687–93).

Kāṇerī/Kaṇerī. Another name of the low-caste Nāth saint Kānhapāda (see *Kānhā*).

Kānhā. The name Kānhā is simply a variant of Krishna and is sometimes used to refer to the avatar Krishna. One human Kānhā was a devotee and poet, probably of Rajasthan. Little is known about him (Nārāyaṇadās 1980: 176; 1982: 969–70). Songs by Kānhā are included in the 1582 C.E. Fatehpur manuscript (Bahura and Bryant 1982). Another human Kānhā is the Nāth and Tāntrik Buddhist saint Kānhapāda or Kāṇerī.

Karamābāī. A famous woman devotee of the god Jagannāth of the city of Puri. She daily fed her god *khicharī* with little concern for ritual purity. She was reprimanded for this by a priest. When she followed all the rules the food preparation was delayed and the God complained to his priests.

Kevaladās (c. 1575). A disciple of Kṛṣṇadās Payahārī in the lineage of Rāmānanda.

Kīlhadev (c. 1575). Another disciple of Kṛṣṇadās Payahārī in the lineage of Rāmānanda.

Kītā. A devotee and poet of the Thorī caste (Nārāyaṇadās 1980: 178–79; 1982: 575–77).

Mādhavāchārya. The identity of the person by this name mentioned in the song attributed to Nābhādās is unclear.

Malūk or *Malūkadās.* There have been at least three poet-saints by this name. The most important of them was born in a Khatrī family from near Allahabad. He died in about 1682. His followers organized a sect.

Mīrābāī or *Mīrā* (died c. 1563). A famous Krishna devotee and poet. She was born in a royal family of Rajasthan and left her royal husband to follow her religious calling.

Moradhvaj or *Mayūradhvaj.* A pre–Kali Yuga king of Ratnapur. Krishna in the guise of a Brahmin tested him by asking him to donate half his body to feed a lion.

Murāridās. Not listed by Nārāyaṇadās or by Chaturvedī.

Nābhā or *Nābhādās* (fl. c. 1600). The author of the famous *Bhaktamāl.* He was the disciple of Agradās in the lineage of Rāmānanda. He is said to have been born in a low-caste, perhaps of Ḍoms.

Nāmadev or *Nāmā* (c. 1260–1350 or later). A famous poet-saint from Maharashtra. He is regarded as a sort of founding father by poets of both the *nirguṇī* and *saguṇī* traditions.

Nānak, Gurū (1469–1539). The first Sikh Gurū.

Nārad. A pre–Kali Yuga sage, the son of Kaśyap. He is the teacher of Prahlād, Dhruv, Ambarīṣ, and other famous devotees. He also narrates parts of the *Bhāgavata-purāṇa.*

Narasī (or *Narasiṃha*) *Mehatā* (1415–81). A devotee and poet from Gujarat. He is closely associated with Mīrābāī and is respected in both *nirguṇī* and *saguṇī* traditions.

Nīmānanda. Not listed by Nārāyaṇadās.

Nine Nāths. A standardized list of the most important early saints of the Nāth Sampradāy.

Palaṭū Sāhab (fl. c. 1850). A saint in the Bhuṛakuṛā lineage. He was born in the Kāndū caste and lived in Ayodhyā. His guru was a disciple of Bhīkhā Sāhab.

Paṇḍharī's King. Viṭṭhal, the form of Vishnu in the temple at Paṇḍharapur, Karnataka.

Parasā or *Paras.* A Rajasthani devotee and poet of the carpenter (khātī) caste. He is said to have been a disciple of Pīpā (Nārāyaṇadās 1980: 196–97; 1982: 225–26).

Pīpā (c. 1450–1500?). A king of Gagaraunagaṛh in Rājasthān. He gave up his throne to follow a religious life. His wife Sītā accompanied him. He is said to have become a disciple of Rāmānanda. Several of his songs attributed to him are still perserved.

Prahlād. The son of the demon king Hiraṇyakaśipu. He became a devotee of Vishnu against his father's wishes. When Hiraṇyakaśipu tried to kill him, the Man-lion avatar killed the demon king.

Priyadās or *Priyādās.* The author of a famous commentary, written in 1712, on Nābhādās's *Bhaktamāl.*

Prostitute (gaṇikā). This bad woman, named Jīvantī, bought a parrot to whom she recited "Ram, Ram" every morning. The day both she and the parrot died, Vishnu's messenger took them to heaven. Another prostitute devotee of Vishnu was named Piṅgalā.

Raidās or *Ravidās* or *Rohidās* (c. 1450–1525). Rāmānanda's famous Chamār disciple from Banaras. Several stories associate him closely with Kabīr.

Rajjab (died 1689). A disciple of Dādū Dayāl and an important poet of the Dādū Panth. He was born in a Muslim family (Nārāyaṇadās 1980: 35–36; 1982: 742–45).

Rambhā. An *apsarā* noted for her seductive beauty. In several legends she is sent to earth to compromise the virtue of powerful ascetics and saints.

Rāmānanda (c. 1425–1500 or earlier). The famous guru of Kabīr, Raidās, Pīpā, Sen, Dhannā, and others.

Rāṅkā and *Bāṅkā.* Two devotees of the potter *(kumhār)* caste.

Rāvaṇ. The famous demon who abducted Sītā and was eventually killed by Rāmachandra. In some versions of his story, he is said to have been saved by the fact that he was killed by Ram.

Ṛṣabhadev. A pre–Kali Yuga king, the son of Nābhi and Merudevī. Ṛṣabhadev married a certain Jayantī. Their eldest son was Bharat.

Sadanā or *Sadhanā.* A butcher devotee who weighed the meat he sold using, unwittingly, the Śālagrāma stones in which Vishnu is thought to be incarnate. Despite this treatment, Vishnu was pleased with Sadanā's devotion.

Sanak, Sanandan, Sanātan, and *Sanatkumār.* Often written as a collective "Sanakādik." These pre–Kali Yuga sages are said to be the four "mind-born" sons of the god Brahmā.

Śavarī. See *Bhīlanī.*

Sayan. Not listed by Nārāyaṇadās.

Sen or *Sain* or *Senā* (c. 1500). A devotee and poet highly respected in *nirguṇī* tradition. He is said to have been a barber who served the court of the Bandhogarh (Rewa) king Rājarām.

Sojhā. A devotee and poet. His wife Sojhī was also a devotee They abandoned their children to become ascetics (Nārāyaṇadās 1980: 174–75; 1982: 573–75).

Sudāmā. A very poor Brahmin who was a friend of Krishna. At the insistence of his wife, Sudāmā took some rice to Krishna and asked for the avatar's help. Krishna ate the rice and rewarded Sudāmā.

Śukadev. A pre–Kali Yuga sage, the son of Vyās.

Sūradās or *Sūr* (c. 1483–1563). A famous Krishna devotee and poet of *saguṇī* tradition. He is said to have been a blind Brahmin who lived in the Mathura-Agra region.

Trilochan or *Tilokan.* A poet-saint of Paṇḍharapur. A few of his *pads* are found in the *Gurū Granth Sāhib.*

Tukārām (1607–49). A famous poet-saint of the Vārakarī Sampradāy of Maharashtra.

Tulasīdās or *Tulasī* (died c. 1623). The famous Brahmin author of the *Rāmacharitamānas* and other *saguṇī* works. In lists of saints, he is sometimes difficult to distinguish from Tulasī Sāhab of Hātharas (born c. 1788) and from Turasīdās Nirañjanī among others.

Turasīdas Nirañjanī (c. late 16th century). One of the more important poets of the *nirguṇī* Nirañjanī Panth of Rajasthan. Since his name is sometimes written "Tulasī," references to a poet by this name in western manuscripts are often ambiguous.

Vibhīṣaṇ. The younger brother of the demon Rāvaṇ. He became an ally of King Rāmachandra and was put on the throne of Laṅka after Rāvaṇ's death.

Vidur. The son of the sage Vyās and a slave girl. He became a minister of Dhṛtarāṣṭra but always tried to protect the Pāṇḍavas.

Vīr Siṅgh Baghel (c. 1470–1530). A ruler of the Baghelkhand region who is said to have become a lay follower of Kabīr.

Viṣṇuśarmā. Not listed by Nārāyaṇadās. A Viṣṇuśarmā is the traditional author of the *Pañchatantra.*

Vulture. The vulture Jaṭāyu, despite his unclean race, was saved because he died trying to save Sītā from being abducted by Rāvaṇ.

Yārī Sāhab (died c. 1684). The first important poet of the Bhuṛakuṛā lineage. He was born as a Muslim and lived and died in Delhi. His guru was Bīrū Sāhab and his disciple Bullā Sāhab.

NOTES

Introduction

1. See, for example, the essays by Wendy O'Flaherty and Frits Staal in the volume on the *sants* edited by Schomer and McLeod (1987).

2. See Lorenzen 1995a. For an able argument, itself from a Marxist point of view, against the idea of a dominant ideology, see Abercrombie, Hill and Turner 1984.

3. Remote but not impossible. R. Tagore's English translation of one hundred of Kabīr's songs was first published in 1915. Trumpp's translation of the Sikh *Gurū Granth Sāhib* was first published in 1877 and Macauliffe's translation in 1909.

4. A full translation of this song is given on p. 213.

5. The amen corner is the section of the church where the most enthusiastic members of the congregation sit, those who respond to the preacher's exhortations with a vocal "amen."

6. The best known such passage is the dialogue in the *Chhāndogya Upaniṣad* (6.13) between Uddālaka Āruṇi and Śvetaketu. There are others as well.

7. White 1952–64, vol. 3, pp. 620–21. This version was collected in about 1927 or 1928. Only one verse is preserved. It reads: "God is at de pulpit, / God is at de do', / God is always over me, / While He is in de middle of de flo'. / *Chorus:* / God is a God; / God don't neber change, / 'Cause He always will be king."

8. For more information about Johnson's life and songs see Samuel Charters' notes to *The Complete Blind Willie Johnson* (Johnson 1993) and also the discussion by Mark A. Humphrey (1993, 107–49).

9. The quotes are taken from the 1952 Revised Standard Version of *The Holy Bible*.

10. On Ikhnaton's hymn and its relation to psalm 104, see Pritchard 1969, 369–70; and Breasted 1933, 281–89, 366–70.

1. Prahlād the Pious Demon

1. In Sanskrit Prahlād's name is pronounced as "Prahlāda" and has been so written here when discussing Sanskrit versions of his story. Hindi texts often write "Prahilād" or "Prahalād," but I have standardized such alternative spellings

as "Prahlād." Hindi spellings of most other personal names have also been standardized in forms close to Sanskrit.

2. *Gurū Granth Sāhib* n.d., 1165 (my translation). See also the translations by Macauliffe (1963, 6:67–68) and by Gurbachan Singh Talib (*Gurū Granth Sāhib* 1984–90, 4:2359). A somewhat different version is edited and translated in Callewaert and Lath 1989, 213–14, 327–28 (no. 118). The other two Nāmadev songs that feature Prahlād's story are found in ibid., 143–44, 254–55 (no. 3) and 218, 333 (no. 127). Two other versions of the *Gurū Granth Sāhib* song are found in Vānakhaṛe Gurujī 1970, 110–11 (no. 46), and 168–69 (no. 254).

3. Here the literal sense is "Let's lengthen his life." Most modern translators claim that this statement is meant ironically.

4. Prahlād gets put "under" a mountain in Jan Gopāl's *Prahilād charitra*, section 12.

5. The *Kabīr granthāvalī* text is found in Kabīr 1985, 370 (*basanta* 2a); the *Gurū Granth Sāhib* version is printed in *nāgarī* in Kabīr 1966, 233–34 (standard edition, p. 1194); the *Sarvāṅgī* version is in Gopāladās 1993, 303 (59.3); the modern bhajan version is in Kabīr 1988, 41–42. Other texts of the *Kabīr granthāvalī* version are published in in Kabīr 1989, 16–17; and Kabīr 1981, 200. The unpublished manuscript versions of the song include no. 12378 (p. 48) of the Rajasthānī Prāchyavidyā Pratiṣṭhān in Jodhpur and Kabīr Chaurā library manuscripts nos. 002 (pp. 155–57), 005 (pp. 341b–42a), 006 (pp. 395–96), 083 (pp. 1–2) (Lorenzen 1994).

6. Kabīr 1966, 155; *Gurū Granth Sāhib* n.d., 856.

7. In their *The Life and Works of Raidas* (1992, 157–59, 224–25). See also Callewaert and de Beeck 1991, 447–48. I have compared this untitled version with a titled *(Prahlād charita)* version in an unpublished 19th-century manuscript from the Rājasthān Prāchyavidyā Pratiṣṭhān in Jodhpur (no. 1882, fol. 68–69). Except for two extra verses in the manuscript version, the two texts are quite similar. Unfortunately all of the texts seem to be somewhat corrupt. A transcription of the manuscript text is included in the appendix to this article. Two other manuscript copies of this text are listed in the catalog of the Rājasthān Prāchyavidyā Pratiṣṭhān in Jodhpur: nos. 13765 (1780 v.s.) and 13497 (19th v.s.). For other published versions, see Rāmānanda Śāstrī and Vīrendra Pāṇḍey (1956) and Jogīndar Siṅgh (1972), neither of which was available to me.

8. Two of these songs are in *Gurū Granth Sāhīb* n.d., 1133, and the third in ibid., 1154. I have translated the first of them below.

9. *Gurū Granth Sāhib* n.d., 67 (my translation). See also the translations by Macauliffe (1963, 2:160) and by Gurbachan Singh Talib (*Gurū Granth Sāhib* 1984–90, 1:140–41).

10. *Mahātmāoṃ kī bāṇī* 1933, 85. It is interesting to note that the word used here for "burst" is *phāro,* while all the Hindi songs about Prahlād found in western manuscripts use cognates of the verb *bidāranā* to refer to the same act.

11. Rajjab 1967, 1390. Nārāyaṇadās, the editor-commentator, identifies Ghūṅghachī with Holikā as in Jan Gopāl's telling of the story (see chapter 2 (13.14) below). I have read *darśā* instead of *daśā* in the last line.

12. For more information on Jan Gopāl and his compositions, see pp. 37–40 below.

13. One of Hopkins' (1968, 20) more interesting claims is that Prahlāda at one point (7.9.12) describes himself as "of inferior birth." Unfortunately this is based on a mistranslation. It is not Prahlāda, but "a man" *(pumān)* who is "low" *(nīcas)*. It is also not quite true (ibid.) that "in the *Bhāgavata* (the sage Nārada) appears as a Śūdra." Verse 1.5.23 states quite clearly that Nārada was a Shudra only "in a former birth" *(purātīta-bhave)*.

14. The fifteen Discourses have the following number of verses: 1(47), 2(61), 3(38), 4(46), 5(57), 6(30), 7(55), 8(56), 9(55), 10(71), 11(35), 12(31), 13(46), 14(42), 15(80).

15. The eighteen sections contain the following number of verses (base and interpolated texts): 1(8 + 0), 2(17 + 13½), 3(13 + 11), 4(18 + 7¼), 5(11 + 7½), 6(21 + 10), 7(7 + 1), 8(8 + 3½), 9(12 + 7), 10(11 + 3½), 11(8 + 2), 12(10 + 3), 13(15 + 5), 14(10 + 7), 15(9 + 1), 16(9 + 2), 17(9 + 9), 18(11 + 4½).

16. One of the most interesting of these parallel passages is one that observes that "half" of our lives are lost in sleep, most of the rest in youth, old age and the cares and responsibilities of life as a householder. This same idea is elegantly expressed in a well-known verse from Bhartṛhari's *Śatakatraya* and is even found in an important Taoist text in China, the *Lièzi* (Lorenzen and Maeth 1979).

17. On the general theme of demon devotees, see — in addition to the already cited works of Hacker, Biardeau and Soifer — the essays in Alf Hiltebeitel's edited volume, *Criminal Gods and Demon Devotees* (1989).

18. It is perhaps fair to say that this sort of minimal role is all that most of the major avatars play in the myths of their "descents," with, of course, the notable exceptions of Rama, Krishna, and perhaps the Buddha.

19. The story of the curse against Jaya and Vijaya and the defeat of Hiraṇyākṣa by the Boar avatar is told in more detail in book three, discourses 15–19, of the *Bhāgavata-purāṇa* (1971).

20. The one significant essay on the presence of Oedipus-like figures in Indian myth and legend is by A. K. Ramanujan (1983). Curiously, Ramanujan nowhere mentions Prahlād, perhaps because Prahlād is responsible for his father's death, however unintentionally, and this goes against Ramanujan claim that the Oedipus myth is typically "inverted" in Indian stories, in the sense that in them the son is typically murdered by the father or submits to him.

21. It is curious, however, that in the *Bhāgavata-purāṇa* (7.2.20–60; 7.3.26–38) Hiraṇyakaśipu is also portrayed as possessing great philosophic and sacrificial erudition, as if he were a Brahmin.

22. See Moffatt 1979. I have elsewhere sharply criticized major aspects of the Dumont-Moffatt replication thesis (Lorenzen 1987a). Here, however, most of this criticism does not apply since the demon society is in fact a construction of the high-caste authors of the Puranas, not a construction of the demons themselves. Even in the myths, however, we can note that the value system of the demons inverts rather than simply replicates the value system of the gods.

23. See chapter 2 below (16.1–6). Monika Boehm-Tettelbach informs me, in a letter, that this hymn forms part of the daily liturgy in the Dādū Panth. A similar *via negativa* hymn appears in the final section of the *Prahilād charitra* (18.1–8). For the Hindi texts, see the edition of the text in this book.

24. *māṃ hi pārtha vyapāśrita ye 'pi syuḥ pāpayonayaḥ / striyo vaiśyās tathā śūdrās te 'pi yānti parāṃ gatim //*

25. See chapter 2 below (2.17).

26. See chapter 2 below (6.16–18).

27. The reading is perhaps पटन (for पइन).

2. Jan Gopāl's *The Deeds of Prahlād*

1. Although the pronoun *tini* seems to refer to Śukra, in the next verse the demons Śaṇḍa and Marka suddenly make their appearance as Prahlād's teachers.

2. In other words, the letters that make the name "Rāma."

3. The meaning of this half-verse is not clear.

4. An alternative translation of the second half-verse is: "As long as the guards are not here, O young princes, you should offer worship." Another is: "As long as the great protector is not here, you should offer devotion to the young prince."

5. The translation here is rather speculative.

6. We read *merī* for *terī* to make the sense.

7. The translation of this line is rather speculative.

8. Another difficult line. If the word is *sarīra,* a possible interpretation is "They got exhausted, his body had no door."

9. The idea seems to be that as hot air cannot blow out a painted lamp, so it has no effect on Prahlād. The air is "hot" because, as we learn in the next verse, they are attempting to burn him to death.

10. It is possible that it is the chains that sink, but *gaye* is clearly masculine not feminine.

11. Also possible: "The world knows that even a rock can be saved." In this case the allusion is probably to the story of Ahalyā who is cursed to be a rock until she is touched by Rāmachandra.

12. Another possibility: "[Prahlād] runs to get bound by the chains that would keep an elephant bound." In this case the chains in question would be the chains of devotion.

13. This interpretation takes *kāṃna* as equivalent to *kāni* (= *lihāj*). If it is taken as equivalent to *kān,* then a possible translation is: "Pay attention to what I have said [lest] your ears get broken." Or: "My ears break when I hear what he has said."

14. From the context *parahas* seems to mean "purpose."

15. Another possibility: "As soon as they are created from Maya, one forgets them."

16. A problem here is that almost all manuscripts read *sahārai,* and none reads *saṃhārai.* If we link this verb with modern *sahāranā,* a possible translation is: "If it causes poisoning, then one must endure everything."

17. Possibly: "They didn't get close to the Inner controller."

18. Possibly: "The devotee Prahlād speaks Ram's truth."

19. Sister Horī is the mythical embodiment of the fire of the Holi festival.

20. The word *jauhar* denotes the Rajput custom in which the women throw themselves on the funeral pyre to avoid being captured by a conquering enemy.

21. The sense of this quarter-verse is not clear.

22. The implied idea seems to be that Prahlād was like gold and the others were like the small seeds sometimes used to weigh it.

23. Since the moon *does* rise in the east, something is obviously wrong here, unless the author is referring to some phenomenon of the mystical yogic anatomy.

24. Literally: "The army of the gods is standing and looking with mind and eyes."

25. We have taken the word *alāhu* as equivalent to *alābhya* or *alābh.* It is also just possible that it refers to "Allah."

26. The readings of this quarter-verse are quite varied and the intended sense is not entirely clear.

3. Singing about Saints

1. In this chapter as elsewhere in this book, I have standardized and partly Sanskritized the names of saints and devotees to make them easier to recognize. All the saints and devotees mentioned are identified in the glossary.

2. On the curious motif of salvation through killing, see W. L. Smith (1992) who discusses the stories of both Rāvaṇ and his nephew Taraṇisena.

3. One exception, important for the very fact that *saguṇī* songs of this type are so rare, is one attributed to Sūradās that mentions Nāmadev. See J. Hawley 1995, 164–65.

4. On this subject see especially the essays by S. Pollock (1989 and 1990).

5. See also the similar discussion in Lorenzen 1995a.

6. This subject still needs much research. Relevant academic studies on the Sufi tradition in India include books by S. A. A. Rizvi (1978–1983) and P. Chaturvedī (1965). Two recent articles that suggest future lines of research in this area are those of F. Mallison (1992) and H. van Skyhawk (1992). For an argument against the importance of Muslim influence on *nirguṇ* bhakti, see W. H. McLeod 1976, 158–61.

7. In the earlier collections of Kabīr's songs and verses, there is one rather ambiguous mention of Rāmānanda and another of Pīpā, both from the *Bījak*

(*pads* 77 and 86). There are also clear though solitary references to the legendary Nāth saints Bharatharī and Gopīchanda (*Kabīr granthāvalī, pad* 48) and Matsyendranāth (*Bījak, ra.* 54). As argued elsewhere (Lorenzen 1991, 11–13), I accept the tradition that Rāmānanda was probably the guru of Kabīr. It also seems likely that Rāmānanda was the guru of Raidās and, somewhat more dubiously, of Sain, Pīpā, and Dhanā.

8. On the "autobiographical" songs attributed to Kabīr, see Vaudeville 1974, 39–48. For an excellent discussion of Mīrābāī's autobiographical songs, see Mukta 1994, 69–154.

9. Anantadās's texts are discussed in Lorenzen 1991. See also Anantadās in the bibliography.

10. One important example of a composition that cannot be easily classified as either a eulogistic song or a hagiographic narrative is attributed to Raidās and dedicated to the demon devotee Prahlād (see above, p. 18). I regard this as an extra-long eulogistic song rather than a sustained narrative. Two unpublished compositions of this type dedicated to Kabīr are a long *pad* called the "*Ādi maṅgal*" or "*Janma maṅgal*" and the "*Chhapai chhanda.*" See Lorenzen 1994.

11. "Dūdhu kaṭorai gaḍavai pānī" (pp. 1163–64); "Hasat khelat terai dehure āiā" (p. 1164); "Sulatānu pūchhai sunu be nāmā" (pp. 1165–66). In the second of these songs Nāmadev makes a strong egalitarian protest against the discrimination he suffers when he is thrown out of a temple because of his "low caste."

12. "Uṭhi re nāṃmadev bāhari jāi" (Callewaert and Lath 1989, 353–54) and "Ā bhaḍai re nauā ā bhaṇai re" (ibid., 354). Different versions of these two songs are found in Vānakhaṛe Gurujī 1970, 29, where the first song is attributed to Kabīr rather than Nāmadev.

13. On the life and songs of Harirām Vyās, see Pauwels 1994; Gosvāmī 1952; and Dube 1968, 31–38. Gosvāmī's book contains a large collection of Vyās' songs. The Hindi text of the song translated here is from Gosvāmī 1952, 195. The article by Pauwels (1994) contains an excellent discussion of several other hagiographic songs by Vyās. These songs mention both *nirguṇī* and *saguṇī* saints including Nāmadev, Rāmānanda, Kabīr, Raidās, Sen, Dhanā, Pīpā, Jayadev, Kamāl, Tilochan, Paramānanda, Khem, Sanātan, Rāghavānanda, Harivaṃśa, Kṛṣṇadās, Haridās, and many pre–Kali Yuga saints. Considering that Vyās was himself a follower of *saguṇ* Krishna, his mention of so many *nirguṇī* saints is quite unusual.

14. The word is "*syām*" which can be equal to *Śyām* (Krishna-Vishnu) or to *svān* (a dog), since the legend claims that God took the form of a dog to eat the bread. Kanhāī, mentioned at the end of the song, is another name of Krishna.

15. For the respective Hindī texts, see Sukṛtadāsajī 1980, 47–50 and *Sandhyā pāṭh* 1977, 149–50.

16. The first line of Malūkadās' song begins "Japo re man keval nām Kabīr" (Kabīr 1988, 61–62).

17. These fifty-two heroes are probably Shiva's *gaṇas.*

18. "Jan Harīdās ānaṃda ihai" (Maṅgaladās 1962, 388–89).

19. "Sultān balakh bukhāre kā" (Kabīr 1988, 168–69). On Ibrāhīm bin Adham and Kabīr, see Lorenzen 1991, 66–67. The song appears in several modern collections of Kabīr bhajans.

20. "Satasaṃga kī hari ne nāv banāī jī" (Khemadās 1989, 94).

21. The translation is of the *Kabīr granthāvalī* text (Kabīr 1985, 165–66 [*pad* 33]). It is possible that this is a Nāth song that somehow ended up with Kabīr's signature.

22. To complete the sense, I have understood an implicit *biralā*.

23. "Mahāśūr tinakā yaś gāūm." In Callewaert and Op de Beeck 1991, 1:567 (no. 116); Sundaradās 1989, 402–3. For other testimonal songs of Sundaradās, see Callewaert and Op de Beeck 1991, 1:570 (no. 131), 552 (nos. 27, 37), 558 (no. 71).

24. "Bhale man rājā khelai ṛtu basaṃta" (*Mahātmāoṃ* 1933, 398; also Gulāl 1983, 66–67). Two published versions of Gulāl's second song, "Chalahu manuām hari ke dhām," are somewhat different (*Mahātmāoṃ* 1933, 288; and Gulāl 1983, 69). The Belvedere Press version mentions Gorakh, Datta, Śukadev, Tulasī, Sūr, Jayadev, Nāmadev, Raidās, Kabīr, Rāmānanda, Dhanā, Sen, Kṛṣṇadās, Chaturabhuj, Nānak, Malūkadās, Yārī, Keśavadās, and Bullā. Gulāl's third song, "Man Basaṃta tum dharahu dhyān" (*Mahātmāoṃ* 1933, 402–3) mentions Prahlād, Nāmadev, Dhanā, Sen, Raidās, nine Nāths, Nārad, Śukadev, Kabīr, Nānak, Kānhā, Sadanā, and Yārī. Bullā Sāhab's Basant song, "Man basaṃta khelai agam phāg" (*Mahātmāoṃ* 1933, 168; and Bullā 1989, 19) mentions Brahmā, Mahādev, Nārad, Jayadev, Dhruv, Prahlād, Śukadev, Hanumān, Arjun, Sahadev, Nāmā, Kabīr, Nānak, Yārī, and Keśav.

25. Kabīr 1988, 42–43.

26. See, for example, the song by Basava cited by R. B. Michael (1992, 7) in his interesting discussion of Vīraśaiva egalitarianism.

27. "Mhāre nanāṃ age rahājo jī" (Mīrābāī 1966: 140). See also her song "Giridhārī śaraṇām thārī āyā" (Mīrābāī 1966, 139).

28. "Mhānaiṃ māhā ko Rāmajī bhavai ho" (Mīrābāī 1972, 125). See also the egalitarian hagiographic song by Tukārām, the great Vārakarī poet of Maharashtra, translated by Anne Feldhaus and Shankar Gopal Tulpule in Lorenzen 1987b, 100.

29. "Manāṃ bhajasi re hari charaṇā." I have used the version found in Rajjab 1990, 130–31 (no. 22.22). A similar version is found in Gopāladās 1993, 145 (no. 9.30). In the *Gurū Granth Sāhib* (n.d., 1293), a variant of this song is attributed to Raidās. This omits the refrain and the verse with the *bhaṇitā* of Pīpā and places verse four ("No one . . .") first. This leaves Raidās as the last saint mentioned, but the verse about Raidās is not a typical *bhaṇitā*. I infer the attribution to Pīpā is probably correct. If so, Pīpā cannot be dated before Kabīr and Raidās as some scholars propose.

30. Only the *Gurū Granth Sāhib* version reads "family" *(kul)*. Rajjab's version has "always" *(nit)*, and Gopāladās' has "and" *(aru)*.

31. This rather enigmatic phrase is usually taken to refer to Kabīr and his father. To me it seems more likely that the reference is to Kabīr and his son Kamāl, who also abandoned the path of their Muslim forebears.

32. "Ganikā giddha Ajāmil Sadanā au Raidās" (Palaṭū 1987–90, 1:91–92. The other song is "Hari ko bhajai so baṛā hai" (ibid., 90–91).

33. "Bhakti jāti ko kyā karai" (Rajjab 1967, 1135–36). For another example, see "Jāti jagataguru dekhe nāhīṃ" (ibid., 1073).

34. In this line I have taken *su* to be a mistake for *(a)ru*.

35. "Saṃta bīlag kab kīnhā saṃto." The only place I have found this song is in manuscript no. 008 of the Kabīr Chaurā Library (Lorenzen 1995). Since it appears to be otherwise unobtainable, it is quoted in full below:

संत बीलग कब कीन्हा संतो ॥ संत बीलग कब कीन्हा ॥ टेक ॥

सेवरी जाति कवन कुल कही ॥ सब सो रहत अधिना ॥

सेवाटहल करे संतन के ॥ राम प्रशादि लीन्हा ॥ **1** ॥

तुलसी ब्राह्म बडे कुलींना ॥ लोग कहे प्रबीना ॥

नाभा जी भंगी के बालक ॥ तासु प्रसादी लीन्हा ॥ **2** ॥

ना पतीआ तो साष बतावो ॥ अजहु समुझ कमीना ॥

सुपच भक्त रईदास चमारा ॥ हरी आपन करी लीन्हा ॥ **3** ॥

कहै कबीर सुनो भाई साधो ॥ अतिना साषि हम दीन्हा ॥

गुरमुष हो ऐसो शाधु के चीन्हे ॥ नीगुरा मति के हीना ॥ **4** ॥

4. Sain's *The Kabīr-Raidās Debate*

1. See Lorenzen 1994, 9. The Kabīr Chaurā monastery has published the *Kabīr-Gorakh kī goṣṭhī* (1937), the *Kabīr-Jogājīt kī goṣṭhī* (n.d.), and the *Kabīr-Sarvājīt kī goṣṭhī* (1930). A *goṣṭhī* between Kabīr and Rāmānanda, the *Jñan tilak,* is published in P.D. Barthwal 1955, 31–37. One of my own future projects is to edit and translate some of these Kabīr Panthī *goṣṭhīs*.

2. The manuscripts used for my edition of the text all spell the author's name as Saiṃnām, Saiṃnā or Saiṃna. I have simplified this to Sain. The spelling Sen is often used in other sources. The different manuscripts of the text consulted for this edition give it the following names (in the numbered order of the list at the end of this introduction): 1. *Śrī Kabīr jī aru Raidās jī kau saṃbādau* and *Kabīr aru Raidās saṃbād,* 2. *Svāmmī jī srī Kabīr jī aru Raidās jī kau saṃbād* and *Śrī Kabīr Raidās saṃbā,* 3. *Kabīr jī aru Raidās jī kau saṃbād* and *Kabīr aru Raidās saṃbād,* 4. *Kabīr aru*

Raidās jī kau saṃbādau, 5. the red ink of the transitions is invisible on the microfilm, 6. *Sāheb Kabīr ko gūsṭa* | | *Raiyedās (?sobha) pāso graṃtha* and *Śrī Kabīr Sāheb au Raiyedās kī guṣta bhayā (?jhaga) ra,* 7. *Kabīr jī Raidās jī kī goṣta* and *Śrī Kabīr jī Raidās jī kī goṣta,* 8. *Kabīr Raidās jī kau saṃbād,* 9. *Goṣta Kabīr Sāhab Raidās kī.*

3. See Sain in the bibliography. John Hawley has written a useful summary and discussion of the text in Hawley and Juergensmeyer 1988, 45–46.

4. B. P. Śarmā (Anantadās 1982) and Shukdeo Singh (Anantadās 1993) have published versions of this text. Singh's book also includes a somewhat rough English translation. On Anantadās and his *parachaīs,* see Lorenzen 1991.

5. On this Raidāsī version of the debate, see Darshan Singh 1981, 9–21 and Hawley and Juergensmeyer 1988, 46.

6. One reason why the story of this debate has been largely forgotten may be that it was not retold by Priyādās in his influential A.D. 1712 commentary on Nābhādās's *Bhaktamāl.*

7. B. P. Śarmā (Raidās 1978, 143) suggests that the real author may have been Anantadās. The only basis for making this suggestion, however, appears to be the presence of the debate in Anantadās' *Raidās parachaī.*

8. On the little studied Nirañjanī Panth, see P. Chaturvedi 1964, 337–56, Mangaladās Svami 1962, and S.H. More 1977.

9. I thank John S. Hawley of Barnard College for this reference.

10. Also possible: "The Spirit is not the Goddess, nor Shiva, nor Vishnu."

11. Gopāl is a name of Vishnu. Mohan is another name of Krishna, the foster son of Nanda and Yaśodā.

12. Literally: "Who is Nanda and who is his son?"

13. The wording and translation of this last *pada* is somewhat uncertain.

14. Literally: "Nanda is everywhere. His son is everywhere."

15. This verse could not be translated. It mentions Ram and Krishna as avatars.

16. The meaning of *pīra mati* is not clear.

17. This seems to imply the work of performing religious sacrifices.

18. Kaṃsa is the evil uncle of Krishna. The demon Hiraṇyakaśipu is the enemy of Vishnu and the father of Prahlād, Vishnu's faithful devotee.

19. Vishnu in his Rāmachandra avatar killed the demon Rāvaṇ and put Rāvaṇ's good brother Vibhīṣaṇ on the throne of Laṅkā.

20. Also possible: "The Spirit is not the Goddess, Shiva nor Vishnu."

21. Also possible: "[If] the Spirit is not the Goddess, Shiva nor Vishnu . . ."

22. The translation here is somewhat speculative.

23. "Añjan" and "Nirañjan" are roughly equivalent to the "Conditioned" *(saṃsār)* and "Unconditioned"(Brahman) respectively. See also Kabīr's song "Rām nirañjan nyārā re" (below, p. 217).

24. The word *nriti (= nirati),* a key term in *nirguṇ* religion, has been translated by W. H. McLeod in the Sikh *B40 Janam-sakhi* as "ineffable beatitude." McLeod comments that the term "connotes the transcendent condition resulting from *surati.*" This latter term that McLeod interprets as "a virtual synonym

for *simran* as used in *sabad simaran* or *nam simaran* (remembrance of the divine Name)" (McLeod 1980, 152). On these two terms, see also the discussion by C. Vaudeville (1974, 135).

25. The word *ūlī* seems to be equivalent to the feminine of *ūrā*, meaning "incomplete" or "imperfect."

26. This first *pada* is repeated in the next verse, but evidently with an inverted sense.

27. Has Raidās misunderstood Kabīr's interpretation of the first *pada?*

28. Also possible: "He is the Lord of the cowherds of infinite worlds."

29. Julāhā is the name of the low caste of Muslim weavers to which Kabīr belonged.

30. Chamār is the name of the untouchable caste of leather workers to which Raidās belonged.

31. The translation of the last *pada* is somewhat speculative.

32. This verse seems to refer to the story of Durgā taking the form of the daughter of the cowherd woman Yaśodā. This daughter is then exchanged for Krishna, the son of Devakī. When the evil king Kaṃsa kills Yaśodā's daughter, Durgā displays her true form and announces she will kill Kaṃsa in the future.

33. Here it is not clear to what myth the text refers.

34. If the translation of the last two *padas* is correct, they refer to Krishna, who was killed by a hunter. Is the whole verse an attempt by Durgā to proclaim her superiority over Krishna and Vishnu?

35. Pīpā is traditionally considered to be a disciple of Rāmānanda like Kabīr.

36. Here it is also possible that it is Kabīr who speaks this verse.

37. The sense of the second *pada* is uncertain.

38. The precise implications of this enigmatic statement are not clear.

39. The meaning of *rālāṃ* is uncertain.

40. The word *ajūṃnī* seems to mean "foolish" or "ignorant."

41. Shiva gave Bhasmāsur ("Demon of Ashes") a boon so that anyone he touched on the head would turn to ashes. When Bhasmāsur tried to do this to Shiva, Shiva fled and Krishna killed the demon. The five manuscripts used for the present edition all read *bhasmāgar* or *bhasmāgir* instead of *bhasmāsur*.

42. The meaning of the second *pada* is uncertain.

43. The translation of the last two *padas* is somewhat speculative.

5. Kabīr's Most Popular Songs

1. This chapter is based in part on a 1991 article by Mariela Álvarez and myself published in Spanish.

2. The better ones include Kabīr 1949; 1953; 1959; 1964; and 1984; I. Gurṭū 1963; and Yugalānanda Bihārī 1982.

3. Some versions begin "Chadariyā jhīnī jhīnī." See Kabīr 1953, 169; 1959, 117–18; 1964, 251; 1984, 35–36; 1987–89, 1:62–63. The translation here is based on the text in Kabīr 1988, 153.

4. The Hindi text specifies "five" *tattvas*, i.e., the five elements, and "three" *guṇas*, i.e., the Sāṃkhya "qualities" of *sattva*, *rajas*, and *tamas*.

5. See Kabīr 1953, 31; 1984, 28–29; 1987–89, 1:15; Gurṭū 1963, 40. My translation here is based on the text in Kabīr 1988, 119 (see also p. 152).

6. See Kabīr 1964, 223; 1984, 36; 1987–89, 1:21; H. Dvivedī 1971, 343. Some versions begin "Soch samujh abhimānī." My translation is based on the text in Kabīr 1988, 156.

7. The *Kabīr bījak* version is *śabda* 73 (Kabīr 1972, 135–36); the *Kabīr granthāvalī* version is *śabda* 241 (Kabīr 1968, 126); and the *Gurū Granth Sāhib* version is *soraṭhi* 2 (Kabīr 1966, 131).

8. See Kabīr 1964, 247; 1987–89, 1:26; 1988, 151. Some versions begin "Phūlā phūlā phirai jagat meṃ." My translation here uses the text in Kabīr 1984, 22.

9. Literally, "arm."

10. Tagore has translated this bhajan (Kabīr 1961, 39–40), and its Hindi text is included in several collections (H. Dvivedi 1971, 261–62, 342–43; Kabīr 1984, 39; 1988, 203; 1953, 66). For an interesting comparison, see two bhajans by Gulāl Sāhab of the Bhuṛakuṛā lingeage that use the metaphor of marijuana intoxication (Gulal 1983, 15–16, 18; *Mahātmāoṃ* 1933, 74).

11. *Kabīr bījak, śabda* 12 (Kabīr 1972, 115). See also the translation by L. Hess and Shukdeo Singh (Kabīr 1983, 47).

12. See Kabīr 1953, 38–39; 1964, 225; 1984, 33; 1987–89, 1:45–46; H. Dvivedī 1971, 272, 345. My translation here is based on the text in Kabīr 1988, 110.

13. Kabīr 1984, 27; 1987–89, 1:29; 1988, 124; H. Dvivedī 1971, 266. Dvivedī's short version is translated by Tagore in Kabīr 1961, 50.

14. See Kabīr 1953, 152; 1987–89, 2:7; 1988, 152. My translation here is based on the text in Kabīr 1984, 26–27.

15. See Kabīr 1953, 64; 1959, 118; 1964, 180; 1984, 35; 1987–89, 1:90–91; H. Dvivedī 1971, 234 . My translation here is based on the text in Kabīr 1988, 111.

16. Kabīr 1984, 48; 1988, 126. My translation here is based on the former text.

17. In some collections this bhajan begins "To ko pīv milaiṅgai." For English translations, see Machwe 1977, 48; Sethi 1984, 490–91; Behari 1971, 227–28; and *The Kabīr Voice* of November 1991. For the Hindi text, see Kabīr 1959, 115; 1964, 209; 1984, 22; 1988, 111; H. Dvivedī 1971, 346–47; and Gurṭū 1963, 40. I have used the text in Kabīr 1987–89, 2:73.

18. This probably refers both to the patchwork robe of an ascetic and to the body constructed from five elements.

19. See Kabīr 1953, 20; 1964, 243; 1984, 38; 1987–89, 2:13; H. Dvivedī 1971, 275. My translation is based on the text in Kabīr 1988, 154–55.

20. See Kabīr 1953, 48; 1964, 247; 1984, 41; 1987–89, 1:38–39; Dvivedī 1971, 310–11. My translation is based on the text in Kabir 1988, 110.

21. See Kabīr 1964, 205; 1987–89, 2:103. My translation is based on the text in H. Dvivedī 1971, 282.

22. *Bījak, śabda* 23 (Kabīr 1972, 119). For the versions in more modern collections, see Kabīr 1964, 167; 1987–89, 2:24; H. Dvivedī 1971, 299–300.

23. The *Kabīr granthāvalī* song is *pad* 336 (Kabīr 1968, 151). I have based my translation on this text. For a modern version, see Kabīr 1988, 182.

24. In works of Kabīr Panthī theology, particularly those of the Dharmadāsī branch, the supreme Satpuruṣ is said to have given birth to the creator Kāl-Nirañjan, who brings death into the world and in turn creates the gods Brahmā, Vishnu and Shiva. Why and how this radical shift in the meaning of *nirañjan* occurred needs further study.

25. See Henry 1991; and 1988, 168–69, 278. I have used the text as sung by Abul Hassān in 1978 (Henry 1988, 278). Its meter seems to be quite uneven. The three versions all begin with somewhat different refrains ("Hīrā ratan," "E ab koi hīrā ratan," and "Ab koi hīrā ratan").

26. See Bhadaīdās 1983, 27–28. The text of his version is considerably different from Henry's, and Bhadaīdās immodestly puts his own name in the signature phrase. My translation here is based on Henry's text.

27. Some versions of this song begin "Chalanā hai dūr musāfir" and others "Chalanā sabere musāfir." See Kabīr 1987–89, 2:36. My translation is based on the text in Kabīr 1988, 191 (see also p. 85).

28. Literally, "With you are the messengers [of Death]."

29. See Kabīr 1964, 144; 1984, 21–22; and 1987–89, 1:55. My translation is based on the text in Kabīr 1988, 149–50. In the next to last line, read *aṅga* for *ag*.

30. In some collections the bhajan begins without the word *avadhū*. For Tagore's translation, see Kabīr 1961, 93–94. For the Hindi text, see Kabīr 1964, 231–32; 1987–89, 1:62; H. Dvivedī 1971, 286. My translation is based on the text in Kabīr 1988, 80.

31. It is not clear to what if anything these numbers refer. "Nine" and "ten" often refer to the "openings" of the body as in "Saiyāṃ nikasi gayo" (above, no. 8), but in this context some other equivalent would be better. The 88,000 are perhaps a variant of the more common 84,000 lives that beings are said to pass through.

6. The Rituals of the Kabīr Panth

1. This chapter is based in part on my 1988 article published in Spanish. See also Lorenzen 1981.

2. It is not my intention here to attempt a general theoretical analysis of ritual behavior. More theoretical studies that I have found useful include those of C. Bell (1992), S. Tambiah (1985), S. Ortner (1986), and V. Turner (1967; 1977).

3. The Hindi text is from *Sandhyā pāṭh* 1977, 9–10.

4. Hindi text from *Sandhyā pāṭh* 1977, 166–67.

5. Hindi text from *Sandhyā pāṭh* 1977, 157–58.

6. The straw in question is the one that is broken during the rite of initiation.

7. Hindi text from Kabīr 1982, 42–43.

8. The places in the text where each night's *pāṭh* begins and ends are specified in Kabīr 1982, 44.

9. See in the bibliography the references under *Mūl saṃdhyā pāṭh, Mūl sandhyāpāṭh,* and *Sandhyā pāṭh.*

10. For the date of this text, see below, p. 238.

11. The Hindi text is the one I edited in *Jñān gudarī* 1988. An earlier English translation is found in *The Path of Spiritual Realization* 1985.

12. The complete Sanskrit text is found in *Sandhyā pāṭh* 1977.

13. Hindi text from *Sandhyā pāṭh* 1977, 11–12.

14. The word *pārakh* or *parakh* normally means "test" or "good judgment." In Kabīr Panthī usage, however, it is given a difficult to define technical sense, sometimes translatable as "perfection."

15. Sanskrit text from *Sandhyā pāṭh* 1977, 12.

16. See Brahmalīnamuni 1960, 84–94, 231–34, 297–301. Portions of pp. 86–94 are translated into Spanish in Lorenzen 1988, 449–50.

17. See Lorenzen 1991 for historical details about these texts.

18. See Sen 1974, 101; K. Dvivedi 1965, 321–22; and Giladā 1985, 156–62. Umā Ṭhukarāl (1979, 36) claims that there is a resemblance between the *chaukā* and the *sekoddeśa vidhi* of the Tantric *Bhairavī chakra.*

19. For the Brahminical cycle of funeral rites, see Kane 1953, 4:179–266; and Pandey 1969, 234–74.

20. The text of the Kabīr Chaurā "Haṃsāvalī" is in *Sandhyā pāṭh* 1977, 158–64. The text of the Dharmadāsī songs is found in Sukṛtadāsajī 1980. "Haṃsāvalī" number five corresponds to Dharmadāsī *śabda (haṃsa gaman ke)* number two.

21. Hindi text in *Sandhyā pāṭh* 1977, 155–56.

22. Hindi text from *Sandhyā pāṭh* 1977, 156–57.

23. This mantra was told to me by the current junior *mahant* of the Kabīr Chaurā. The verse is found in the *Sumiran bodh* (Yugalanand 1953, 10:23). The initiation mantra of the Dharmadāsīs is known as the *pāñcha-nām* (five name) mantra. As written out for me in 1985 by Gṛndhamuni Nām Sāheb, the then *mahant* of the Damakheda branch, it is as follows:

ādi-nām ajar-nām amar-nām
patāl śabda sindhu nām
akāse adalī nīr-nām
yahī nām haṃsa ko kām
kholo kuñjī khol kapāt
pāñjī chaḍhe mūl ke ghāṭ

Dharmadās ajar mukh bolā, kahe Kabīr pramāṇ
pāñchanām le haṃsā satyalok payān

This mantra — minus the last two lines and with somewhat different readings — also appears in the *Sumiran bodh* (ibid., 22).

24. The sense of this first line is not clear.

25. Hindi text from *Sandhyā pāṭh* 1974, 154–55.

26. See here the chapter on Kabīr's popular bhajans. The three older collections of Kabīr's compositions are the *Kabīr bījak*, the *Kabīr granthāvalī* (parts translated in Sethi 1984), and that found in the Sikh *Gurū Granth Sāhib*. See also various modern collections of bhajans such as those in H. Dvivedī 1971 (partly translated in Kabīr 1961), and Kabīr 1988 and 1987–1989.

27. See L. Hess 1987.

28. Hindi texts from *Sandhyā pāṭh* 1977, 148–54. See also the versions in Gaṅgāśaraṇ Śāstrī 1983, 36–39 and in Kabīr 1988, 14–20. If the *chaukā* is performed on a night other than that of a full moon, a sixth song, not translated here, is substitued for the first one.

29. Literally, "a scissors in the armpit."

30. Hindi texts from *Sandhyā pāṭh* 1977, 158–64. See also the versions in Gaṅgāśaraṇ Śāstrī 1983, 41–43 and in Kabīr 1988, 32–34.

31. Read *ghaṭavār*.

32. Also possible is "takes birth in age after age," but this goes against the context unless we assume that rebirth is being taken as something positive.

33. Although the term "six faiths" *(ṣaṭ daraśan)* traditionally refers to the six schools of classical Hindu thought, modern *nirguṇī* commentators often claim that the term indicates six religions. The list varies, but Buddhism, Jainism, Vaishnavism, and Shaivism are usually included.

34. Other versions read "he" *(soī)* in place of "cries" *(roī)*.

35. Or, "on the shining island."

36. The translation the enigmatic *surati karo* as "remember the Name" is admittedly somewhat arbitrary.

37. The "city at the root" *(mūl nagar)* is probably the *mūlādhāra-chakra* of the mystical yogic anatomy.

38. This verse refers to the yogic anatomy of the *sahasrār-chakra*, the *nāḍis*, and the *brahma-randhra*.

Epilogue

1. See Nāmadev 1989; Kabīr 1972 and 1985; Callewaert and Friedlander 1992; *Gurū Granth Sāhib* n.d.; Dādū Dayāl 1966; Sundaradās 1989; Callewaert and Op de Beeck 1991; Rajjab 1967 and 1990; Gopāladās 1993; Maṃgaladās

Svāmī 1962, Dariyā of Bihar 1962, Nābhādās 1969; Rāghavadās 1969; Anantadās 1989, 1991 and 1993; Jan Gopāl 1988; and *Mahātmāoṃ kī bāṇī* 1933.

2. See Lorenzen 1987a; 1987b; 1987c; and 1995a for further discussion of these points.

BIBLIOGRAPHY

Abercrombie, Nicholas, Stephen Hill, and Bryan S. Turner. 1980. *The Dominant Ideology Thesis*. London: George Allen and Unwin.

Álvarez, Mariela and David N. Lorenzen. 1991. "Las canciones populares de Kabir," *Estudios de Asia y Africa* 26, 1:139–57.

Anantadās, 1982. *Raidās-parachaī*. Edited in B. P. Śarmā 1982, 34–51).

———. 1989. *Nāmadev parachaī*. Edited and translated by W. Callewaert and M. Lath in Nāmadev 1989, 37–54.

———. 1991. *Kabīr parachaī*. Edited and translated in Lorenzen 1991, 93–254.

———. 1993. *Raidās-parichaī*. Edited and translated by Shukdeo Singh (Śukadev Siṃha). Varanasi: Viśvavidyālay Prakāśan. Also contains a Hindi text of Sain's *Kabīr-Raidās kā saṃvād*.

Arya, U. 1968. *Ritual Songs and Folksongs of the Hindus of Surinam*. Leiden: E. J. Brill.

Bahura, Gopal Narayan and Ken Bryant (eds.). 1984. *The Padas of Surdas*. Jaipur: Maharaja Sawai Man Singh II Museum. A facsimilie edition of the 1582 C.E. Fatehpur manuscript.

Baṃsūdāmajī. 1948. *Chaukā-vidhān*. Baroda: Svasaṃved-kāryālay, Sīyābāg.

Barthwal, P. D. (Pītāṃbar Datta Baṛathvāl) (ed.). 1955. *Rāmānaṃda kī hiṃdī rachanāeṃ*. Varanasi: Nāgarīprachāriṇī Sabhā.

———. 1978. *Traditions of Indian Mysticism Based upon Nirguna School of Hindi Poetry*. New Delhi: Heritage Publishers.

Behari, Bankey. 1971. *Sufis, Mystics and Yogis of India*. Bombay: Bharatiya Vidya Bhavan. Contains texts and translations of bhajans of several saints including Kabīr.

Bell, Catherine M. 1992. *Ritual Theory, Ritual Practice*. New York: Oxford University Press.

Benedict, Ruth. 1934. "Ritual." In *Encyclopedia of the Social Sciences*. New York: Macmillan.

Bhadaīdās. 1983. *Anupam kīrtan mālā*, vol 4. Damakheda: The author.

Bhāgavata-purāṇa. 1971. Sanskrit text with an English translation by C. L. Goswami. Gorakhpur: Gita Press. The cited passages are my own translations.

Bhaṭṭa, Kāntikumār. 1975. *Kabīr-paramparā (Gujarāt ke saṃdarbha meṃ)*. Allahabad: Abhinav Bhāratī.

Bhīkhā Sāhab. 1985. *Bhīkhā Sāhab kī bānī*. Allahabad: Belvedere Press. Reprint.

Biardeau, Madeleine. 1975. "Narasiṃha, mythe et culte." In *Puruṣārtha: récherches de sciences sociales sur d'Asie du sud*. Paris: Centre d'études de l'Inde et de l'Asie du sud.

Brahmalīnamuni. 1960. *Sadguruśrīkavīracharitam*. Baroda: Svāmī Srī Brahmalīnamuni.

Breasted, James Henry. 1933. *The Dawn of Conscience*. New York: Charles Scribner's Sons.

Bullā Sāhab. 1989. *Bullā Sāheb kā sabdasār*. Allahabad: Belvedere Press. Reprint.

Callewaert, Winand M. and Peter G. Friedlander. 1992. *The Life and Works of Raidās*. Manohar. With an edition and translation of 111 *pads*.

Callewaert, Winand M. and Bart Op de Beeck (eds.). 1991. *Devotional Hindī Literature: A Critical Edition of the Pañc-vāṇī or Five Works of Dādū, Kābir, Nāmdev, Raidās, Hardās with the Hindī Songs of Gorakhnāth and Sundardās and a Complete Word-index*, 2 vols. New Delhi: Manohar Publications.

Chaturvedī, Paraśurām. 1964. *Uttarī Bhārat kī saṃta-paraṃparā*. 2nd ed. Allahabad: Bhāratī Bhaṇḍār.

———(ed.). 1965. *Sūfī-kāvya-saṃgrah*. Allahabad: Hindī Sāhitya Sammelan.

———. 1990. *Saṃta kāvya*. Allahabad: Kitāb Mahal. Reprint. First published in 1952.

Dādū Dayāl. 1966. *Dādūdayāl (graṃthāvalī)*. Edited by Paraśurām Chaturvedī. Varanasi: Nāgarīprachāriṇī Sabhā.

Dariyā of Bihar. 1962. *Dariyā-granthāvalī*. Patna: Bihār-Rāṣṭrabhāṣā-Pariṣad.

Dasam Granth Sāhib. 1983–86. 4 vols. in Nāgarī script with a translation into modern Hindi. Lucknow: Bhuvan Vāṇī Trust.

Dasgupta, Shashibhusan. 1962. *Obscure Relgious Cults*, 2nd ed. Calcutta: Firma K. L. Mukhopadhyay.

Dharmadās. 1985. *Dhanī Dharamadāsajī kī śabdāvalī*. Allahabad: Belvedere Press. Reprint.

Dharanīdās. 1976. *Dharanīdās jī kī bānī*. Allahabad: Belvedere Press. Reprint.

Dowson, John. 1961. *A Classical Dictionary of Hindu Mythology and Religion, Geography, History, and Literature*, 10th ed. London: Routledge & Kegan Paul.

Dube, Lālatā Prasād. 1968. *Hindī bhakta-vārtā sāhitya*. Dehra Dun: Sāhitya Sadan.

Dūlanadās. 1985. *Dūlanadās jī kī bānī*. Allahabad: Belvedere Press. Reprint.

Dumont, Louis. 1986. *Homo hierarchicus: le systéme des castes et ses implications*, rev. ed. Paris: Gallimard. First edition published in 1966.

Dvivedī, Hajārīprasād. 1971. *Kabīr*. Delhi: Rājkamāl Prakāśan. In Hindi. An appendix contains the Hindi texts of 256 popular songs attributed to Kabīr. The first one hundred are translated by R. Tagore in Kabīr 1961.

Dvivedī, Kedāranāth. 1965. *Kabīr aur Kabīr-pantha: tulanātmak adhyayan*. Allahabad: Hindī Sāhitya Sammelan.

Freed, Ruth S. and Stanley A. Freed. 1980. *Rites of Passage in Shanti Nagar*. New York: The American Museum of Natural History.

Gaṅgāśaraṇ Śāstrī. 1976. *Kabīr jīvan charitra*. Varanasi: Kabīravāṇī Prakāśan Kendra.

———. 1983. *Āchār saṃhitā*. Varanasi: Kabīravāṇī Prakāśan Kendra.

Garga, Gaṅgārām. 1963. *Saṃkṣipta Oxford Hiṃdī-sāhitya parichāyak*. Delhi: Oxford University Press.

Garībadās. 1985. *Garībadās jī kī bānī*. Allahabad: Belvedere Press. Reprint.

Genovese, Eugene D. 1974. *Roll, Jordan, Roll: The World the Slaves Made*. New York: Pantheon Books.

Gilaḍā "Śaivāl," Ved Prakāś. 1985. *Kabīr Paṃtha par paṃthetar prabhāv*. Meerut: Anu Books.

Goetz, Hermann. 1966. *Mira Bai: Her Life and Times*. Bombay: Bharatiya Vidya Bhavan.

Gold, Daniel. 1987. *The Lord As Guru: Hindi Sants in North Indian Tradition*. New York: Oxford University Press.

Gopāladās. 1993. *Sarvāṅgī*. Edited by W. H. Callewaert as *The Sarvāgī of Gopāldās*. New Delhi: Manohar.

Gosvāmī, Vāsudev. 1952. *Bhakti-kavi Vyās jī*. Mathura: Agravāl Press. Contains an edition of 757 of Harirām Vyās's *pads*.

Gulāl Sāhab. 1983. *Gulāl Sāhab kī bānī*. Allahabad: Belvedere Press. Reprint.

Gurṭū, Indranārāyaṇ (ed.). 1963. *Hindī ke janapad saṃta*. Delhi: Motilal Banarsidass.

Gurū Granth Sāhib. n.d. 4 vols. in Gurmukhī and Roman script with an English translation. Translation and edition by Pritam Singh Chahil. Published by the editor-translator. No address given. Uses the standard pagination.

Gurū Granth Sāhib. 1984–90. Translated to English by Gurbachan Singh Talib in 4 vols. Patiala: Publication Bureau, Punjabi University. Each volume has separate pagination but the standard pagination is also indicated in the margins.

Hacker, Paul. 1959. *Prahlāda, Werden und Wandlungen einer Idealgestalt: Beiträge zur Geschichte des Hinduismus*, 2 vols. Mainz: Verlag der Akademie der Wissenschaften und der Literatur in Mainz. Abhandlungen der Geistes- und Sozialwissenschaftlichen Klasses, no. 9, 13.

Harirām Vyās. See Vāsudev Gosvāmī.

Hawley, John Stratton. 1984. *Sūr Dās: Poet, Singer, Saint*. Seattle: University of Washington Press.

———. 1989. "Author and Authority in the Bhakti Poetry of North India." *Journal of Asian Studies* 47:269–90.

———. 1992. "Creative Enumeration in the *Vinaya* Poetry of Sūrdās." In McGregor 1992, 225–36.

———. 1995. "The Nirguṇ/Saguṇ Distinction in Early Manuscript Anthologies of Hindi Devotion." In Lorenzen 1995c, 160–80.

Hawley, John Stratton, and Mark Juergensmeyer. 1988. *Songs of the Saints of India*. New York: Oxford University Press.

Henry, Edward O. 1988. *Chant the Names of God*. San Diego: San Diego State University Press.

———. 1991. "Jogīs and Nirgun Bhajans in Bhojpuri-Speaking India: Intra-Genre Heterogeneity, Adaptation, and Functional Shift," *Ethnomusicology* 35,2:221–42.

———. 1995. "The Vitality of the Nirguṇ Bhajan: Sampling the Contemporary Tradition." In Lorenzen 1995c, 232–52.

Hess, Linda. 1983. "The Cow is Sucking at the Calf's Teat: Kabir's Upside-down Language." *History of Religions* 22:313–37.

———. 1987. "Three Kabir Collections: A Comparative Study." In K. Schomer and W. H. McLeod 1987:111–41.

Hiltebeitel, Alf (ed.). 1989. *Criminal Gods and Demon Devotees: Essays on the Guardians of Popular Hinduism*. Albany: SUNY Press.

Hopkins, T. 1968. "The Social Teaching of the Bhāgavata Purāṇa." In Milton Singer (ed.), *Krishna: Myths, Rites, and Attitudes*. Chicago: University of Chicago Press, pp. 3–22. First published in 1966.

Humphrey, Mark A. 1993. "Holy Blues: The Gospel Tradition." In Lawrence Cohn (ed.), *Nothing But the Blues: The Music and the Musicians*. New York: Abbeville Press.

Jagajīvan Sāhab. 1983–90. *Jagajīvan Sāhab kī bānī*, 2 vols. Allahabad: Belvedere Press. Reprint.

Jan Gopāl. 1947. *Dādū janma līlā*. Edited by Sukh Dayāl Dādū as *Śrī Dādū janma līlā paracī*. Jaipur: Śrī Svāmī Lakṣmīrām Trust.

———. 1988. *Dādū janma līlā*. Edited and translated by Winand M. Callewaert as *The Hindī Biography of Dādū Dayāl*. Delhi: Motilal Banarsidass.

Jñān gudarī. 1988. Trans. to Spanish and edited in Hindi by Mariela Álvarez and David N. Lorenzen as "El edredón del conocimiento (Jnan gudari)," *Estudios de Asia y Africa* 23,1:166–87.

Jogīndar Singh. 1972. *Santa Raidās*. New Delhi: Akṣar Prakāśan.

Johnson, Blind Willie. 1993. "God Don't Never Change." A 1929 recording on the compact-disk set *The Complete Blind Willie Johnson*. Sony Music Entertainment, Inc. With nineteen pages of written notes by Samuel Charters.

Kabīr. 1949. *Kabīr padāvalī*. Edited by Rāmakumār Varmā. Allahabad: Hindī Sāhitya Sammelan.

———. 1953. *Śabdāmṛt sindhu*. Edited by Hanumānadāsajī Sāhab. Gujarātī Sāhitya-premī maṇḍal. No place indicated.

———. 1959. *Kabīr-saṃgrah*. Edited by Sītārām Chaturvedī. Allahabad: Hindī Sāhitya Sammelan.

———. 1961. *One Hundred Poems of Kabir*. Trans. by Rabindranath Tagore. London: Macmillan. First published in 1915.

———. 1964. *Kabīr vachanāvalī*. Edited by Ayodhyāsiṃha Upādhyāy "Hariaudh." 12th reprint. Varanasi: Nāgarīprachāriṇī Sabhā.

———. 1966. *Santa Kabīr*. Edited by Rāmakumār Varmā. 5th imp. Allahabad: Sāhitya Bhavan. A Nāgarī edition of the compositions by Kabīr in the *Gurū Granth Sāhib* with paraphrases in modern Hindi.

———. 1968. *Kabīr graṃthāvalī*. Edited by Śyāmasuṃdaradās. Varanasi: Nāgarī Prachāriṇī Sabhā. By custom this edition is used for references, but the editions of M. Gupta (Kabīr 1985) and W. M. Callewaert and B. Op de Beeck (1991) are more useful.

———. 1972. *Kabīr bījak*. Edited by Śukadev Siṃha. Allahabad: Nīlabh Prakāśan.

———. 1981. *Sabad*, vol. 2 of *Kabīr vāṅmay*. Edited by Jayadev Siṃha and Vāsudev Siṃha. Varanasi: Viśvavidyālay Prakāśan. With paraphrases in modern Hindi.

———. 1982. *Bījak*. Edited by Gaṅgāśaraṇ Śāstrī with an introduction by Śukadev Siṃha. Varanasi: Kabīr Prakāśan Kendra.

———. 1983. *The Bijak of Kabir*. Trans. by Linda Hess and Shukdeo Singh. San Francisco: North Point Press.

———. 1984. *Bhajan śatak*. Edited by Vichār Dās. Varanasi: Kabīravāṇī Prakāśan Kendra.

———. 1985. *Kabīr-graṃthāvalī*. Edited by Mātāprasād Gupta. Allahabad: Lokabhāratī Prakāśan.With paraphrases in modern Hindi.

———. 1987–89. *Kabīr Sāhib kī śabdāvalī*, 4 vols. Allahabad: Belvedere Press. Reprint.

———. 1988. *Kabīr śabdāvalī*. Edited by Gaṅgāśaraṇ Śāstrī. Varanasi: Kabīravāṇī Prakāśan Kendra.

_____. 1989. *Kabīr-granthāvalī*. Edited by Pārasanāth Tivārī. Allahabad: Rākā Prakāśan. This is Tivārī's own collection, not the Dādū Panthī *granthāvalī*.

Kabīr-Gorakh kī goṣṭhī. 1937. Edited by Bābā Śrī Lakhanadās in *Viparyay śabda gūṛhārtha saṭīk tathā Gorakh goṣṭhī*. Kabīr Chaurā, Varanasi: the editor.

Kabīr-Jogājīt kī goṣṭhī. n.d. Edited by Lakhanadās as *Kabīr Sāhab aur paṃḍit Yogājīt kī goṣṭhī* in a small booklet with a missing title page. Kabīr Chaurā, Varanasi. Booklet also contains *Dādū jī dvārā stuti* and several short Kabīr Panthī compositions.

Kabīr-Sarvājīt kī goṣṭhī. 1930. Edited by Bābā Lakhanadās as *Paṃ. Sarvājīt kī goṣṭhī*. Kabīr Chaurā, Varanasi: the editor.

The Kabir Voice. A monthly magazine published by the Kabir Association of Canada, 5858 150th St., Surrey, B.C., Canada V3S 5L5. Edited by Dr. J. Das.

Kabīropāsana-paddhati. 1979. Bombay: Śrīveṅkaṭeśvar Press.

Kalyāṇ: saṃta-vāṇī-aṅka. 1955. Gorakhpur: Gītā Press.

Kamāl-bodh. 1953. In Yugalānanda Bihārī 1953, 10:1–17.

Kane, Pandrang Vaman. 1953. *History of Dharmaśāstra*, vol. 4. Pune: Bhandarkar Oriental Research Institute.

Keay, F. E. 1931. *Kabīr and His Followers*. Calcutta: Association Press.

Khemadās (ed.). 1989. *Santa sudhā bāṇī*. Koliyā, Rajasthan: the editor.

Leavitt, John. 1992. "Cultural Holism in the Anthropology of South Asia: The Challenge of Regional Traditions." *Contributions to Indian Sociology* (n.s.) 26,1:3–49.

Lessa, William A., and E. Z. Vogt (eds.). 1972. *Reader in Comparative Religion: An Anthropological Approach*, 3rd. ed. New York: Harper & Row.

Levine, Lawrence W. 1977. *Black Culture and Black Consciousness: Afro-American Folk Thought from Slavery to Freedom*. New York: Oxford University Press.

Lorenzen, David N. 1981. "The Kabīr Panth: Heretics to Hindus." In D. N. Lorenzen (ed.), *Religious Change and Cultural Domination*, pp. 151–71. Mexico City: El Colegio de México.

———. 1987a. "Traditions of Non-Caste Hinduism: The Kabir Panth." *Contributions to Indian Sociology* 21,2:263–83.

———. 1987b. "The Social Ideologies of Hagiography: Śaṅkara, Tukārām and Kabīr." In M. Israel and N. K. Wagle (eds.), *Religion and Society in Maha-*

rashtra, pp. 92–113. Toronto: Centre for South Asian Studies, University of Toronto.

———. 1987c. "The Kabir Panth and Social Protest." In K. Schomer and W. H. McLeod 1987, 281–303.

———. 1988. "El chauka del muerto en el Kabir Panth." *Estudios de Asia y Africa* 23,3:445–68.

———. 1991. *Kabir Legends and Ananta-das's Kabir Parachai*. Albany: SUNY Press.

———. 1994. *A Catalog of Manuscripts in the Kabīr Chaurā Monastery*. Mexico City: El Colegio de México.

———. 1995a. "The Historical Vicissitudes of Bhakti Religion." In Lorenzen 1995c, 1–32.

———. 1995b. "The Lives of *Nirguṇī* Saints." In Lorenzen 1995c, 182–212.

——— (ed.). 1995c. *Bhakti Religion in North India: Community Identity and Political Action*. Albany: SUNY Press.

———. 1995d. "The Life of Kabir in Legend." In A. Entwistle, M. Shapiro, and C. Salomon (eds.), *Early Literature in New Indo-Aryan Languages*. Delhi: Manohar.

Lorenzen, David and Russell Maeth. 1979. "El Lièzi y el Śatakatraya de Bhartṛhari: Descubrimiento de una relación entre dos textos clásicos de China e India." *Estudios de Asia y Africa* 14,4:696–707.

Lutgendorf, Philip. 1990. "La búsqueda del Tulsidas legendario." *Estudios de Asia y Africa* 25,1:8–29.

Lynch, Owen M. 1990. "The Social Construction of Emotion in India." In Owen M. Lynch (ed.), *Divine Passions: The Social Construction of Emotion in India*, pp. 3–34. Berkeley: University of California Press.

Macauliffe, M. A. 1963. *The Sikh Religion*. 6 vols. in 3. Reprint. Delhi: S. Chand and Co. First published in 1909.

Machwe, Prabhakar. 1977. *Kabir*, 2nd ed. New Delhi: Sahitya Akademi.

McGregor, R. S. (ed.). 1992. *Devotional Literature in South Asia: Current Research, 1985–1988*. Cambridge: Cambridge University Press.

McLeod, W. H. (trans.). 1980. *The B40 Janam-sakhi*. Amritsar: Guru Nanak Dev University.

Mahātmāoṃ kī bāṇī. 1933. Bhuṛakuṛā, Gazipur district: Bābā Rāmabaran Dās Sāheb.

Mahendra. 1969. *Kabīr kī bhāṣā*. Delhi: Śabdākār.

Mahipati. 1982. *Bhaktavijaya*. Translated from Marathi by J. E. Abbott and N. R. Godbole as *Stories of Indian Saints*, 2 vols. bound as 1. Reprint. Delhi: Motilal Banarsidass. First published in 1933.

Mallison, Françoise. 1992. "Muslim Devotional Literature in Gujarati: Islam and Bhakti." In R. S. McGregor 1992, 89–100.

Malūkadās. 1988. *Malūkadās jī kī bānī*. Allahabad: Belvedere Press. Reprint.

Maṃgaladās Svāmī. 1962. *Śrī mahārāj Haridāsajī kī vāṇī saṭippaṇī apar niraṃjanī mahātmāoṃ kī rachanā ke aṃśāṃśa*. Jaipur: Nikhil Bhāratīy Niraṃjanī Mahā Sabhā.

Marriott, McKim. 1989. "Constructing an Indian Ethnosociology." *Contributions to Indian Sociology* (n.s.) 23,1:1–39.

Michael, R. Blake. 1992. *The Origins of Vīraśaiva Sects.* Delhi: Motitlal Banarsidass.

Mīrābāī. 1966. *Mīrāṃbāī kī padāvalī.* Edited by Paraśurām Chaturvedī. Allahabad: Hindī Sāhitya Sammelan.

———. 1972. *Narasījī ro māhero.* Edited Jeṭhālāl Nārāyaṇ Trivedī. Jodhpur: Rājasthān Prāchyavidyā Pratiṣṭhān.

———. 1988. *Mīrābāī kī śabdāvalī.* Allahabad: Belvedere Press. Reprint.

Mishra, Vijay C. 1987. "Two Truths are Told: Tagore's Kabir." In K. Schomer and W. H. McLeod 1987, 167–80.

Moffatt, Michael. 1979. *An Untouchable Community in South India.* Princeton: Princeton University Press.

More, S. H. 1977. *Sevādās Niraṃjanī: vyaktitva evaṃ kṛtitva, ek anuśīlan.* Mathura: Javahar Pustakālay.

Mukta, Parita. 1994. *Upholding the Common Life: The Community of Mirabai.* Delhi: Oxford University Press.

Mūl saṃdhyā pāṭh. 1982. Maūsahāniyāṃ, Chhatarapur district: Kabīr Ashram.

———. 1983. Edited by Bhadaīdās Sāheb. Dāmakheḍā: The editor.

Mūl sandhyāpāṭh. 1982. Varanasi: Kabīr Kīrti Mandir.

———. 1974. Edited by Rāmasvarūpadās. Burhanpur, M.P.: Śrī Kabīr Nirṇay Mandir.

Nābhādās. 1969. *Śrībhaktamāl.* With the commentaries of Priyādās and Sītārāmaśaraṇ Bhagavānprasād Rūpakalā. Lucknow: Tejakumār Press.

Nāmadev. 1989. *The Hindi Padavalī of Nāmdev.* Edited and translated by Winand M. Callewaert and Mukund Lath. Delhi: Motilal Banarsidass.

Nārāyaṇadās of Ajmer. 1979. *Śrī Dādū Paṃtha paricay,* vol. 2. Jaipur: Śrī Dādū Dayāl Mahāsabhā.

———. 1980. *Rājasthānī saṃta sāhitya parichay.* Jaipur: Śrī Dādūdayāl Mahāsabhā.

———. 1982. *Śrīsaṃtamāl.* Jaipur: Śrī Dādū Dayālu Mahāsabhā.

Ortner, Sherry B. 1986. *Sherpas through Their Rituals.* Cambridge: Cambridge University Press.

Palaṭū Sāhab. 1987–90. *Palaṭū Sāhib kī bānī,* 3 vols. Allahabad: Belvedere Press. Reprint.

Pandey, Raj Bali. 1969. *Hindu Saṃskāras: Socio-religious Study of the Hindu Sacraments,* 2nd ed. Delhi: Motilal Banarsidass.

Paramānanda-dās. 1984. *Kabīr manśūr.* Bombay: Lakṣmīveṅkaṭeśvar Steam Press. New imp. The longer version.

The Path of Spiritual Realization. 1985. Edited by Jagadish Das. Surrey, B.C., Canada: Kabir Association of Canada; and Jamnagar, Gujarat: Kabīr Ashram.

Pauwels, Heidi. 1994. "The Early Bhakti Milieu as Mirrored in the Poetry of Hariram Vyas." In Alan W. Entwistle and Françoise Mallison (eds.), *Studies in South Asian Devotional Literature,* pp. 24–50. New Delhi: Manohar.

Pollock, Sheldon. 1989. "Mīmāṃsā and the Problem of History." *Journal of the American Oriental Society* 109,4:603–10.

———. 1990. "From Discourse of Ritual to Discourse of Power in Sanskrit Literature." *Journal of Ritual Studies* 4,2:315–45.

———. 1991a. "The Divine King of the *Rāmāyaṇa*." In vol. 3, *Araṇyakāṇḍa*, of Robert P. Goldman (ed.), *The Rāmāyaṇa of Vālmīki: An Epic of Ancient India*, pp. 15–54. Princeton: Princeton University Press.

———. 1991b. "Rākṣasas and Others." In ibid., pp. 68–84.

Pritchard, James B. 1969. *Ancient Near Eastern Texts Relating to the Old Testament*, 3rd ed. Princeton: Princeton University Press.

Rāghavadās. 1969. *Bhaktamāl*. With a verse commentary by Chaturadās (c. 1800 C.E.) and a modern prose commentary by Nārāyaṇadās of Ajmer. Jaipur: Śrī Dādū Dayāl Mahāsabhā.

Raidās. 1978. *Sataguru Ravidās-vāṇī*. Edited by B. P. Śarmā. Delhi: Sūrya-Prakāśan.

———. See also Callewaert and Friedlander 1992.

Rajjab. 1967. *Śrī Rajjab vāṇī*. Edition and Hindi commentary by Nārāyaṇadās of Ajmer. Ajmer: Nārāyaṇasiṃha Śekhāvat.

——— (ed.). 1990. *Sarabaṃgī*. Edited by Dharmapāl Siṃhal. Jalandhar: Dīpak Publishers.

Rāmānanda Śāstrī, Svāmī and Vīrendra Pāṇḍey. 1956. *Santa Ravidās aur unakā kāvya*. Lucknow: Navabhārat Press.

Ramanujan, A. K. 1983. "The Indian Oedipus." In Alan Dundes and Lowell Edmunds (eds.), *Oedipus: A Folklore Casebook*, pp. 234–61. New York: Garland.

———. 1989. "Is There an Indian Way of Thinking? An Informal Essay." *Contributions to Indian Sociology* (n.s.) 23,1:41–58.

Rizvi, Saiyid Athar Abbas. 1975–83. *A History of Sufism in India*, 2 vols. New Delhi: Munshiram Manoharlal.

Sain (or Sen). 1978. *Raidās-Kabīr kā saṃvād*. Edited by B. P. Śarmā in Raidās 1978, 143–46.

———. 1986. *Kabīr-Raidās kā saṃvād*. Edited by Shukdeo Singh in his (ed.), *Ravidās*, pp. 37–40. Varanasi: Ravidās Smarak Society.

———. 1993. *Kabīr-Raidās kā saṃvād*. Edited by Shukdeo Singh in Anantadās 1993, 39–54.

Sandhyā-pāṭh. 1974. Edited by Rāmanandanadās. Varanasi: Ādi Mūlagādī Kabīr Chaurā Maṭh. An earlier Kabīr Chaurā text.

———. 1975. Edited by Bālakṛṣṇadāsajī Sāheb. Kharsiyā, M.P.: Śrī Udit Nām Sāhab. A Dharmadāsī text.

———. 1977. Edited by Vivekadās. Varanasi: Kabīravāṇī Prakāśan Kendra. The current Kabīr Chaurā text. A second edition was published in 1984.

Śarmā, B. P. 1982. *Śrī guru Ravidās charitam*. Chandigarh: Śrī Guru Ravidās Saṃsthān.

Sax, William S. 1991. *Mountain Goddess: Gender and Politics in a Himalayan Pilgrimage*. New York: Oxford University Press.

Schaller, Joseph. 1994. "Sanskritization, Caste Uplift, and Social Dissidence in the Sant Ravidās Panth." In Lorenzen 1995c, 95–120.

Schomer, Karine, and W. H. McLeod (eds.). 1987. *The Sants: Studies in a Devotional Tradition of India*. Berkeley: Berkeley Religious Studies Series.

Sen, Kshitimohan. 1974. *Medieval Mysticism of India*. 2nd ed. New Delhi: Oriental Reprint Corporation.

Sethi, V. K. 1984. *Kabir: The Weaver of God's Name*. Dera Baba Jaimal Singh, Punjab: Radha Soami Satsang Beas.

Singh, Darshan. 1981. *A Study of Bhakta Ravidāsa*. Patiala: Punjabi University.

Smith, W. L. 1992. "Taraṇisena: A Parochialised Devotional Motif." In R. S. McGregor 1992, 261–67.

Soifer, Deborah A. 1991. *The Myths of Narasiṁha and Vāmana: Two Avatars in Cosmological Perspective*. Albany: SUNY Press.

Sudhādās "Sukavi" Dehalavī. 1970. *Chaukā paddhati*. Damakheda, Raipur District: Vaṃśa Pratāp Gaddī.

Sukṛtadāsajī, Barārī. 1980. *Chaukā-chandrikā arthāt kaṃḍahārī bhed*, 4th ed. Kharsiya, Raigarh district: Kabīr Dharmasthān Kharsiyā. First published in 1947.

Sundaradās. 1989. *Sundar granthāvalī*. Edited by Nārāyaṇadās of Ajmer. Jaipur: Śrī Dādū Dayāl Mahāsabhā.

Tambiah, Stanley Jeyaraja. 1985. *Culture, Thought, and Social Action: An Anthropological Perspective*. Cambridge, Mass.: Harvard University Press.

Tapasvī. 1976. *Kabīr satya prakāś—saṭīk*. Līmbaḍī, Gujarat: Śrī Tapasvī Sāheb.

Thiel-Horstmann, Monika. 1983. *Crossing the Ocean of Existence*. Wiesbaden: Otto Harrassowitz.

Ṭhukarāl, Umā. 1979. "Kabīr panthī sāhitya kā ālocanātmak adhyayan." Ph.D. thesis, Rājakīya Snātakottar Mahāvidyālay, Koṭadvār, U.P.

Turner, Victor Witter. 1967. *The Forest of Symbols*. Ithaca, N.Y.: Cornell University Press.

———. 1977. *The Ritual Process: Structure and Anti-Structure*. Ithaca, N.Y.: Cornell University Press.

van Skyhawk, H. 1992. "Ṣūfī Influence in the Ekanāthī-bhāgavat: Some Observations on the Text and Its Historical Context." In R. S. McGregor 1992, 67–79.

Vānakhaṛe Gurujī, K. G. 1970. *Saṃta Nāmadev tathā unakā hindī sāhitya*. New Delhi: Publishing Division, Information and Broadcasting Ministry, Government of India.

Vaudeville, C. 1974. *Kabīr*, vol. I. Oxford: Clarendon Press, 1974.

———. 1993. *A Weaver Named Kabir*. New Delhi: Oxford University Press.

Wescott, G. H. 1953. *Kabir and the Kabir Panth*. Calcutta: Susil Gupta. First published in 1907.

White, Newman Ivey (gen. ed.). 1952–1964. *The Frank C. Brown Collection of North Carolina Folklore;* the folklore of North Carolina, collected by Dr. Frank C. Brown during the years 1912–1943. 7 vols. Durham, N.C.: Duke University Press.

Wilson, H. H. 1972. *Religious Sects of the Hindus*. Varanasi: Indological Book House. First published in *Asiatick Researches*, vols. 16 (1828) and 17 (1832).

Yugalānanda Bihārī (ed.). 1953. *Kabīr sāgar*, 11 vols. Bombay: Lakṣmīveṅkaṭeśvar Press. Volume 11 contains Yugalānanda's own *Kabīr charitra bodh*. Reprint.

——— (ed.). 1982. *Kabīrapaṃthī-śabdāvalī*. Bombay: Gaṃgāviṣṇu Śrīkṛṣṇadās.

Index